BECOMING A MASSAGE
THERAPIST AT AGE 70

BECOMING A MASSAGE THERAPIST AT AGE 70

NOTES ON LEARNING
WESTERN MASSAGE AND CHINESE TUINA

For Rosemary Maxwell,

With Best Wishes,

SAm wong 5/2/2015

Samuel Wong

AUTHOR OF *INTIMATE WITNESSES: COPING WITH CHALLENGES*

FOREWORD BY LESLIE A. YOUNG
Editor-in-Chief, *Massage & Bodywork*

Library of Congress Control Number:		2015902658
ISBN:	Hardcover	978-1-5035-4519-9
	Softcover	978-1-5035-4520-5
	eBook	978-1-5035-4518-2

Print information available on the last page.

Rev. date: 02/26/2015

To order additional copies of this book, contact:
Xlibris
1-888-795-4274
www.Xlibris.com
Orders@Xlibris.com
656874

Dedicated to

Alvin Yabes, Sarah Rines & Elizabeth Javier-Wong

and

Isabel, Imogen, Maximus & Caroline

with whom I share the joy of East meeting West

Blessed are the flexible, for they shall not be bent out of shape.
– Robert Wong, age 67, as I began writing this book in December 2013.

Just relax, be calm, be peaceful, and most of all, have fun!
-- Isabel Yabes, age 7, before she gave me, her *gonggong*, a relaxation massage in her imaginary Dance Spa, in 2011.

Contents

Foreword

Leslie A. Young, Ph.D.
Editor-in-Chief, *Massage & Bodywork*

I first met him through a flurry of emails in November of 2012. A Virginia bodyworker named Samuel Wong had developed a modality and he wanted to script a magazine feature about it and have the manuscript published in *Massage & Bodywork* magazine. Space is quite limited in the nation's largest trade journal for bodyworkers which I edit, but fresh voices inspire us and our readers, and I was keen to learn more.

He submitted a very strong feature story about his modality— Yin Yang Touch, a product of Eastern wisdom meeting Western applications. It didn't take long before I realized the modality was a wonderful reflection of Sam himself—the perfect blend of Chinese wisdom rooted in Singapore and Western tenacity. In working with Sam on the edits, I found him and his work to be innovative, intuitive, flexible, honest, and open.

For me Sam's story unfolded in reverse. It was some months before I learned he was in his 70s and had only recently embraced bodywork as a career. I'm someone who isn't fazed by age. By some quirk of math and fate, I myself am in my 50s, some of my best friends are in their 70s and 80s. They inspire me, so I was delighted to meet someone in my chosen career field who continues this trend and has so much to offer.

I was fortunate some months later to meet Sam and his charming wife quite by chance when we were seated next to each other in a Boston restaurant in April 2013. As luck would have it, we were all in town to learn and grow at the International Massage Therapy Research Conference. His warmth and depth were even more apparent in person; his dark eyes shined as he talked about his fascination for massage therapy and the evidence-based conversations at IMTRC.

So, of course I'm honored to preview his text and write this foreword. It takes great strength to allow yourself to be vulnerable and that's exactly what Sam Wong has done in here, for our benefit. He writes his story with a level of detail reflective of not only an autobiography, but a how-to manual for those interested in tracing his footsteps. You'll learn that from age 8 or 9 he knew his hands had a gift, but he spent a lifetime and a career touring worldwide before settling in Virginia and attempting massage school. He's very transparent here about how and why he's finally manifested his talents. I find it stunning that someone with his life experience and common-sense Chinese roots looks at the profession with such wide eyes and an inquiring spirit.

Even though I had been married for 30-some years, raised three children, had had countless skin-on-skin contacts with people of diverse background, and had seen bodies in various stages of nakedness, I was still unprepared for touching another body or being touched for massage practice.

Sam is very soft spoken and understated, but he's the kind of person who inherently inspires others if they're paying attention at all! Don't you dare stereotype this "senior" bodyworker because his insights will humble you. So, instead, I suggest you allow him to educate you. It's clear he's a lifelong learner. Quietly tenacious, he immersed himself in the massage therapy profession deftly moving from fan to student to practitioner to educator. His reward is apparent:

It is an avenue of service that blesses both the giver and the receiver, the service that brings wholeness to others and to you.

So journey with Sam as I have as he shares his very personal and ultimately professional story with you. Marvel at how he ventured to China to learn tuina and integrate it into his Yin Yang Touch modality. For others this would be a reach to go across the world to study such an in-depth topic in an exotic land, but with Sam's aptitude and background, it's clear he was destined for this study. Indeed bodywork is his calling.

Of course you can learn much about the traveler by reading between the lines. Those of us at Associated Bodywork & Massage Professionals are dedicated to students' success. We hear so much about contemporary students' struggles and work hard to help them alleviate test anxiety, so I was moved by Sam's very transparent stories about negotiating massage school obstacles such as test anxiety and navigating distance learning. Formidable for anyone, then consider having the scenario amplified by some 35 years since he'd been in graduate school.

Sam's is the best voice to represent his bodywork endeavor, so I won't approach that subject here, but I'm struck by his drive to create his own modality with so little experience in the profession and his subsequent determination to claim his own seat at the bodywork table. He's endeavored to make his work immediately relevant and applicable for populations in need, such as veterans struggling with posttraumatic stress syndrome and individuals suffering from fibromyalgia.

In the end I remain touched by his deep respect for the body and its innate ability to heal given a chance and appropriate touch. So whether you're a client, a student, or a bodyworker, enjoy Sam's story and the lessons it holds for us all. And think then about your story. How would you write it? Would you write it? If so, what obstacles would it reveal? Who would benefit from your story? Are you manifesting your given strengths? Are you answering your calling?

What do you have to lose? So what if you fail? At least, you would know that you have tried!

Preface

When I began learning massage therapy, I was merely interested in gaining the skills so that I could give my family members the relaxing and pleasurable sensations I had when I received massage. It was for family bonding; my wife and children were all supportive of my venture. I was focused on what I could do. I was unaware of the body's inherent power of healing, neither was I aware of my potential as a medium for healing. I remember a niece's delight when the numbness of her thigh had vanished after I gave her a few minutes of rhythmic compression and sustained gliding. I also remember the amazement of a young mother that her panic attack had subsided after I cradled her head in my hands for a while.

I discovered I could help a body to heal through the movements known as therapeutic massage and through the interplay of my inner energy with that of the receiver. I was not the healer. I was a medium that elicited the healing power from within me and from the person I touched. That discovery launched me onto an exciting career after I was well into my retirement. When I retired in 2004, I thought I had done my life's work and my future was behind me. Message therapy set a totally unexpected future ahead of me. It is still unfolding. Instead of rehashing nostalgia, I am engaged in learning and writing about alternate routes of healing. I don't live in what I had accomplished in the past. For me, the best is yet to be!

Since becoming a massage therapist at age 70, I live a full and exciting life, arguably more enjoyable than many experiences in my previous careers. I have come across so many new discoveries that I feel obliged to share now instead of waiting for their maturation. The fact is, I have no assurance for how many more years I shall live, and I don't want my findings to vanish so that other therapists could not learn from them, build on them, or use them as points of departure. So, I decided to write down what I have learned.

Some of what I have discovered is worth sharing especially with people who are similarly retired. I am not a member of the baby boom generation. I was born ahead of them. However, my new career as a massage therapist may offer some of the baby boomers and older retirees ideas for a rewarding pursuit in their golden years. If you have graduated from playing golf, tending a garden, messing around in your garage, fishing, travels, cruises, volunteer services, doting on grandchildren, nurturing family pets, and other worthwhile activities, or wish simply to add more spice to your life, to do more than what you have been doing, or if you are pondering what you might do for the next 20 or more years of your life, I invite you to consider learning massage therapy. It is an avenue of service that blesses both the giver and the receiver, the service that brings wholeness to others and to you. I feel more energetic and more aware of my posture, and I take better care of myself since I became a massage therapist.

We know the platitude that time heals. What I discovered in massage therapy is that time really heals, with a slight twist: the time we spend touching someone actually promotes healing. The passage of time allows the body to heal itself, but that is different from "touching time" incurred in massage. Touching time is intentional. It can be the standard massage sessions of 30, 45 or 60 minutes or intensive sessions that last 90-120 minutes. The simple act of sustained touching in a relatively calm and quiet setting releases the body's potential for healing. Touching unhurriedly is what most retired people can do and what many therapists might re-learn to do. Retirees have time on their hand and they might use it deliberately for healing. All they need is to spend some time learning to touch with healing intention. They can help to reduce the cost of healthcare and improve their own quality of life and that of their clients, without negative side effects. A small investment with a big reward, individually and societally!

What seasoned therapists might find in this account are some timely reminders that massage is an investment of quality and quantity time. At age 70, many practitioners would have earned their retirement, and some have probably burned out many years before that. I am not asking them to emerge from their retirement. I just want to remind those who are still active in the profession that massage is both bodywork and brainwork and to share what I have discovered from my study of Chinese massage to keep them from early burnout. Most students of Chinese massage, known variously as *tuina* or *anmo*, learned the trade through serving as apprentice to a master practitioner in China or attending workshops in the U.S. I had the rare opportunity of learning it in a classroom setting in China, along with other Chinese practitioners, following a standard curriculum. Since what I had learned (am learning) about Chinese *tuina* and traditional Chinese medicine is providing a complementary way of doing Western massage and my learning experiences are different from most Western practitioners, I feel I have an obligation to share them.

As a brainworker, I do not follow traditions blindly. I am not wedded to this school or that school. I have no qualms about deviations from traditions, but I want to document my deviations. I love to navigate uncharted waters in the pursuit of healing. Total immersion in Chinese massage for three months had helped me to further refine my own method of bodywork, a practice that even an older person can do. I want to share that.

Becoming a therapist requires formal training. I would like older and younger people considering choosing massage therapy as a career to have a feel of the rigors of training and to highlight the learning community of massage therapists as a nurturing community. I am a recipient of care and nurture from my massage instructors and classmates. They are partially responsible for what I have become. I recount my learning experiences as a tribute to them and as an introduction for prospective massage students. Of course, my formal learning experience is limited since I have attended only the massage programs at Northern Virginia Community College and Guangzhou Medical College. However, both these programs follow standard curriculum; what you might learn in other programs is likely similar. My experience might give you a heads up of what to expect. However, what I have written are *notes on learning Western Massage and Chinese Tuina*, not instructions. **You need to have formal training to become a therapist; reading these notes will not make you a qualified therapist!** Nonetheless, I have included a number of completed assignments and class notes, marked off from the main text, to give you a flavor of learning massage therapy. Most of them have been edited but are real and authentic materials. I hope that they entice you to enroll in a massage training program at whatever age you are.

What is not adequately reflected in the book is the support of a myriad of people who wished me success and helped me to succeed in my emerging career as a massage therapist. Foremost among them is my wife Mercedes Javier-Wong, who was usually the first person to experience the exuberance of my discovery. Initially, she was skeptical about my involvement with a new career and uncertain about my association with a much younger crowd, mostly younger women. However, she became a true believer after I helped her recover from the numbing effects of piriformis syndrome that emerged after our driving trips to Toronto and from New York City. She even tried Yin Yang Touch on her bedridden older brother in the Philippines and was amazed at its results. I cannot thank her enough for the many ways she supports me in my process of becoming a therapist and I want to thank her especially for proofreading this book and for taking many of the massage pictures in the book.

Next to my wife, my children, grandchildren, relatives and family friends had been my willing and quasi–willing subjects for my class assignments. Most of them found time for me to practice on them. Some of them yielded to my constant reminder that "it is time for a massage" in the days when I had to fulfill my quota of massages. The grandchildren had their massages while they were babies and two of them became caring therapists when they were seven and five! The unique role of my niece Angela (not her real name) in the case study of fibromyalgia is indelible. Without her initial interest and continuing cooperation, I doubt that I would have embarked on the road of massage research. I thank them all for their contribution to my new career.

In my professional development as a massage therapist, I am indebted to Jennifer Sovine and Heidi Peña-Moog, outstanding teachers at Northern Virginia Community College (NOVA), for their initial and abiding faith in my healing potential. Despite their hectic schedules, Sovine found time to discuss my ideas and expanded them for better connection between theory and practice, and Peña-Moog gave me opportunities to work with her and provided valuable feedback on my touch and tableside manners. I had enjoyed my status as the most *senior* student in their classes at NOVA.

Other instructors and former classmates at NOVA have also been my cheerleaders. Many of them led me to believe that I could be a professional therapist even in the days when I could not locate C7 and my draping technique was clumsy. Self-fulfilling prophecy still works!

I am grateful to: Huang Fengqin of the Chinese Medicine Clinic in Guangzhou who trusted my massage method and encouraged me to follow my gentler way; Betty Chen, also of Guangzhou, who spent many hours to discuss and practice Yin Yang Touch with me and shared her learning of Guangzhou Motion; Sharon Fussell of Solace Clinical Massage, who provided me a professional base for doing massage research and allowed me to partner with her in promoting massage therapy, and Philip Javier-Wong for taking some of the pictures in this book.

Shortly after my graduation from NOVA, I was blessed with knowing Leslie A. Young, Editor-in-Chief of *Massage & Bodywork*. The foreword she wrote for this book speaks volume of her caring and supportive personality and her outreach to an unknown in the profession. I stand in the shadow of her generosity.

Elizabeth Javier-Wong, the mother of Caroline (the youngest of my grandchildren) is an astute and meticulous editor. Just as she did for my book *A Chinese from Singapore*, she devoted many hours reading and editing this book, asking penetrating questions to make it more intelligible. She honored me by asking for pre- and post-natal massages. She gave this book its gestation massage. The trade was definitely in my favor.

I am indebted to: Nancy Crippen for securing a grant for doing case studies on fibromyalgia; Deanna McBroom for helping to write Chinese sounds as English words; Timothy Sovine for designing the poster on using massage to treat fibromyalgia; and several friends for reading different chapters and sections of this book and making valuable suggestions for clarification. I am grateful to the Kuang Jianhong family in Guangzhou for hosting me when I studied tuina in China. Due to privacy issues, I have used pseudonyms or just first names for many of the people I worked or studied with in various projects and classes, but my appreciation for their contributions and camaraderie is real and full.

I appreciate the efficient management of the publication of this book by Xlibris. The staff Amanda Escano and Angelica Merlas have been most supportive and patient.

For permission to use their materials, I wish to thank: Angela for "What did Angela Think?" (Chapter 11), Associated Bodywork and Massage Professionals for "East Meets West: Yin Yang Touch," (Chapter 14), Rebecca Mayfield for her evaluation of the case study on fibromyalgia (Chapter 25), Guinevere Meyer for "sequence of massage," (Chapter 3), Deborah Wedemeyer for her account of a treatment process of using massage to treat fibromyalgia (Chapter 25), and Master Xue Anri for the use of "Eight Moves for Health," (Appendix 1).

In Part II of this book, especially Chapter 16, you will come across many Chinese words in Romanized forms. Before you read that section, you might read Appendices 2 to 4 for an overview of Chinese words to give you a feel of the language. As you read about pressure points, you might refer to Appendix 5 to get a feel for their locations on the body. After you read these appendices, you may find my *notes* on learning Chinese tuina much less confusing. In the text, I have italicized most of the Chinese words, except for "yin, yang, qi, tuina, anmo, sanjiao, Du and Ren" because through frequent use, they have become an integral part of my massage vocabulary.

When you feel tired from reading, you might do the Guangzhou Motion (Appendix 1) to get refreshed. When you wish to discuss your ideas on massage, you might send an email to drsamwong39@gmail.com. I would love to hear from you and to meet you in a research conference to compare notes.

An accomplished classmate remarked that I was her role model. That was compliment extraordinaire. I did not set out to be a role model, but I am glad to have become a massage therapist at age 70!

Prelude

Chapter 1

DESTINED TO BE A THERAPIST

Dumgwat (a Cantonese expression meaning "to pound the bones') was a leisure activity my aunt enjoyed, an activity for me to earn extra pocket money when I was eight or nine years old in Singapore. My aunt, single and in her late 50s, looked old to me. She led a sedentary life. Often after an evening meal, she would lie sideways on the floor of our apartment chatting with her friends, while I sat by her side to pound on her hip, thigh and lower leg with my small fists. After a few minutes, she would roll over, and I would continue to pound the other side until I asked whether she had had enough. The whole pounding lasted ten to fifteen minutes, but it seemed much longer. For all the tiring exercise, I probably got no more than a dollar. Not a lot of money, but enough for some delicious snacks. I don't recall who taught me how "to pound the bones," but I must have been a good service provider. Many of her friends wanted to have the same service. I made more money. Little did I know my training in bodywork had begun decades before I became a certified massage therapist or that I was a child prodigy in the practice!

In the interim, graduated from college, married and working for the U.S. Government (and I am skipping a big chunk of my life that was not directly related to my development as a massage therapist), I had opportunities traveling and vacationing in Asia, Europe and Africa, and I had massages in Japan, Korea, China, Hong Kong, Singapore, Malaysia, Thailand, the Philippines and Morocco. From these massages, I improved my massage skills. At home, I gave massages to my family members and they gave the same to me. I taught my three children, when they were little, massage games, and they became proficient in doing the "monkey pounds," "elephant walk," "tiger crawls," and a number of other games. To play their game, my wife and I had to pay according to their fee schedule; it was quite reasonable, I might add. As they grew up, they encouraged me to become a massage therapist, not without vested interest, of course!

My wife loves to regale our friends with the story of the most humorous massage experience I have had. Our family was returning home from the Philippines via Japan and I wanted to try the pampering massage Hotel Otani offered. We had a late appointment; 11:00 p.m. was the only time available. I bathed, wrapped in a fluffy bathrobe and anticipated the gentle touches of a petite, pretty-looking practitioner, whose picture was on the hotel brochure, to relieve the fatigue of travel. When the practitioner arrived, I had a minor shock. She was a stern-looking, small-framed, wrinkle-faced older woman. Clad in her kimono, she directed me with military precision to lie prone on the bed. She pummeled me, revealing she was a sumo wrestler disguised as a shiatsu practitioner! Paying for pain was not what I bargained for, but I did not speak Japanese to protest. I was certain she planted the sore spots on my back; I had pain there after her massage. My wife was chuckling at my predicament, mumbling that I should have listened about foregoing the massage. Thank goodness I survived. It was ordained that I was not meant to be a shiatsu master.

In contrast, the gentlest massage experience I had was by the edge of a hot spring pool in Los Baños in the Philippines. As I did not speak Tagalog, my wife arranged for a young Pinoy, lean and bony, to give me a massage. That was after an afternoon of soaking and bathing in the hot spring. With soft breezes drifting over me, I lay prone in public, clad in my swimming trunks, with my head turned toward the sloshing water, without a care in the world. Not far from me were my relatives and other massage clients, similarly on the ground, their chatters muted by the water and the breeze, being attended to by other Pinoys and Pinays. The gentle gliding of hands of rough texture on my back was a pleasant sensation. The young Pinoy, clad in baggy shorts, topless, began with pouring warm spring water over me and cleansed me with soap from neck to toes, and then began to knead the muscles on my shoulders, my back, my hands, my legs and my feet. After a few minutes, he poured warm water on me again. It was total relaxation and cleansing. My wife woke me up from the massage when it was time to go home. Except for my relatives, the hot spring was practically deserted by then.

In Hong Kong, I had my first experience of having practitioners walking on and scrubbing my back. In Bangkok, I discovered a new definition of body massage. In Korea, I had the whispering touch that sent chills down my spine. Ah, memories!

In just about every city my wife and I visited in Asia, I had offers of "extra services," or was told where to get them. Apparently, the practitioners had their defined scope of practice. The ones offering "extra services" were in the same building, but usually on a different floor from where we had our massage. Alas, I was not affluent enough to afford the extras. I did hear enough about them to affirm that the negative association between massage and "sex for sale" was well founded. Conversations with some of the practitioners helped me to understand why their peers engaged in extra services. They could make four or five times more money in less time than they made providing regular services! Sometimes, my informants would add a note of caution: the practitioners of "extra services" had backstage (underground) support and they were strictly for business. Caveat emptor!

<>

In the final years of my Government Service, between 1999 and 2003, I was stationed in Guangzhou, China working in the U.S. Agricultural Trade Office, under the U.S. Consulate. Among the most enjoyable aspects of my four-year tenure in China was my weekly massage. Shortly after my arrival, Maggie, the wife of a consular colleague, introduced me to the pleasure of facial and foot massage. She and her husband were frequent customers of a facial massage shop within walking distance from our residence and they enjoyed their experience. They also discovered foot massage at a teahouse a short taxi ride away, and they enjoyed their regular visits. Both facial and foot massage were refreshing and rejuvenating. Either one of them was the perfect antidote to a day of office work in a dusty city. It did not take me much time to become addicted to both. Like the TV commercial featuring L'Oréal hair products, I kept telling myself, "I'm worth it!"

When my wife joined me in China a few months later, I had already become a massage aficionado. She attained that rank in no time at all. We knew more massage establishments than Maggie and her husband! When consular colleagues and visitors wanted to know where they might get a good and inexpensive (or expensive) massage, they asked us. Wherever we traveled in China, we made it our business to seek out massage facilities for our enjoyment. Some massage operators were surprised that I brought my wife along. They did not know she was my bodyguard (pun intended)!

Practically all the massage facilities we visited in China had separate shower areas for men and women. A typical massage experience for men and women in Guangzhou begins with a shower and a change of underwear and wrap. You can opt for disposables too. In some facilities, men can have a body scrub after the shower, sit for a sweat in the sauna or soak in a whirlpool of steamy water. After the shower or whatever other post-shower activities in the men's room, you wear a pair of pajama tops and bottoms and adjourn to a lounge where both men and women (similarly clad) wait for the practitioners. In the lounge, you have the pleasure of having your ears cleaned, nails trimmed and upper shoulders pounded while sipping a cup of tea with pieces of fresh fruit. You can also order a snack of noodles or sweets. Would you believe Guangzhou was designated as a hardship post by the State Department?

When a practitioner is available, you are led to a communal room with four or six massage tables. There are partitions screening off clusters of tables. Sometimes you are led to a smaller room with only two tables. After you settle on the massage table, in either supine or prone position, the practitioner helps you remove your pajama top and cover you with a big towel. As Guangzhou is a humid city, the massage room is usually air-conditioned and chilly. You can ask for an extra towel to keep warm. I could predict how good a practitioner might be when she asked me if I needed an extra towel! The good ones always covered me with an extra towel.

Before the practitioner begins working on you, she usually asks which body area you need more work and what amount of pressure you prefer for the session. Sometimes she uses oil or baby powder with her initial work. At other times, she finishes the session with a rubdown using oil. You then return to the men's room to take another shower, to sweat again in the sauna or simply to change into street clothing. Each visit takes two or three hours. Our local friends, both men and women, usually continue to use their ubiquitous cell phones to conduct business while they are in the shower room, the lounge or the massage room. They have yet to learn how to really enjoy life!

In the early days, my wife and I usually shared the same massage room and I was her interpreter. As it was unusual for a couple to be in the same room, the practitioners were always curious about us. They wanted to find out about us and engaged me in conversation. That was anything but relaxing. Often I would grunt in short phrases to ward off further questions -- not polite, I knew. Sometimes I spiced up the uncommon situation by telling the practitioner that the woman in the same room with me was merely my traveling companion! That remark always made them want to know more details. I spin a fantastic story!

As my wife became more proficient in communication with the locals, she joined our women friends in their own room and I joined our men friends in our communal room. I had total relaxation without interruption. Both my wife and I usually had a companion with us because our local friends were ever conscious of our safety and wellbeing. On several occasions, we had six or more friends, men and women, in the same room, our massage tables right next to each other. It was like having a massage party!

Before the session, I would usually inform the practitioner that I could not hear well and therefore would not be talking to her during the session. Most of the time, she worked in silence and I snored on the massage table until it was time for me to turn over. My companions knew I wanted quiet and they seldom engaged me in conversation. However, some of them would banter with their attending practitioners all through the session. I heard despite being hard of hearing!

From the countless hours I was worked on and the conversations I had with massage technicians, I learned more about giving massage. While my manual skills were less than professional and my practice was infrequent, my wife thought I was becoming a proficient practitioner. She said that probably because she was getting free service. I had become a massage practitioner without a license.

<>

Upon returning from China in August 2003, we asked our friends about good massage facilities in our neighborhood, but they did not know of any. We visited spas occasionally, but the China experience had spoiled us. The infrequent visits to spas were like scratching an itch over socks -- not very satisfying. I don't remember how the idea came, but I thought of getting referrals for good practitioners from teachers of local massage schools. That meant I needed to attend massage schools. I entertained that idea when I retired in May 2004, but I did not follow through. I was then caught up with several other projects. My massage addiction was held in remission.

By 2010, the projects had run their courses. I had completed writing *A Chinese from Singapore*, essentially the story of an immigrant's life in the US; and *A Diplomat in Guangzhou*, an account of my China experience. I had terminated my language teaching and testing due to my hearing problem and I was no longer spending frequent time with my grandchildren. Travels, formerly a business necessity and arguably pleasurable, had become less interesting and more burdensome due to the post 9-11 security checks and the seemingly endless hours of waiting for transit in airport lounges. I refrained from travel unless I had to. Thus, I had more free time at home. My dormant massage addiction resurged to the foreground. I resumed my search for massage schools and found several in the Metro Washington area such as the Potomac Massage Training Institute and the Northern Virginia School of Therapeutic Massage, but the lump sum financial requirements were quite expensive. I recall one six-month training program requiring an upfront payment of almost $8,000 for tuition, plus other fees for certification. That was too steep for a hobby; I was not training for a new career.

In my continuing search, I came across the massage therapy program in Northern Virginia Community College. The College, known affectionately as NOVA in the community, is one of the schools in the Virginia Community College System. It has six campuses most of which are within easy driving distance from my house. The massage therapy program had classes at both the Springfield and Woodbridge campuses. I decided to apply for admission to the program at the Springfield campus because it is less than ten minutes from my house, and it did not require a lump sum payment upfront.

Chapter 2

BIOLOGY FOR A THERAPIST

Before I could enroll in the massage therapy program, I had to be admitted to the college. I applied online. I discovered that it was to be a re-application. My wife and I had attended a non-credit exercise class at the Annandale campus in 2004 and that attendance had established us as students of the community college. Thus, all I needed was to activate my old records. That was more difficult than applying from scratch because I did not remember what I had submitted before. Even though I intended to take only the three hands-on classes on massage, I had to apply for study in a certification program. Typically, the application called for information on prior educational attainment and other biographical information.

Whoever processed my application might be forgiven for questioning my sanity. I was then already 71 years old, had retired from 30-some years of work as a church worker, college teacher, and U.S. Government employee. I had completed my formal graduate training in Northwestern University 35 years before. Why did I want to study in a community college? The primary student population of a community college is high school graduates en route to a four-year college or involved in vocational training. I was much older and had already completed my career in life. Why would I want to become a massage therapist at age 70? In fact, that was exactly the question a young classmate in China asked me when I studied tuina there in 2013. Regardless of what they thought of my sanity, the college admitted me to "General Studies."

Actually, despite my involvement with other projects, I would have applied for training in massage therapy earlier but for the prerequisite of satisfactory completion of the course on Human Biology. That requirement had deterred me from moving forward. Natural science, regrettably, was not my strength in secondary school. I had difficulty in just about every branch of that field, be it physics, chemistry or biology. Human Biology was for me an insurmountable obstacle. I was certain I could never pass it. There was no use to try. So, I put off applying until I finished the projects on my to-do list and my inner voice increased its agitation asking: "What do you have to lose? So what if you fail? At least, you would know that you have tried! Dilly-dallying is unbecoming!" Ouch!

By that point in my life, my hearing had deteriorated. I had lost total hearing in my right ear and had retained partial hearing in my left ear. That was the primary reason why I quit teaching and quit being a tester of Chinese language, even though I enjoyed doing that immensely. I rationalized with myself that I could be excused for not trying to study a new subject since I could not hear well what's said in class. But NOVA foiled me. The Human Biology class was an online course of the Extended Learning Institute (ELI). I could take it in the privacy of my home, without classroom noises. Being able to hear well was not crucial to learning that subject. I could pace myself, study within a fairly flexible timetable, and fulfill the science requirement for the massage therapy program. I enrolled. The class roster showed it started with 20 students. I don't know if anyone dropped out.

Tools for Study

Just as I expected, the course was tough, but it was made easier through the outstanding guidance of Huey-Jane Liao, the online (and therefore invisible) instructor. She was a master in the use of computer technology and prompt in responding to inquiries. I had at least 13 individual email exchanges with her. The primary textbook we used was *Essentials of Human Anatomy and Physiology* (9th edition) by Elaine N. Marieb. As befits a college textbook, it has 592 pages and weighs 2.9 lbs.[1] In addition, I had to work with a companion study guide, a coloring workbook and a book on chemistry for biology students.[2] Liao led her students to a number of very useful online study tools, including the interactive CD that came with Marieb's textbook. Her course plan was clear and informative. She encouraged group discussions through the Discussion Board and gave good pointers on how to take exams.

In the first few months of 2010, I learned about life functions, survival needs, atoms, molecules, cells, tissues, organs, organ systems and organisms. I became acquainted with new terms and concepts such as homeostasis, adenosine triphosphate, cytoplasm, synovial joints, and resting membrane potential. Practically all of them were polysyllabic and tongue twisters. To talk biology, you don't say fingers; you need to specify whether you are referring to their bones or muscles, whether you mean metacarpals, phalanges, tendons of flexor digitorum profundis or tendons of extensor digitorum or whatever it is you want to talk about. Precision has a price!

I had fun coloring various body systems in the workbook and appreciated the simple skill of doing coloring and how it brought out salient features for clearer visual learning. I enjoyed the clinic exercises in the workbook. They made me apply what I learned in the lessons. However, the written practices of matching, answering questions, filling in the blanks, and providing definitions were as difficult as the textbook. As I was entirely on my own, even though NOVA had free tutoring, I often would look up the answers first and then figure out why the answers were what they were. I am sure my study method was not what Marieb had planned, but it helped me to "know" the answer. At its worst, I "force-connected" the question and answer. I knew all I needed was to get a passing grade to meet the admission requirements. I did not need to learn and understand everything in the textbook. And I still don't understand everything in that textbook, or any textbook I have used in the process of becoming a massage therapist. Re-reading the various textbooks is one of my continuing learning activities.

The online study tools gave me more drills. I did crossword puzzles, hangman, labeling, matching, true/false, and other games

---

[1]   Foolishly, I sold the textbook back to the college bookstore thinking that I would have no further use of it. I had to buy another one, a different edition, when I needed to refresh what I had learned.

[2]   *Introduction to Chemistry for Biology Students*, 9th Edition (2008), by George I. Sackheim.

for hours. What I did not understand in one exercise was sometimes resolved in one of the games. I had quite a few "aha" moments. I could not help but feel that if I had had the same repertoire of study tools when I was in secondary school, I would have been channeled into the study of science and medicine. What an interesting retrospect! Wishful thinking aside, I applied myself to the rigor of learning human biology. The discipline was probably more important than all the tools I had at my disposal. If learning new ideas was the way to stimulate the brain, I gave that amazing organ a thorough workout. I proved that old dogs could learn new tricks and skills acquired from one situation could be transferred to another. What it requires is time, patience and concentration!

Study Strategy

As I was a distance learning student, Liao did not really know who I was and what experiences I might have had in life; I was just another student. In one of her notes to me, she inquired if she might share with my fellow students what I wrote about how I studied for Chapters 3 and 4 so that they might benefit from my approach. She felt they might listen to their peer more readily than they would pay heed to what a teacher said. What she did not know, of course, was that I was hardly a peer to my fellow students. But, at the basic level, I was just like most of my classmates; much of what I had to learn was as novel to me as to them. Many of them had in fact an advantage over me in their memory power and their computer skill. I was slow and obsolete; how could I be their peer? Nonetheless, I agreed to share my study strategy.

* * * * *

At the beginning of my distance learning, I had discovered my learning style relied more on visual and tactile rather than auditory skill. Since most of the technical terms were new to me, I decided to familiarize myself with them by writing them down in a notebook. That was using visual and tactile skills. It also helped me to remember the terms a bit better.

I found the section on "anatomy of a generalized cell" more difficult than the other sections and I read it several times. As suggested by Dr. Liao and the study guide, I read through each figure as carefully as I could and tried to visualize how they look in my mind. The most vivid ones were the various phases of mitosis and cytokinesis; I almost could see the movement of the different organelles.

Instead of trying to digest the whole chapter, I went at it section by section, tested myself after each section and proceeded with the next section only after I was satisfied I knew the subject reasonably well. All the materials in the study guide were useful. The self-tests and quizzes also helped me to catch points I missed in reading the text or class notes.

I do not recall any prior experience that helped me understand the subject of cells, tissues, skin and body membranes. However, the recent illness of a friend's daughter made me understand better the role of dehydration in a child's overall health. From the child's symptoms (dry lips, sunken eyes, loss of appetite, and drowsiness), I felt she was showing the signs of "viral enteritis," as described in the case study in the coloring book. I even wrote my friend about my understanding of how the virus worked and concluded that the virus had to run its course. As the child was under medical care, I was not playing doctor in any sense. I felt better for "understanding" the condition, even though I received no payment for my "diagnosis."

* * * * *

Among the requirements of the course was the completion of exercises in the study guide designed by the program head of the biology department. Working through the exercises was like listening to the more important points of a lecture that the instructor was drawing out. Following my practice of "using diligence to overcome slow learning," I worked through every problem in the guide. I learned the subject well and was quite turned on by the new knowledge. I did not realize the human body could be such a fascinating subject! It did not bother me that I took an inordinate amount of time to grasp the essential points of a lesson. I did not have to keep up with my classmates. Neither did I have to listen to the chatters of discussion that I did not understand because I could not hear what was said. All I had to do was to keep up with the course demand. Periodically, I went to the test center of NOVA in Springfield to take the required tests and I passed all of them.

Perhaps the most satisfying experience in that course was my exchange with Liao about answers in the companion study guide. Sometimes, they were different from what I worked out. I double- and triple-checked the process and the product and concluded each time that the guide had the wrong answers! Without exception, Liao did not comment on whether the study guide was right or wrong. She simply informed me my answers were correct and gave me extra credit for pointing out the discrepancy.

Low Back Pain

One of the course requirements was to write about a medical condition of our choice. I chose "low back pain" to bridge the biology course with the introductory course on massage therapy and I wrote about the experience of my friends, Tom, Sara and Dennis.

* * * * *

Tom had just moved from Geneva back to the United States. Before he was to take up his new assignment, he requested sick leave. He reported he probably overused his back muscles while packing and supervising the shipment of his household effects. His condition was so severe that he had to get cortisone shots and was ordered to take bed rest for a couple of weeks. Sara had been working long hours in her computer security job since she moved to a new office a year ago. In the last few weeks, she complained of having headaches and low back pain, and her sleep was frequently interrupted by back pain as she rolled in bed. She tried to take dancing to exercise her muscles, but the stress of learning a new skill had worsened her back problem. Dennis had been taking classes in the evening while holding down a full-time job. In the recent snow days, he had been shoveling the sidewalk in front of his house. It was after one of the more labor-intensive exercises that he complained about tight muscles in his back. He seemed to have lost his spontaneous joviality.

These three friends experienced a medical condition that affects up to 85% of Americans[3] and is estimated to cost between $25 billion to $50 billion annually in the United States.[4] Low back pain is centered in the lumbar region on the posterior side of the body. While the focus of the problem is the muscular system, the integumentary system, the skeletal system and the nervous system are directly affected and the

---

3   *Prevention*, January 2010.
4   *C Health*, January 23, 2010, "Low Back Pain."

other organ systems of the human body are indirectly affected.[5] Pain, as the Merck Manual of Medical Information states, "is an unpleasant sensation signaling that the body is damaged or threatened with an injury."[6] In the parlance of Human Biology, lower back pain is a condition of homeostatic imbalance. It can be the result of unusual exertion on the musculoskeletal system such as house-moving, working in a sedentary environment with your eyes glued to the computer screen without regard to your sitting posture, or doing several demanding tasks concurrently, thereby adding stress to the support structure of the body, creating a psychosomatic condition.

In a typical situation of homeostatic imbalance in the low back, the sensory receptors in the lumbar region receive the electrical impulses signaling something is misaligned. The impulses pass through the nerves in the spinal cord to the brain for corrective action. The brain fires off a number of immediate responses, ranging from getting the sufferer to support his lumbar vertebrae with his hands (almost a reflex action) or to stretch his whole spinal column to relieve the pressure on the vertebrae, to getting home remedies such as taking aspirin or Advil or putting heat pad and medicated ointment on the sore spot, and to getting professional evaluation and treatment. These measures are using different forms of energy – mechanical, chemical, electrical and radiant – to alleviate the "unpleasant sensation" and to restore the internal environment of the human body to homeostasis. The sufferer will be able to ease up on over-compensation for the pain, such as favoring some parts of his body, and to move his lower back more freely, gradually regaining a sense of wellness. However, the effect might be short-lived.

One of the more effective, drug-free, ways to alleviate low back pain is the use of acupuncture to stimulate the nerve endings in various pressure points in the human body.[7] Another effective way is the practice of Yoga.[8] And a third way is the use of therapeutic massage.[9] Apparently, acupuncture works on the nervous system to release the congestion in muscles and nerves and excite the nervous network for efficient circulation of the "innate force of healing." Yoga stretches the muscles and bones to release the muscle-bone adhesion

---

[5]   *MedicineNet.com*, "Lower Back Pain."

[6]   *Merck Manual of Medical Information,* Home Edition (1997), Chapter 61, "Pain."

[7]   Reported in *American Journal of Nursing*, October 2009.

[8]   *Harvard Women's Health Watch*, November 2009.

[9]   *The Journal of Family Practice*, September 2001.

for an unimpeded flow of essential nutrients. And, therapeutic massage improves tissue pliability by reducing fascia adhesion and thereby increasing blood and lymph circulation.

Once the human body is restored to its homeostatic condition, it will gradually slip back into imbalance again unless the sufferer deals with the root cause of the problem, which is the adhesion of the fascia and the muscles in the lumbar region and the squeezing out of breathing space between the vertebrae.

The muscles and vertebrae of the lumbar region are like a suspension bridge without the suspension cables and the anchors on the terminus of the bridge. It is a flesh and blood object wrapped in fascia and suspended in space, working against the downward pull of gravity. As the lumbar region is in the inferior region of the human body, the lumbar vertebrae, the fascia and the muscles in the abdomino-pelvic cavity are involved in providing support to all the organs superior to the region as well as the small and large intestines in the abdominal region. This support structure "carries" every organ superior to the pelvic girdle.

For this movable support structure to maintain its optimal pliability, it has to be in shape, the vertebrae are stacked just right and the muscles are layered with sufficient breathing space for blood and lymph circulation. The steps to keep the structure in shape are relatively simple. They include drinking sufficient amount of water, doing aerobic and isometric exercises (with special attention to strengthening and loosening the muscles of the lumbar region), having a proper diet, and taking sufficient rest. In addition, one must cultivate a sensible lifestyle to ensure all the other organ systems are functioning optimally so that they do not add undue burden on the movable support structure. One needs to tune up the whole body to prevent the recurrence of low back pain.

* * * * *

The paper was completed before I had more exposure to the study of human body in my massage classes. What I wrote then I did not have to retract or amend in subsequent semesters.

With dogged efforts and attention to details, I completed the course on Human Biology, glad that I did not have to repeat it. I was totally and delightfully surprised on September 1, 2010 when I received a letter from ELI that I had been selected to receive a scholarship and that I was nominated by my ELI instructor "who felt [I] had done exceptional work." If Liao was surprised by the appearance of a senior citizen at the award ceremony, she did not show it.

Chapter 3

INTRODUCTION TO MASSAGE

Another prerequisite for enrollment in the massage therapy program was completion of the one-credit introductory course on massage. I enrolled in it in the same semester I studied human biology. The course was available at the Springfield campus, taught by Guinevere Meyer, a therapist active in the massage profession. It met once a week for six weeks in early 2010 and it required in-person attendance. There were six or seven students in that class. We were expected to miss no more than one class session; otherwise, we would be "administratively withdrawn" (expelled) from the class. We had three tests (no make-up) and one final exam.

Tappan's Handbook

I had no problem reading and understanding the textbook, *Tappan's Handbook of Healing Massage Techniques*, by Patricia Benjamin or hearing what Meyer said in class. She covered essentially what was in the textbook and the handouts she distributed.

The class began with an introduction to the skeletal system of the human body -- how bones were connected to each other. The rest of the short course (made shorter by cancellation of one session because of inclement weather) was devoted to reviewing the first seven chapters in *Tappan's Handbook*. We learned about the history of massage, its effects, benefits and clinical applications, the endangerment sites, contraindications and cautions and the guidelines for giving massage. We also discussed professional boundaries and ethics. The focus of the class was basic Western massage techniques.

Meyer began each session with a quick test, followed by a review of what we had read (what Benjamin designed as "Memory Workout") and the quiz in the textbook. My classmates and I took turns to answer the questions. I later found out that mastery of the key terms in Tappan's book was useful for taking the test of the National Certification Board for Therapeutic Massage and Bodywork (NCBTMB).

Meyer's Sequence for Swedish Massage

We learned how to set up the massage table and how to do draping. In addition to the massage sequence in Tappan's, Meyer shared her own "Sequence for Swedish massage." It included neck and shoulders, arms and hands, front of the legs and feet, back of the legs, and back. It was a scaled down version of a full body massage. The neck and shoulders sequence,[10] which I still follow these days, includes:

- *Recipient supine (face up)*
- *Place bolster/pillow under recipient's knees*
- *Sit/stand behind recipient's head*
- *Spread cream on hands*
- *Scoop under neck and apply sweeping motion from base of neck to skull – repeat for several minutes*
- *Turn head to the left – cradle skull in palm of hand and assist head turn with other hand*
- *Stretch neck – one hand on base of skull, other hand on shoulder*
- *Use repetitive strokes from base of neck at shoulders to base of skull – use firm traction on these strokes – repeat several minutes*
- *Return head to neutral. Turn head to other side*
- *Repeat steps 6, 7, and 8.*

---

[10]   Used with permission.

I also follow quite closely her sequence for arms and hands:

- *Spread more cream on hands and apply to recipient from shoulder to hand*
- *Holding hand at wrist, perform several effleurage strokes along the entire length of arm from hand to shoulder*
- *Hold wrist and apply stretch to side of neck*
- *With sweeping motion, extend arm overhead and scoop under the lumbar section of the back to stretch the torso – bring arm back to neutral*
- *Place both hands on shoulder – one anterior and one posterior – rock and rotate the shoulder*
- *Proceed from shoulder down to the hand with a combination of effleurage, petrissage and tapotement*
- *Proceed from the wrist down the hand, spreading bones of the hand. Corkscrew massage of the fingers from distal to proximal*
- *Turn hand over and interlace your fingers with those of the recipient. Apply pressure on back of recipient's hand spreading the palm*
- *Complete the arm by applying several effleurage strokes along the entire length of the arm from shoulder to hand*
- *Repeat with other arm*

The other sequences were outlined in detail, similar to the ones for neck and shoulders and arms and hands. I practiced them on my wife and my children and tried to remember them as much as I could. Initially, I kept the handouts right by the massage table as I worked on my "clients," but I was able to remember the routines by the end of the short course. Practices form habit!

Sports Massage

In addition to class attendance, tests and exam, we were required to have a professional massage in a modality that we had no prior experience. I had tried many forms of massage but not sports massage, and so I asked Meyers for a referral. She suggested Jane Taylor (not her real name), a therapist with extensive experience in sports massage. The following is what I wrote about the experience.

* * * * *

Sports massage is "the science and art of applying massage and related techniques to maintain the health of the athlete and to enhance athletic performance."[11] It is event specific and it involves the pre-event, event and post-event phases. In the pre-event phase, sports massage may involve tuning up the body for the wear and tear of the upcoming strenuous competition. It serves primarily as a warm up and preventive function. In the event phase, sports massage is focused on accelerated recovery. In the post-event phase, sports massage involves helping the muscles to recover and, as necessary, to rehabilitate them from injuries.[12] It is an intervention. All three phases, with varying intensity, are applicable for athletes and physical fitness enthusiasts.

The primary purposes of sports massage are to help an athlete get in shape faster, with less stiffness and soreness, to recover faster from heavy workout, and to relieve conditions that may cause injury. It counteracts the tearing effects of exercise and enhances muscle recovery and rebuilding.[13] Athletes should use general massage for overall conditioning and sports massage for special treatments.

A sports massage therapist uses the full range of Swedish massage techniques to work with athletes. However, stretching to increase muscle pliability and joint movement and deep pressure to focus on treating trigger points are applied more often in sports massage than general massage. Also, sports massage therapists generally work on isolated muscles or muscle groups, with particular attention to the sports an athlete is engaged in.[14]

I had my massage session in Jane's massage studio, which was in the basement of her home. It appeared that the studio, dimly lit but warm and ventilated, was set aside solely for massage. It was saturated with soft instrumental music from a television set (sound only, no picture). The massage table was in the center of the studio. It was covered with a sheet and a blanket. Directly on top of the massage table was a heating pad with adjustable temperature control. In one corner of the studio was a side-table on which were several bottles of massage cream. A bathroom was close by the studio.

---

[11]   Tappan's *Handbook of Healing Massage Techniques* (2010) by Patricia J. Benjamin, p. 440.
[12]   The way I treat sports massage is different from Patricia Benjamin's scheme.
[13]   See *Holisticonline.com*, "Sports Massage."
[14]   From a conversation with Jane Taylor. Also, see *Holisticonline.com*, "Sports Massage."

After a review of my health history, prior massage experience and a general overview of sports massage's expected effects, Jane excused herself for me to get ready. I disrobed and settled under the top sheet/blanket, lying supine as instructed. Upon her return and after washing her hands, Jane began working on my feet, first the left and then the right, focused on the ankle region. She alternated using effleurage and petrissage to massage the plantar and dorsal areas of both feet. She also used stripping on the metatarsals.

She covered my feet after the massage and moved on to working on the cervical lumbar, the occipital, and the trapezius regions. Her main techniques were effleurage and direct pressure. She used passive touch to complete working on that area. She next worked on my legs, first the left and then the right. She draped me snugly before she began working on the tibia region and then the femur region. Her techniques were mainly effleurage and frictions, and I sensed that she used cross friction on the femur region. If my sense was correct, Jane was standing on the left side of my body while she worked on my right femur region. That seemed to be an effective use of body mechanics.

Jane then created a tent for me to roll over to a prone position. I rested my face in the head cradle. She worked on the posterior area of my legs and the gluteal region, using broad effleurage and petrissage strokes mainly, but she added pressure at various points. After she completed working on the legs and re-draped them, she bent them one at a time toward the inguinal region to stretch the adductor muscles and then she did touch-without-movement on my hip and ankle for a few seconds.

After that Jane worked on my back. Her initial focus was on the trapezius region. She used direct pressure along the edges of both scapulae and stayed at different spots for several seconds. She also used direct pressure on the muscles parallel to the spinal column. She completed the back massage with passive touch and asked me to roll over again.

After I resettled in the supine position, Jane reached under my back to work on my trapezius, cervical, and occipital regions again, with effleurage and deep pressure. She then worked on my arms and hands, using effleurage, petrissage, frictions and joint movement. I particularly enjoyed the thumb friction on my palms. When that segment was over, she put her hands on my head and rested there for a few minutes. And the session was over.

Jane was cordial, friendly, confident, and relaxed. Her whole demeanor was professional and helpful. Her hands-on expressions (what she did with her hands) made me feel thoroughly comfortable. She consistently warmed the massage cream before she applied it on me and her massage pace was steady and unhurried. I trusted her expertise and my massage experience proved I was right. She did not seem to mind my asking her a lot of questions for clarification.

I took sports massage primarily to fulfill a classroom assignment. However, I felt my body was in a more relaxed mode and some of the knots in my muscles and low back were less tight after the treatment. I expected the massage would make me feel good and it did. Due perhaps to the nature of my assignment, Jane did not use tapotement on me, and I did not pick up if she used vibrations in the session.

It seems to me sports massage is more rigorous than general Swedish massage, but not as gymnastic as Thai massage. The deep pressure applied by Jane was not as deep or painful as shiatsu pressure or as pinpoint needling as acupuncture therapy. The whole session took an hour and a half, but the table time was 60 minutes.

* * * * *

Moving Ahead

As I did not know what to expect from the introductory class, I felt what we covered was adequate. More than a year later, when I had the opportunity to observe a similar class being taught at the Woodbridge campus and to have "trades" with my classmates, I realized that I did not learn some of the strokes my Woodbridge classmates used on me, nor the seated (chair) massage. I re-read Tappan's, practiced what I could, and consciously imitated what my classmates showed me unintentionally. Learning from my classmates was one reason why I wanted to trade with as many classmates as I could in my other massage classes. They were my reliable critics and teachers in disguise.

When the introductory class was about to end, I had an overview of the placement and program requirements of the massage therapy program at NOVA with Meyer. Placement requirements and program requirements were not the same. I met or could meet all of the placement requirements: on admissions, I had already been admitted to NOVA; on minimum age, I was 18 years of age or older; on completion of pre-requisite courses with passing grades, I was completing Introduction to Massage Therapy and Human Biology satisfactorily; on English proficiency, I could qualify for waiver of College Composition; on health condition, I could provide evidence of good physical and mental health; on legal background, I had no problem to disclose fully my law-abiding status; and on attendance at an orientation session, I was ready.

As I was not planning to become a massage therapist, I paid little or no attention to program requirements other than the three theoretical and practical courses dealing with therapeutic massage. I did not plan to enroll in courses on cardiopulmonary resuscitation, interpersonal communication, coordinated internship, concepts of disease, lifetime fitness and wellness, and entrepreneurship for massage therapist. I discussed my interest in taking only massage classes with Meyer and she allowed me to register for Massage I, anatomy and Swedish massage, in the following semester, Summer 2010.

Images

Picture 1. Fire Therapy (Chapter 5).

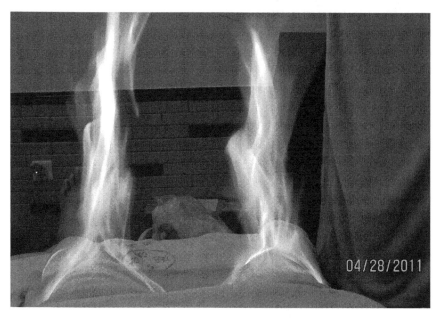

Picture 2. Fire Therapy (Chapter 5).

Picture 3. The Virginian Stretch (Chapter 8).

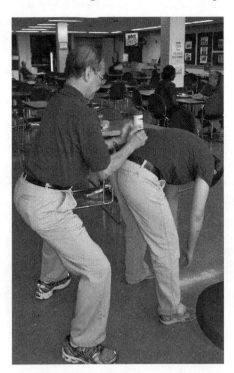

Picture 4. The Virginian Stretch (Chapter 8).

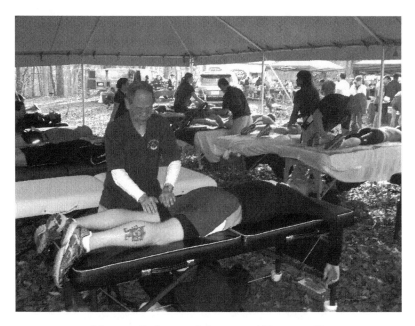

Picture 5. Sports Massage (Chapter 8).

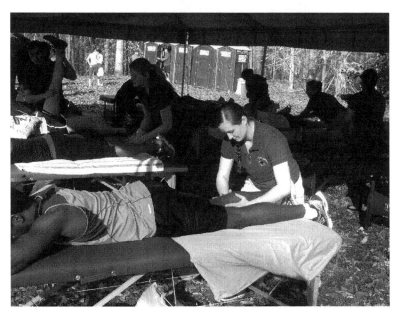

Picture 6. Sports Massage (Chapter 8).

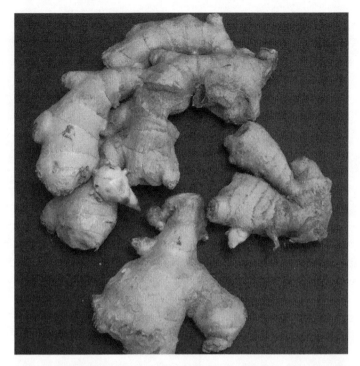

Picture 7. Ginger for Fibromyalgia Treatment (Chapter 11).

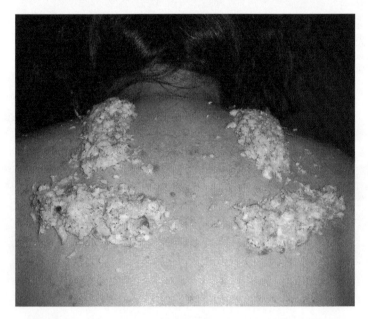

Picture 8. Fibromyalgia Treatment (Chapter 11).

Picture 9. Yin Yang Touch (Chapter 14). Yin on Yang.

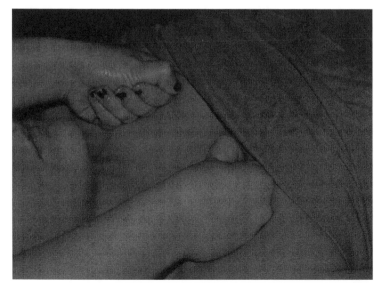

Picture 10. Yin Yang Touch (Chapter 14). Yang on Yin.

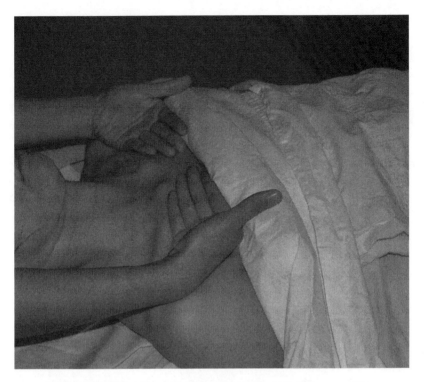

Picture 11. Yin Yang Touch (Chapter 14). Yang on Yin.

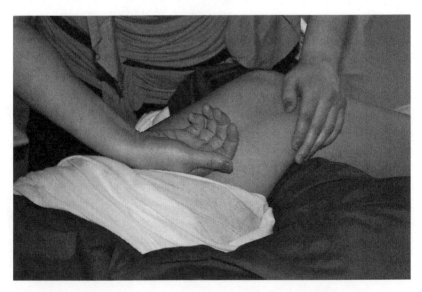

Picture 12. Yin Yang Touch (Chapter 14). Yang on Yin.

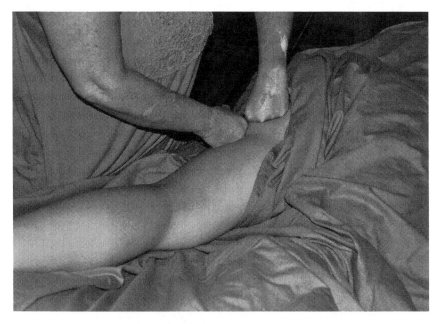

Picture 13. Yin Yang Touch (Chapter 14). Yang on Yin.

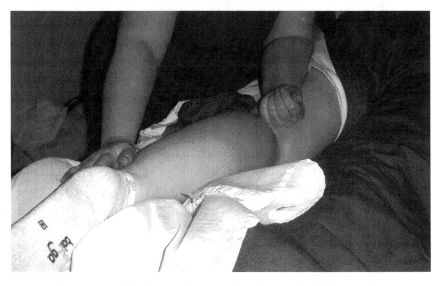

Picture 14. Yin Yang Touch (Chapter 14). Yang on Yin.

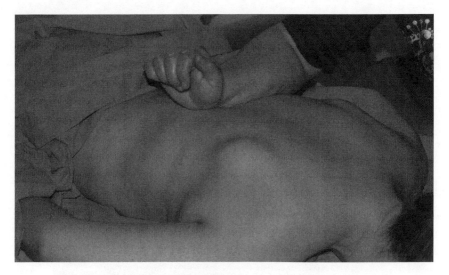

Picture 15. Yin Yang Touch (Chapter 14). Yin on Yang.

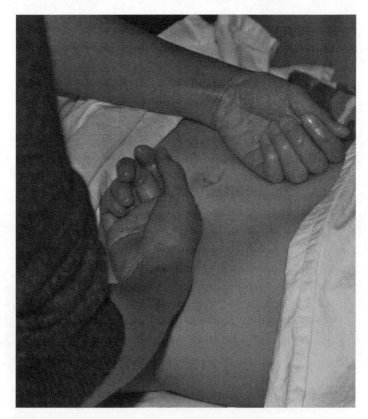

Picture 16. Yin Yang Touch (Chapter 14). Yang on Yin.

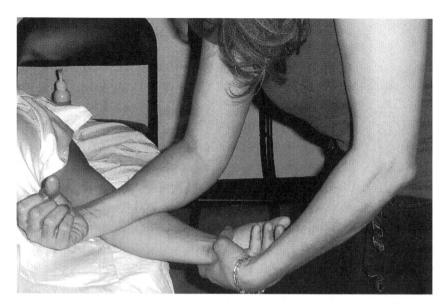

Picture 17. Yin Yang Touch (Chapter 14). Yang on Yin.

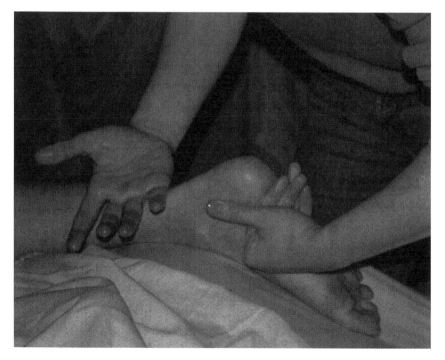

Picture 18. Yin Yang Touch (Chapter 14). Yang on Yin.

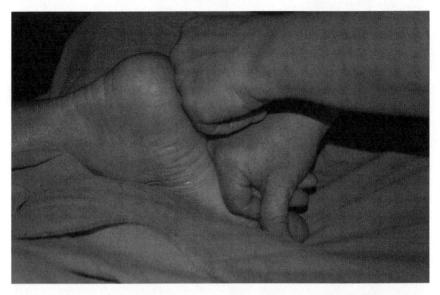

Picture 19. Yin Yang Touch (Chapter 14). Yang on Yin.

Picture 20. Yin Yang Touch (Chapter 14). Yang on Yin.

Picture 21. *Huangdi Neijing* (Chapter 14).

Picture 22. Chinese Textbook (Chapter 15).

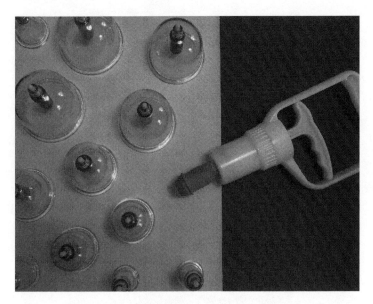

Picture 23. Cupping tools (Chapter 18).

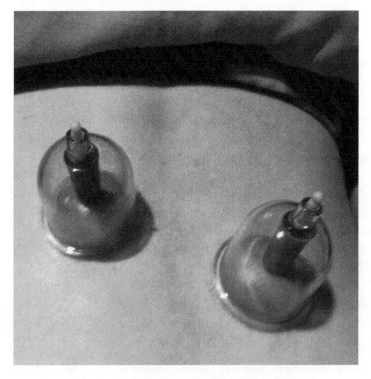

Picture 24. Cupping (Chapter 18).

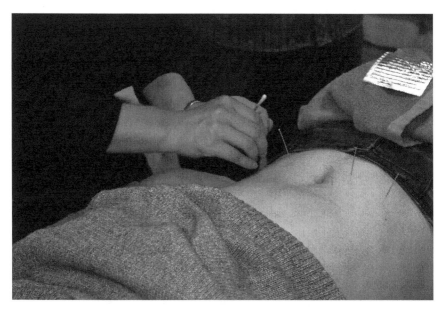

Picture 25. Acupuncture (Chapter 18).

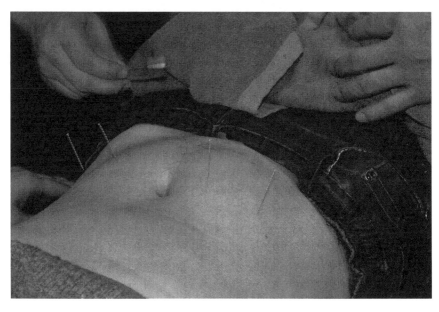

Picture 26. Acupuncture (Chapter 18).

Picture 27. Guasha tools (Chapter 18).

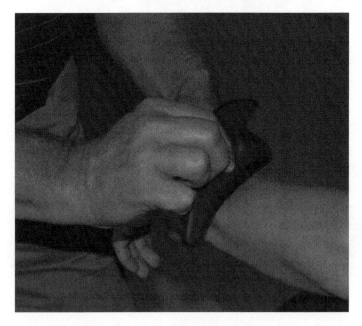

Picture 28. Guasha (Chapter 18).

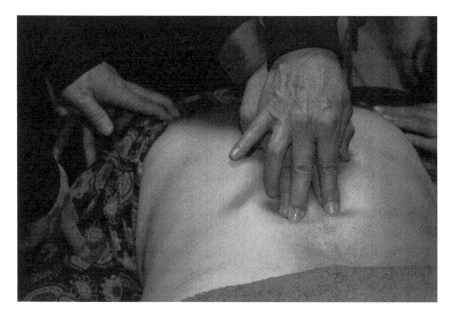

Picture 29. Spinal Tuina (Chapter 18).

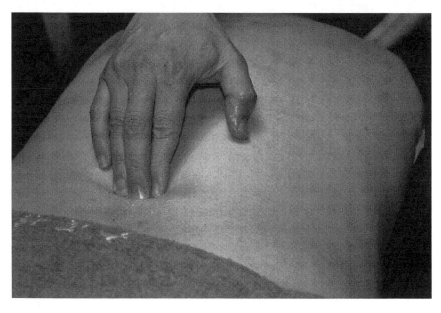

Picture 30. Spinal Tuina (Chapter 18).

Picture 31. Certificate of Completion (Chapter 20)

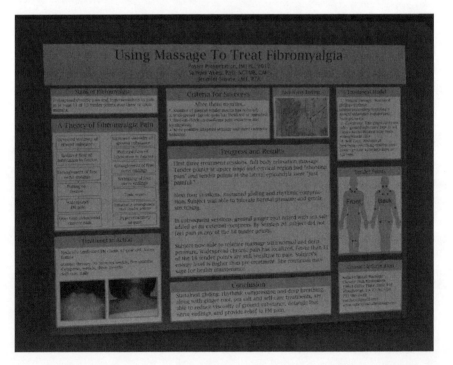

Picture 32. Poster for the Boston Conference (Chapter 24).

Picture 33. With Jeanette Ezzo at the
Boston Conference (Chapter 24).

Picture 34. With Leslie Young at the Boston
Conference (Foreword & Chapter 24).

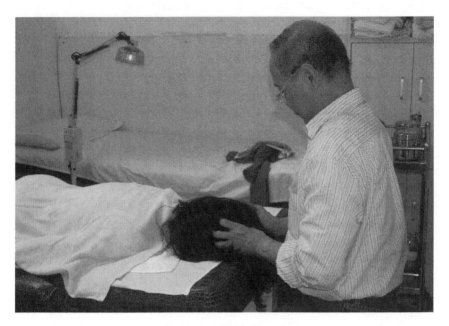
Picture 35. Head massage.

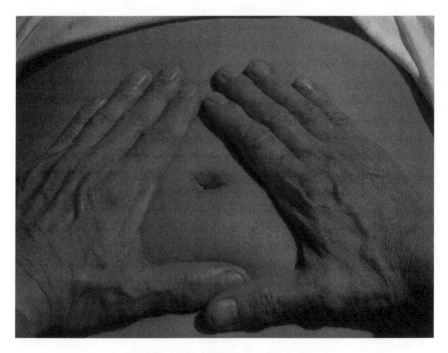
Picture 36. Abdomen massage.

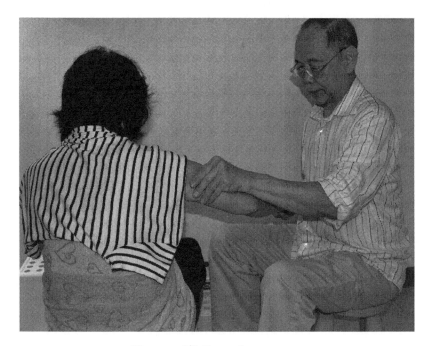

Picture 37. Seated massage.

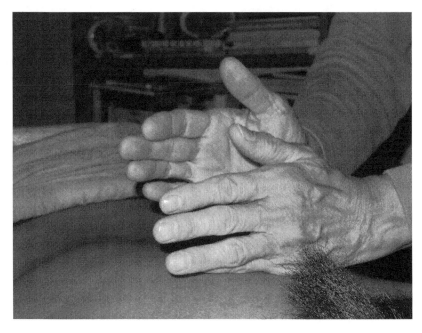

Picture 38. Tapotement.

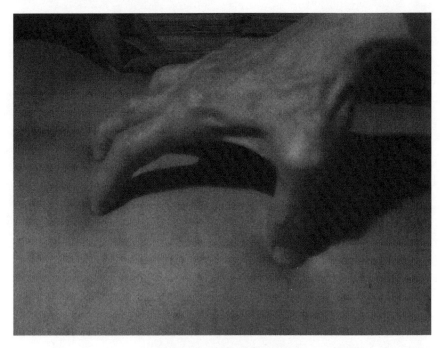

Picture 39. Vibration.

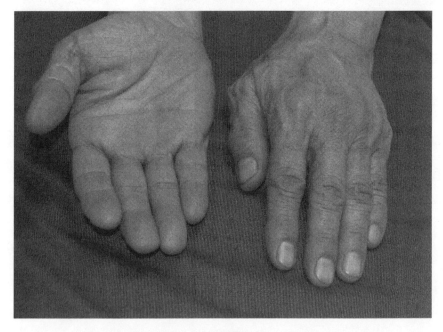

Picture 40. The Yin Yang Touch trademark.

Part I

TRAINING IN THE UNITED STATES

Chapter 4

ANATOMY AND SWEDISH MASSAGE

Inauspicious Beginning

Therapeutic Massage I, the first course in the massage curriculum, was on anatomy and Swedish massage. My instructor was Connie Doyle. The classroom had six or eight massage tables that doubled as study desks. Each table had two chairs or stools underneath it. A partition screen, situated diagonally across from the raised AV projection platform, provided privacy for students to undress for hands-on practice, but my classmates and I had made no use of it. When one of us needed to undress for in-class practice, the rest of the class excused themselves and waited outside. Facing the massage tables and stools was a desk and a chair, typical classroom furniture, to which the instructor could anchor her activities. Charts of human anatomy were posted on the walls and a broken model of a human skeleton was hung lopsidedly in one corner of the classroom. The room could comfortably accommodate 12-16 students, but the class I attended had only four: Lisa, Emily, Sean and me, two women and two men. Too bad we were few because Doyle had prepared an elaborate course plan.

On the first day, I was the first one to arrive and Doyle was already seated in the classroom engrossed in reading a textbook. After I introduced myself, I had a conversation with Doyle about why I was interested in learning massage. She was probably annoyed that the first student to show up was an older man not really interested in becoming a massage therapist! She told me the class might be canceled because of low enrollment. I don't recall if my future classmates were present that day, but instead of waiting for the school to confirm whether the class would be canceled, I contacted the administrative office the next day. Someone by the name Joanne told me that the class would indeed be canceled. Thus, I withdrew from it. However, a couple of days later, Joanne telephoned me that the class was being offered as scheduled and asked if I would be interested in re-registering for it. I did and reported for class the next week, but the school had yet to resolve some administrative issues. Finally, on June 10, four weeks after the starting date, Doyle confirmed that NOVA had decided the class would continue regardless of its size. That meant we were behind in our contact hours and we needed to make up for lost time. She told us to bring to class our work schedules for the months of June and July so that we could schedule extra sessions. The intent of extra sessions was good, but they preempted my personal study time, making it more difficult for me to digest and integrate the mass of materials. Early in that semester, I became mentally fatigued with information overload.

We had three textbooks for that course: Andrew Biel's *Trail Guide to the Body*, Patricia Benjamin's *Tappan's Handbook*, and Lauriann Greene's *Save Your Hands*, but Doyle was teaching primarily from *Graf's Anatomy*. Biel's *Trail Guide* had a student handbook that was as dense as the textbook itself. The handbook, I discovered early in the classroom experience, was the source of many of Doyle's quizzes, and I focused on working through the handbook, just as I worked on the study guide for Human Biology. Often, I used the "find the answer first" method, but the new information kept eluding me.

Novice's Anxiety

When I had the first quiz in that class, I discovered all the questions knew me and I understood what they wanted from me, but I could not give them the right answers. The first quiz had 20 questions on identifying structures and 24 multiple-choice questions. I recognized gastrocnemius, calcaneal tendon, plantaris, popliteus, soleus, and other muscles of leg and foot, but I did not remember their names. I recognized most of the options in the multiple-choice section, but I could not decide which one matched what was asked. The guesswork I did in the first quiz produced dismal results.

In the next quiz, I was fully prepared to differentiate tibialis anterior from peroneus brevis, and hamstrings from quadriceps, and I was confident about the different shapes of muscle bellies, be they convergent, biceps, fusiform, unipennate, bipennate or multibelly, but Doyle gave 13 multiple-choice questions on pelvis and thigh. My brain by then had a cacophony of names such as coxal and sacroiliac joints, vastus lateralis, and tibial tuberosity, names I knew in Human Biology, but what I knew would not connect with what's on the quiz. The random matching brought another disappointment.

When I sat for the first two quizzes, I was aware my hands were icy cold. That was an unmistakable sign of stress. All through my academic life, I had never been good at taking tests. At age 70, I still suffered from test anxiety. The evening before a quiz, I usually studied hard, well after midnight. I adapted the study tools I had used in the Human Biology class, but they did not help me to produce the right answers on demand. "Why are you putting yourself to this torture?" I asked myself. My wife asked the same question, but refrained from telling me what to do.

By the third week of the semester, the class had begun hands-on learning. The four of us rotated among ourselves, initially I worked with Emily, and later with Lisa and Sean. Our first hands-on lesson was not about how to massage but about how to drape a client for massage. Because full body massage involves some degrees of disrobing, draping is an essential skill to keep clients from being exposed unnecessarily. Clients are informed that "only the areas of the body being directly treated are uncovered at one time" in the consent statement for massage. Thus, we had to be scrupulous about draping. (I found out later in my other classes that every instructor was punctilious about draping.) I paid close attention to draping, but too fastidiously, according to Doyle. She insisted I did one-touch draping. The more I fussed with keeping the drape neat, she explained, the more uncomfortable my client would be. So, I practiced one-touch draping with Emily, Lisa and Sean, and repeated the process again and again. In actual practice, as I discovered months later, no one does one-touch draping!

Even though I had been married for 30-some years, raised three children, had had countless skin-on-skin contacts with people of diverse backgrounds, and had seen bodies in various stages of nakedness, I was still unprepared for touching another body or being touched for massage practice. Sean appeared nonchalant and wisecracked through the practice, and he allowed his body to be poked, probed and drawn on for locations of bones and muscles. Lisa was almost as "cool." Emily appeared as awkward and uneasy as I was. Her touch was as tentative and hesitant as mine, yet she told me my massage strokes were too fast and too mechanical. When Lisa and Sean worked on me, they would both tell me to relax, and the moment they said, "Relax," I tensed up further. (I have learned later in my practice that it is better for me to simply ask clients to breathe deeply instead of asking them to relax!) When I worked on Lisa and Sean, I could feel tension in my hands and shoulders, and my stomach would chime in with rumbling. As a sign of nervousness, I went through the motion of working on my classmates in tempo presto. Doyle would signal to me to slow down and start all over with tempo adagio. I tried, but I was back to tempo presto in no time.

To develop fluidity and strength in my strokes, Doyle showed me how to use the body to move the hands and coined the term "washer movement" to help me visualize how I might move my wrist as I massaged the leg. I thought of the warm up exercises I used to do in one of my many incomplete Taiji (Taichi) classes and adjusted my stance and strokes accordingly. She also coached me to work on one section of the body at a time and to use linkage strokes to transition from one section to the next. It was one-on-one instruction! As she observed my classroom practices, Doyle commented that I looked bored. She said I should enjoy giving massage instead of treating it as a class assignment to be completed as quickly as possible. What she did not realize was my anxiety! She also chided me for grabbing Emily's leg in the first in-class exchange I had with her. "Grabbing?" That was a comment I heard from my wife often enough in our everyday life and I had dismissed it as nonsense. Now that Doyle had made the same comment, I had to re-examine my assumption. I asked her to show me what she meant. I did not realize I had accumulated bad habits and was glad that massage therapy gave me a chance to reform myself!

Change of Status

The first course in massage was evidently too difficult for me. I had been out of practice as a classroom student for too many years and I could not handle the course demands, notwithstanding my successes with Human Biology and Introduction to Massage. The body landmarks were supposed to help me find muscles and tendons, but I had not found them even on my own body. The technical aspect of massage was so rigorous that all my joints ached from classroom exercise. "Does it make sense to do all the requirements or simply do what I could? How would I know I have learned the materials if I don't take the tests? How can I take the next class if I don't pass this one?" I discussed my dilemma with Doyle and decided to lift the pressure of test anxiety by switching from taking the course for credit to taking it for audit. I would still do all the class requirements, but the grades would no longer be a part of my academic record at NOVA. I would learn for the fun of learning!

Sometime before midterm, an incident happened in class practice that seemed to affirm the wisdom of switching my academic status from credit to audit. I was engrossed with working on Lisa when I felt Doyle tap my shoulder. "Sam, Lisa wants you to lighten up on your pressure," Doyle said. I obviously did not hear Lisa's request. She was lying in prone position and she was speaking to the floor. Doyle stood by the head of the massage table to watch me as I continued working. After a little while, she said to me again, "Sam, Lisa wants you to press harder on her QL." That was the second time I missed hearing what my massage partner wanted. I do not remember how many times Doyle relayed to me what Lisa wanted in that brief practice session, but I do remember asking myself, "If I cannot hear what a client wants in a massage session, how can I work as a therapist?"

I laughed at myself for imagining that I could pursue massage therapy as a new career. When I first enrolled for massage, I was interested in finding where my wife and I could get a good massage and the names of some good therapists in the area. I had already known where to find reliable and legitimate massage facilities and I had found three professional therapists and two budding practitioners. I should quit after I have accomplished my mission.

Unfortunately or fortunately, I was already hooked to massage therapy. The subject had become too interesting to give up. Biel's *Trail Guide* is right. The human body is like a landscape for one to explore. In fact, it is more alive and it has more surprises. In hands-on practices, I had worked on ten different bodies and I found the contours and textures of the bodies vastly different from each other and the movement beneath the skin amazing. Besides, massage therapy had become a form of exercise for me. I had a good work out with each massage I gave to my classmates or my family members. More importantly, the healing potential of massage that Doyle talked about in class, and Benjamin wrote about in her book, was appealing to me. I felt I should learn massage to serve the under-served populations, groups such as premature babies in hospitals or clients in hospice facilities.

I doubled my efforts to study Biel and Graf's, with endless writing and rewriting of the vocabulary of body parts. I moved glacially into the groove of test taking and paper writing. I tackled each assignment with patent perseverance. Whatever was unclear, I asked Doyle, Sean and Lisa. I had three teachers instead of one.

Professional Massages

In addition to classroom activities, my classmates and I were required to have two professional massages to fulfill the course requirements. The assignment confirmed my intuition from the beginning that you learn massage by getting massage! I gladly fulfilled the requirements by having massages at Pro Massage and Healing Massage (not their real names), two facilities in Northern Virginia.

* * * * *

Pro Massage looked clean and neat from the street and it was indeed clean, uncluttered, bright and cheerful inside. Its front area was laid out efficiently. The reception area was in the center. To the right was a waiting area where I filled out an intake form. To the left was a chair massage room. Soft instrumental music drifted from a central system. I heard it in the massage room and in the reception area.

An Indian-looking young woman managed the reception area and brought me to the massage room after I completed the intake form. As I was in the mood for indulgence, I opted for deep tissue and eye soothing treatments, and chose eucalyptus oil for the massage.

The massage room was furnished simply. In addition to the massage table in the center, a small cabinet was in one corner and a chair was placed diagonally across from it. Next to the chair on the wall was a small scenic picture. On top of the cabinet was a small warmer. A bolster lay by the cabinet.

I was introduced to a fresh-looking therapist. She was probably in her early 20s. After she confirmed my treatment selections, she excused herself. I undressed and lay supine under the sheets. The therapist began the session with putting the bolster under my knees, followed with effleurage over my head and neck muscles and my shoulders. Before she worked on my upper chest area, she put cool, cucumber-scented, patches on my eyes. That was a special treatment. She then did light effleurage over my body on top of the drape before she undraped me and worked on my chest. She continued with effleurage, petrissage and deep tissue on my anterior thighs and legs.

Before I turned over, the therapist removed the eye patches and did light friction in the temporal region. She then worked on my back, hands, posterior thighs, legs and feet. She used effleurage, petrissage, friction and compression in different areas of the body but not tapotement or vibration. Her hand pressure was firm and I enjoyed especially her work on my scapulae.

The whole session was invigorating. Perhaps, due to my request for muscle workout, most of the strokes of the therapist were brisk. Some of my back muscles were sore after the massage and I felt a little discomfort in the evening as I lay on my back, but they were all right the next day.

<>

Healing Massage was housed in the basement of a one-story building in an office complex. The therapist's name was Cathy, and she was probably in her late 40s. When she reviewed the intake form with me, she was particularly interested in my status as a massage therapy student. She was surprised that NOVA offered training in massage therapy.

The massage room was cozy. As one entered the room, on the left was a rocker, a wooden desk and a chair. It was at that location where Cathy and I reviewed the intake form. Across from the entrance was the exterior wall of the building. It was lined with bookshelves on which were bottles of essential oils, CDs, books and artifacts. Across from the interview area was another wall. It had a shelf-full of essential oils and massage cream, a hot towel cabinet, a filing cabinet and two floor lamps. To the right of the entrance were two closets. The massage table was in the middle of the room.

Cathy began the massage process by gliding along my left thigh and leg, then my right thigh and leg. She then worked on my shoulders, the acromion regions, and the chest. After I turned over, before she worked on my legs and thighs, she covered me with a hot towel to relax the back muscles. She used the full repertoire of Swedish massage, except tapotement, on me. I could feel different techniques being applied to my body and was aware of the long strokes along the ITT and the peroneus muscles. I liked especially the stretching of my legs and the toes, and the compression on my deltoid area. I felt quite restful during and after the massage. However, after I returned home, I felt some aches in the posterior cervical muscles.

* * * * *

Classroom Learning

In the classroom, Doyle continued to drill us in what Tricia Grafelman had distilled in her book, *Anatomy Guide for Therapeutic Massage* (*Graf's Anatomy*). Even though Graf's was not a required textbook, I bought a used copy to keep up with Doyle's lesson plans. I learned to write SOAP notes, tackled weekly projects, midterm project and the final project as though I were a regular student. I completed 12 projects, far exceeding the course requirements. I wrote about downward facing dog (a yoga pose), stretches during massage (lateral flexion of the neck, horizontal flexion of the shoulders, flexion and hyperextension of the wrists, elongation stretch of the whole body), stretching of the quadriceps and hamstrings, muscles involved in running, swimming and tennis; muscular injuries in baseball, basketball, bicycling, football and soccer; the modalities of myofascial release, reflexology and trigger point therapy; the benefits of massage (reduction of pain, stress and anxiety, emotional release and feelings of general well-being), contraindications, ethics (challenges and solutions), NCBTMB requirements, Board of Nursing certification requirements and the requirements for massage permits in Fairfax and Arlington counties.

For our practical exam, Lisa, Sean and I massaged the same client (Emily had dropped out before mid-term). In my interview with the client, I discovered she was an active woman. She walked a lot for exercise. She informed me she was on medication for diabetes and high blood pressure and she had arthritis on her fingers. She wanted a relaxation massage, focused primarily on her shoulders. When I massaged her in the prone position, I noticed her legs were not swollen (as one might expect from a client with diabetes) but they had some patches of grey spots below the knees. She had brown knobs inferior to both her patellae and slightly swollen knuckles on her left hand. Given my observation and her health status, I decided to use light pressure for the session and made conscious efforts to use a liberal amount of unscented massage cream so as not to aggravate her delicate skin or her sensitivity to scent. I used effleurage and petrissage for the entire session. After the massage, I asked the client about the spots and knobs on her legs. She thought that the spots were a reaction to the sun and the knobs were the result of kneeling while gardening, and she promised to check with her physician about them. She told me my hand pressure was not hard enough even though she felt good when I worked on her toes and fingers. She thought the massage was comfortable; in fact, she fell asleep on the massage table! If I were to work on her again, I would ask for feedback about hand pressure as I massaged her. I should not assume just because she was older that I needed to use light pressure.

<>

The practical exam was the culmination of massage exchanges I had with Sean, Emily and Lisa, and massages I gave to family members and friends. My massage log showed I had completed 21 massages in ten weeks. My wife was the most frequent, semi-willing, but exacting "client." She made sure I was customer-oriented. Shortly after I enrolled in the massage class, she wanted a full body massage. My learning goals for that session were to develop a slower tempo to massage and to use my whole body rather than just my hands in massage.

* * * * *

My wife was in prone position when I began the massage. After I checked her initial draping, I rested my hands on her shoulders and breathed quietly with her for a few seconds. Then I applied several light effleurage strokes over her draped back. After that, I folded the drape down to her hip, warmed up the massage lotion in my hands, and applied basic effleurage on her back, making sure I rounded at her shoulders.

I was aware of my body posture as I glided my hands over her back and I reminded myself to keep my hands in contact with her back and pull back with my waist. After the initial up and down motions, I used effleurage on her thoracic region transversely. Then I re-draped her upper back, undraped her right leg, and draped her right thigh using as few movements as I could and applied contract and stretch joint movements to her coxal and tibiofemoral joints. I repeated the process on her left leg and thigh.

She then turned over and I worked on her shoulders, neck and upper pectoral muscles. After I draped her upper chest with a towel, I undraped the sheet down to her hip and massaged her abdomen. By that point, the 60-minute session was up and I knew I had achieved my goal of slow motion. Mercy's observation that my hand movements were smoother led me to believe I had achieved my goal of using my whole body for massage. She felt that my hand pressure was lighter than what I used to have.

* * * * *

As the final grade of the course was derived from class projects and practice massages as well as tests, where I did not excel in one area, I could compensate with doing well in other areas. So, I was able to get a passing grade for the course. However, despite passing the course, I did not yet make a good connection between anatomy and massage. I only had many bits of fascinating information for short-term memory.

After I completed the course on anatomy and Swedish massage, I did not enroll for the course on physiology and deep tissue massage in Fall 2010 because it was not offered at the Springfield campus. The next opportunity I had to enroll for the latter course was in the summer semester at the Woodbridge campus, one year after completing the anatomy course. Registration for it was by permission of the instructor only. As I did not know the instructor and had no prior contact with the Woodbridge campus, and I was unable to reach Doyle for information, I contacted my first massage teacher, Meyer, for assistance. She gave me the email address of the instructor, Jennifer Sovine.

Chapter 5

PHYSIOLOGY AND DEEP TISSUE MASSAGE

In my email to Jennifer Sovine on March 25, 2011, I wrote:

I request your permission to enroll in HLT 280, which is being offered at the Woodbridge campus this summer. I have completed and passed HLT 180 as an audit student last summer. My interest in therapeutic massage is to develop skills for volunteer service and for treatment of family members and friends. My previous instructors are Meyer and Doyle, both at the Medical Education campus.

Sovine replied on March 27:

I think this is going to work out just fine but I do have a few questions for you. When you audited 180 did you participate in the written tests? For a class in deep tissue you need to be very solid in your gross anatomy. We will be working deep muscles and working directly into endangerment areas for therapeutic treatments. Would you be auditing 280 as well and if so do you intend to take the weekly quizzes?

I replied the next day:

I took all the written tests and my overall grade was 95 out of 100. I think I will take HLT 280 for credit and I will take the weekly quizzes.

Thus, with Sovine's permission, I proceeded to register for the class, but did not take it for credit, since I was not planning to be a professional therapist. As a senior citizen and a longtime resident of Virginia, I was eligible for free tuition and I exercised that option. I even had free parking on campus.

The Woodbridge campus, located in the fast-developing Prince William County, is an oasis in Northern Virginia. Its main teaching and administrative building, the Seefeldt Building, is situated along a man-made lake and the whole campus is nestled in a wooded area. It has ample parking space, but the lots are usually full.

Physiology and Massage

The course on physiology and deep tissue massage, was listed simply as Therapeutic Massage II in the curriculum. We met every Friday for 12 weeks. Full attendance was required. We had lectures in a full-size, multi-use classroom in the morning, and lab in the college gym in the afternoon. The textbooks we used were *Graf's Physiology – Physiology Guide for Therapeutic Massage* by Tricia Grafelman, and *the Ethics of Touch* by Ben Benjamin and Cherie Sohnen-Moe. I found out later that Sovine is a graduate of the NOVA Massage Therapy Program. From the SOAP notes she prepared for campus clinic, I also discovered she was meticulous and thorough in her student days (see Chapter 10). I did ask if she was Grafelman's star pupil, but she declined to disclose the information. Grafelman was a former instructor of anatomy, physiology and massage at NOVA.

At the first session, Sovine handed out a six-page, no-nonsense syllabus and she went over each section to ensure we understood what the course required. She had every session planned, with deadlines for projects clearly stated. While she listened to students' questions and responded to them empathetically, she wasted no time in digression. Neither did she tolerate inattention or what she considered as disruptive behaviors. I liked her style of classroom management. She was poised and confident, and yet not overbearing.

My first impression of Sovine was that she had excellent rapport with my classmates. There were nine of them, one man and eight women. I subsequently discovered that all of them were her students in the anatomy and Swedish massage class in the previous semester. Although I was a newcomer to that circle of friends, I felt comfortable among them. The professionalism that Sovine required of us was, in fact, carried out without further reminder. The students acted as professionals. The requirement that we trade massage with each person in the class at least once would have been difficult had my classmates acted differently.

Our overall course grade came from nine quizzes, one mid-term exam and one final exam, a massage log, two reports on professional massages and one on alternative therapy, two practical exams and class attendance. Even though I was on audit, I decided to tackle all the course requirements to gain maximum benefit. Sovine had skillfully organized the materials on physiology into digestible portions. I could follow along without any problem, even though I had already forgotten most of what I had learned in Human Biology and anatomy and Swedish massage. Using Graf's as her main text, she presented the lectures in PowerPoint and made her notes available via the online Blackboard after each lecture. I could check my notes with what she put on Blackboard and what was in Graf's. Her enthusiasm for physiology was contagious, and there wasn't a muscle in the body she did not like!

Each of the sessions began with a quiz in the computer lab. That was good practice for students taking the NCBTMB certification exam, which was done entirely by computer. I was especially glad that I had Human Biology through distance learning, which required using a computer for regular testing. I had become proficient in navigating that medium.

Tricia Grafelman, whom I heard everyone refer to simply as Graf, wrote *Graf's Physiology* especially for massage students. She had distilled what were important in anatomy and physiology for massage in a pair of highly readable and useful textbooks. Her marks as an outstanding massage teacher were revealed in the content on which she focused students' concentration. Not too much and not too little, but just the right amount to establish you firmly in the discipline and point you in the right direction for more information if you want it. She also provided a rationale for why massage students needed to study muscular, skeletal and other body systems. Sovine was just like

Graf. She knew anatomy and physiology and was crystal clear in her classroom presentation.

Both Graf and Marieb use the same terminology for six levels of body organization and they both list 11 major body systems. However, Graf writes of six life processes, but Marieb has eight life functions. Both of them have movement, responsiveness, metabolism, reproduction, and growth as vital life processes or functions, but Marieb includes maintaining boundaries, digestion and excretion in her list of functions and Graf emphasizes differentiation (evolution of cells) in her processes. Since Graf wrote extensively about boundaries in the chapters on cells and skin, I was surprised she did not have boundary maintenance as a primary life process.

The differences between Graf and Marieb reminded me, in the early stage of my training as a therapist, that people select objective facts to fit their explanatory models and selectivity is essential for explanation. Otherwise, we would be paralyzed by a vast array of variables. Thus, an explanatory model for chronic pain might be an entanglement of free nerve endings or impasse of yin-qi and yang-qi, or other seemingly more sophisticated explanatory models. One model does not provide all the answers. The crucial test is whether the explanatory model makes sense and whether it leads to effective treatment. I was also reminded of the famous saying of the Chinese leader Deng Xiaopeng that "It does not matter whether a cat is black or white. If it catches mice, it is a good cat." Arguing over the exact number of life processes or functions or the efficacy of different evidence-based treatments is meaningless, at least most of the time.

Both Graf and Marieb hold up homeostasis as a key concept and the feedback loop as a vital mechanism in life. Graf links homeostasis to "stress," which is what massage can help alleviate. She writes, "If homeostasis is interrupted, we refer to that as stress."[15] What a succinct but pregnant definition! Reducing stress is restoring homeostasis to what Marieb calls its "dynamic equilibrium." If I were Graf, I would have added "Interruption of homeostasis takes many forms of which the most important one is an impasse between two forces, yin and yang, creating stagnation and, subsequently, cessation of movement. That impasse is stress." However, adding that discussion might be too much information for beginners. Her observation that "massage helps the body maintain the feedback loop and deal with stress" brought me back to the role of physiology in massage therapy.

---

[15]   *Graf's Physiology* (2001), p. 7.

As the locus (and focus) of massage is tissues and muscles, Sovine set aside four weeks for their study, and Graf devoted 41 pages of her book on that. While Marieb had extensive coverage of tissues and muscles in her book, she did not deal explicitly with the thixotropic process, a concept crucial for understanding the effects of massage.[16] In those four weeks, our class was inundated with fascia, cartilage, tendon, ligament and bone, muscle bundles, muscle fibers, myofibrils and myofilaments. Even though I was not good at handicraft, I created a masterpiece of a human muscle cell with lotus root, vermicelli, and human hair. Unfortunately, I did not have the foresight of photographing the work.

Sometime during those four weeks, I had an epiphany from what Graf wrote. She stated, "Two substances, ACh (acetylcholine) and $Ca++$ (calcium) must be removed from the contraction process in order for relaxation to take place."[17] In order to remove ACh, the peripheral nervous system (PNS) needs to reduce the frequency of releasing ACh into the synaptic cleft and PNS can be induced to reduce the frequency of release through relaxing touch. Thus, relaxation is not purely a muscle action. It is external kinetic energy converted into internal chemical and electrical energy. The therapist controls the frequency of energy conversion. Relaxation is not about working with muscles at the organic or systemic level as it is at the cellular level. Massage is working on cells, nerve cells as well as muscle cells, and physical strength is not a crucial factor in therapeutic massage. Massage therapists work with skin, and skin is formed from the same tissue layer as the brain. Therefore, when we touch skin, we touch the brain. We are brainworkers, not just body workers! This epiphany became the guiding light for my professional development as a therapist.

In addition to physiology, Sovine spent time every week lecturing on the ethics of touch. We learned about dual relationship and setting boundaries and discussed management of ethical practices and business ethics. We also had a brief introduction to chakras (the "major energy centers in the body, located at specific areas in the spinal column"[18]). In lab sessions, we had demonstrations on PNF stretching, AIS stretching, Muscle Energy Technique, three

---

[16]   See especially *Job's Body* (2003) by Deane Juhan.

[17]   *Graf's Physiology*, p. 58.

[18]   See *Your Body Speaks Your Mind* (2006) by Deb Shapiro, pp. 56-64, for a brief introduction of this energy system.

phase ischemic compression and postural analysis. We had written handouts for lab work.

As I continued reading Graf's, listening to Sovine's lectures and watching her demonstrations, I felt I was on an exciting intellectual journey. Who needs to wander in a foreign land when you can explore the human body? Quizzes were no longer classroom exercises but exchanges between my mentor and me. They were about what I knew, not what I did not know. My level of test anxiety dropped (the fact that I was just an auditor removed whatever anxiety I might have had). The other class assignments had become means for me to sort out what I knew and to identify gaps in my learning. I allowed my mind to roam for connections between what I read and heard and what I knew before, especially from the practice of Chinese folk medicine among my relatives in Singapore. I jotted down insights such as "sensory deprivation is similar to malnutrition," "massage calms down the electrical impulses by interrupting their firing," "pains come from soft tissues, not from joints," "body fluid is a collection of ions and massage hastens the chemical reactions," "muscle energy is the effect of sub-atomic particles trying to complete its outermost shell to maintain stability," "micro tears are electrical disconnections," "to touch the surface (skin) is to stir the deep (brain)," and other nuggets for rumination.

I was to complete 36 massages for the semester, but I did considerably more than that. I was fortunate to have a teacher who encouraged students to develop their own styles instead of someone who insisted on orthodoxy or fixed routine.[19] I adapted what was taught in class about deep tissue massage and what I understood about relaxation to develop my own routine of running the fascia, feathering, compressing, fractioning and stretching. I traded massages with David, Jeno, Tracy, Jen, Susan, Meron, Katie, Kim and LaVerne. All of them focused on what I did well, rather than what I did poorly. A couple of them felt I should join them to go professional. Friends I worked with for my class assignments observed that I was becoming more fluid in my touch. I usually thought through what I needed to do and wrote down a treatment outline before each massage.

---

[19] As I discovered later when I studied tuina in China.

Treatment Outline

An example of my thinking through was the treatment outline I developed for a friend who had pains in her lower back, legs and shoulders. She was highly tense and stressed and her entire posterior muscles, especially muscles inferior to L1, were extremely hypertonic. Because we had limited time for me to work on her, I had to decide ahead of time which body parts I should focus on and I chose her lower back and legs, especially the muscles inferior to L1. Before I began, I informed her that progress on the balancing of her muscles would dictate subsequent treatments for her shoulder soreness. I recommended to her the option of acupuncture to accelerate muscle tone balance.

I also told her that she needed to pay attention to self-care by stretching her legs daily, drinking more water and not wearing high heels unless absolutely necessary. I suggested that she soak her feet in warm water every evening before sleep to promote vasodilation and better circulation of body fluids; and that before each treatment session, she take a hot shower to warm up and relax her muscles. Clearly, I had begun practicing my understanding that massage was not merely what I did for a client. It involved the client's active participation! For me, healing requires involvement, more than just a passive relaxation on the massage table!

<>

I wrote out a treatment outline for treating a tight back, with emphasis on doing it slowly and gently.

- Seated. Soak feet. Massage head, neck and shoulder muscles. To ease tension and unwind muscles. To warm up leg and feet muscles.
- Supine. Warm back muscles with dry heat. Breathing (abdominal) exercises. Rocking. To increase oxygen intake for ventilation and increase flow of body fluid. To ease tension. To let go. Client may cry or need to go to the bathroom.
- Supine. Massage anterior thigh, leg and feet muscles. Long strokes to feather the fascia. Feathering muscles to reduce adhesion. CFF (cross fiber friction) and stretching to reduce tension and to increase hip range of motion. Try foot-on-shoulder stretch.

- Side-lying. Massage lateral thigh, leg and glut muscles to balance muscle tone and to treat lower back. Long strokes to feather the fascia. Feathering muscles to reduce adhesion. CFF to reduce tension. PNF (proprioceptive neuromuscular facilitation) for adductors and abductors.
- Supine. After completing thigh, leg, glut and feet muscles, do a modified iliopsoas stretch to further treat lower back.
- Supine. Massage neck and shoulder muscles. Focus on shoulder joints. Relax TMJ. Lengthen (stroke and CFF) serratus and pectoral muscles. Deep tissue arms and hands. Stretch. Massage rotator cuff muscles. Abdominal strokes.
- Prone. Massage trapezius, latissimus dorsi, QL, and deep muscles beneath them. Long strokes followed by short stretches. Focus on separating muscle groups through CFF. Compress nodes. Squeeze knots.
- Prone. Massage posterior thigh, leg and feet muscles. Run the fascia, feathering, long stroke, stretch.
- Full body tapotement. Full body relaxation stroke.

<>

Music and Insomnia

My continuing immersion in the study of massage therapy led me to suggest to a musician friend to collaborate with me in using massage and music to treat insomnia. Both her husband and my son had been complaining about having insomnia despite having time for sleep, keeping their bedrooms at the proper temperature and choosing bedding that was dedicated to sleep. Neither of them had a physical or mental disorder that might contribute to their insomnia.

One of the factors associated with insomnia is stress, the sensation that something is out of balance. This something can be of a chemical or electrical nature and it acts on the brain.

Music has been associated with influencing a brain's wavelength. I think of it as kinetic change bringing about chemical change, and chemical change bringing about electrical change. It can move a person to act faster or slower, to gear up or to relax. The vibration of music produces an overtone that elicits a resonance from both the sympathetic and parasympathetic nerves. This is both an electrical and a chemical reaction, or electrical reaction transforming into chemical reaction.

Music of low frequency, low amplitude, in rhythms of two or four beats and slow tempo (what I call Type B music) can relax the parasympathetic nerves, and music of high frequency, high amplitude, in odd or syncopated rhythms and fast tempo (what I call Type A music) can stimulate the sympathetic nerves. The two nerve systems respond differently to different types of music. The electric impulses of Type B music and the electric impulses of parasympathetic nerves are similar. Likewise, the impulses of Type A music and the impulses of sympathetic nerves are similar.

Parasympathetic nerves are the regulators of sleep. They resonate with Type B music helping a person fall asleep and stay asleep. Organ, viola, cello, or woodwind music played primarily in low octaves, in 2/4 or 4/4 time, at piano or pianissimo amplitude, and at andante or largo tempo would be most effective in producing Type B music with which parasympathetic nerves can resonate.

Typically, relaxation music is used to accompany massage in clinical practice. It is Type B music, the same kind for helping people to fall asleep and stay asleep. Moreover, massage as a physical activity induces chemical and electrical reactions that influence biological functions, and the physical activity of massage can be characterized in the musical terms of frequency (pressure), rhythm (evenness), amplitude (depth of pressure) and tempo (pace).

The massage that can help a person to relax might follow the model of Type B music: sonorous pressure, even rhythm with a strong beat followed by a weaker beat (just like breathing in and out), deep pressure and slow pace. Massage generates electrical impulses and an electromagnetic field, both of which interact with the impulses of the parasympathetic and sympathetic nerves (Not to short-circuit the electrical impulses and the electromagnetic field is why we ask clients to remove jewelry and clothing when they receive massage).

Type B massage synchronized with Type B music can create harmonic consonance with the parasympathetic nerves to release the knots in the nerve (neural) network and to revitalize dormant nerve endings. It is like charging a rundown battery with a booster. This jumpstart helps the body to regain balance – free of stress -- and allows the body to let go and fall asleep.

Due to other commitments, my friend did not have time to locate or record the pieces of music and thus was unable to try out the experiment with me. As I did not have the necessary tools, I did not pursue investigating further the use of music and massage to treat insomnia or to use music to develop more effective massage. As I found out later when treating clients with chronic pain, insomnia is a common problem across many disorders. Solving the sleep problem is a critical way to manage pain. Thus, using music (sound) and massage to treat insomnia remains a vital interest for me even though I am hearing impaired. I did not realize that in my exploration of music and insomnia, I was already into the study of yin and yang, a vital principle in traditional Chinese medicine. Neither was I aware that I was on the verge of developing the NOVA-S Method, central to the treatment of fibromyalgia and posttraumatic stress disorder (PTSD).

Professional Massage

Like other massage-specific courses in the program, physiology and deep tissue massage required students to have two professional massages. I asked Gerry (not her real name), a therapist in private practice, to give me one of the massages and went to Eastern Massage (not the real name), a day spa, to have the other one.

* * * * *

The massage session with Gerry was held in her friend's house in Springfield. It was to minimize my travel time to her place in Alexandria. She set up the massage table in the living room. A bathroom was adjacent to it. There was no one in the house and we had privacy for the session. The setting looked comfortable.

As Gerry knew me from previous meetings, she did not ask me to fill out an intake form. She did ask about my health history and current health condition. We had some discussion over the differences between Swedish massage and deep tissue massage. After Gerry excused herself, I undressed and lay prone under the sheets on the massage table. Before she began, she inserted a CD of mood music in the player at the foot of the table.

Probably because I mentioned my sore shoulder, Gerry did effleurage and deep tissue of the muscles of the upper trapezius, the deltoids, the splenii and suboccipital muscles and the rotator cuff muscles. She also stretched the rotator cuff muscles and the deltoids and did some frictions on the splenii and suboccipital muscles. After that she used long strokes to effleurage and deep tissue my legs and thigh.

After she finished working on my posterior muscles, she asked me to turn over to work on the upper chest area. She did some stretching of my arms and shoulders and scooped up my trapezius to create a wave sensation. She then worked on my anterior thighs and legs and feet, using effleurage, deep friction, friction and compression in different areas of the body. She did not use tapotement or vibration. Her pressure was firm and I enjoyed especially her work on my deltoids. Toward the end of the session, her strokes were more brisk, as though to wake me from my nap. After a gentle touch-without-movement for about ten seconds, the session was over.

The whole session was both relaxing and stimulating. The shoulder tightness had dissipated. If I did not have to think about writing the report, I would have enjoyed the experience much more.

<>

The other professional massage I had was at Eastern Massage, in an office park in Northern Virginia, on the second floor of a two-story building. The spa was understated, with no storefront advertisement, almost like a doctor's office. I had to ring the doorbell for admission. The facility was clean, simply furnished, no frills, but brightly lit. The small reception area had framed registration and other permits mounted on the wall. Soft instrumental music played in the background.

Unlike a more elaborate massage establishment, Eastern Massage did not maintain a file on its clients. The receptionist/manager only asked if that was the first time I visited the spa and what kind of massage I wanted. My choice was a Chinese full body massage. She led me to a massage room (one of three or four), brought me a cup of water, told me to undress and excused herself.

The massage room was also furnished simply. In addition to the massage table in the center, a small cabinet was in one corner and a chair was placed diagonally across from it in the other corner. On top of the cabinet was a pile of towels, a table lamp, and a couple of bottles of massage oil.

I undressed and lay prone under the cover, which was just a beach towel, not the usual top sheet. I rested my feet on a roll of towel, not the usual bolster. The therapist entered the room shortly thereafter. After she found out that I needed work on my shoulders, she proceeded to work on them right away. Her warm up routine consisted mainly of compression over the towel. I was pressed rigorously from shoulders to feet and squeezed medially. She then sat on my thighs and used her feet and legs to compress my back and her knees to friction my glut muscles. She also stretched my trunk laterally and diagonally. Much of what she did was similar to Thai massage. Some of her techniques were probably adapted from Chinese tuina.

After ten minutes of warm up, I was massaged with oil and the sensation was deep tissue massage with gusto. (The spa's menu has deep tissue massage; I wondered what that might feel like!) She first undraped me to the glut area and worked on my upper trunk. Perhaps, because I told her I needed work on my shoulders, she massaged my upper traps as though she were using a rolling pin. It was exquisitely painful! After the upper trunk, she worked on my thighs and legs, but did no work on my feet. She did some stretching of my legs and arms while I was in the prone position.

After I moved to a supine position, the therapist massaged my abdomen over the towel and worked on my thighs and legs again. A series of her hand movements over the thigh elicited a tingling sensation. She did not work on my head or neck muscles.

The whole session was stimulating. Most of the strokes of the therapist were brisk and energetic. There was no slow movement or deep tissue stripping. I thought some of my back muscles might feel sore. Instead, I felt relieved! As I dressed, I noticed that over the massage table was a set of hanging bars. They were probably holders for therapists who walk on their clients' back. That is a massage technique I have not encountered in America though I have had it several times in Hong Kong and China. I planned to return to the spa to try that, but I have not followed through yet!

* * * * *

Fire Therapy

Earlier in the semester, I had told Sovine about my experience with fire therapy when I was in China in 2011. She found it fascinating and wanted my classmates to know about it. She told me to write it up as my project. Using fire as a therapeutic tool might sound esoteric or bizarre, but it is one form of traditional Chinese medicine still in practice today. I received this treatment, twice, in the teahouse where I used to have foot massage when I was stationed in China (Chapter 1). The first fire therapy session was practically perfect. The second session singed me a little, but I recovered the next day.

* * * * *

The therapist told me fire therapy was effective for treating discomforts of the back, stomach and the extremities. I chose the leg and foot treatment. She first draped two towels over my thighs and then rubbed my knees and legs for a while. After that, she layered two damp towels and a damp cloth over them and sprayed 80 proof alcohol on the cloth. She then set fire to the alcohol to create a blanket of flame (Pictures 1 and 2). She allowed the fire to burn for about ten seconds, smothered it with a wet towel and left the steaming towels on the legs for another ten seconds. She then repeated the process five or six times. When the flaming and smothering process was finished, she rubbed the knees and legs to even out the blood circulation.

The therapist also told me that my tolerance of the heat and the color of the flame were indicators of my internal body condition. If I could stand the heat or if the flame was orange in color, that meant my body had a high amount of toxin and I was consequently fatigued. If I could not stand the heat or if the flame is blue, then my body is in good shape. By that standard, I was in fairly good shape. I could not stand the heat.

I told the therapist the heat was unbearable several times. Each time, she merely lifted the damp towels off my legs to release the discomfort and put them back on again a few seconds later. She told me to endure as much discomfort as I could, so the treatment could be more effective. I did not understand her logic and I was in no position to argue with her. At the second session, the therapist was so insistent on giving me the maximum benefit of my treatment that she singed my legs.

Why do people use fire therapy? What is it for? Is it effective? When I read the brochure on fire therapy, I was intrigued by the claim that it was a fast way to "expel toxins and release fatigue" from the body. I was eager to give it a try. All of us have some toxins in our body and most of us feel fatigued sometimes. If this alternative therapy works and works fast, why not try it?

Actually, despite its bizarre appearance, the form of fire therapy I tried is similar to a steam sauna although the heat was much more intense and focused. It was like having an extremely hot towel on your skin. Despite the flame over the body, the heat is indirect, mediated in the form of steam through the layer of damp towels. A variation of this steam treatment is to soak the towels in herbal medicine and layer them over the treatment sites. When steam penetrates the skin, it opens up the pores and allows the essence of herbal medicine to seep into the body.

Yuxitang,[20] an entrepreneurial group for Chinese massage therapies, states that fire therapy has a long history. It cites from the ancient treatise on Chinese medicine, *Huangdi Neijing*, dated more than 2,200 years ago, the comment that "if using acupuncture needles cannot bring about the desired effect, using *jiu* is a proper alternative."[21] *Jiu* in that text is often translated as moxibustion, but it can be defined as "to cauterize or to raise blister by burning moxa or the dried tinder of the Artemisia on the skin."[22] In other words, use fire. Yuxitang and several other massage centers attribute the source of fire therapy to Tibet.

"Fire therapy and clinical applications," a Chinese article on the website xywy.com and Yuxitang state that fire therapy is effective for treating rheumatism, arthritis, periarthritis, joint ache, cervical vertebral disease, muscular strain, stomachache, abdominal pain, menstrual irregularity, dysmenorrhea, insomnia and excessive perspiration. In addition, some practitioners and clients claim that fire therapy is effective for weight control. The Kemi Spa in Singapore advertises that fire therapy is "the most amazing heat therapy for all your leg problems," and at least one of its clients uses fire therapy to lose weight. The Blue Water Day Spa in the Philippines reports that fire therapy will "melt away body pain as you burn excess fat."[23]

In a more primitive environment, fire is readily available. Its use as therapy is relatively simple, inexpensive and effective. That's why it persists as an alternative treatment. However, the same ancient treatise on Chinese medicine implies that fire therapy should be used only as a treatment of last resort. When all else fails, use fire.

Was my treatment effective? It was. That was why I went for a second session. Of course, I could not measure how many toxins were removed, but I did feel my muscle aches had vanished. I believe the

---

[20]   See www.yxt08.com, a website in Chinese, for information about this group.

[21]   The comment is my translation of the Chinese phrase, "*zhen suo bu we, jiu zhi suo yi,*" as quoted by Yuxitang, from *Huangdi Neijing*.

[22]   From *A Complete Chinese-English Dictionary*, (1980), China Publishers Co., Hong Kong.

[23]   See http://www.camlawblog.com/articles/health-trends/fire-therapy-treatment-for-weight-loss, and www.bluewaterdayspa.com, accessed on June 5, 2011.

treatment works essentially on the same principle as other bodywork techniques. It uses external heat to warm up the body to open up the tissues for internal chemical reaction, and to accelerate and sustain thixotropy for cleansing and healing.

A practitioner of fire therapy in the Philippines explains the treatment process this way: "Heat, combined with the right traditional Chinese herbs and essences, aids in melting away acid buildup, toxins and fatty deposits." Another practitioner explains that "fire opens the way to the sick organ, allowing the active principles in the herbs to work at full power in order to regenerate the tissue."[24] A client in Singapore feels that by burning off the excessive water element in his body, fire therapy eases his digestive problems, which helps him to lose weight.

Besides the steam treatment, there are other forms of fire therapy. In Taiwan, a therapist strokes naked flame on his patient's back. In Thailand, a therapist practices "hot foot massage" (my term). He dips his foot into a pan of aromatic oil and then holds it over an open flame or a mound of smoldering charcoals. The flame or the smoke swirls up to the dripping oil to warm the foot, which is then applied to the body.[25] That massage is a combination of heat, aroma and pressure.

Unlike moxibustion, cupping, acupuncture and acupressure, fire therapy is not taught in Chinese medical schools in Guangzhou or Hong Kong, two of the prime centers of Chinese medical practices. I am not aware whether it is formally taught in any medical schools. It is a technique usually learned from a master therapist. In America and other countries with strict fire safety codes, high insurance costs and stringent licensing requirements, fire therapy may take many years to evolve into a popular therapeutic alternative, if it ever does so. The National Center for Complementary and Alternative Medicine (NCCAM)[26] provides no information on fire therapy on its website. The National Certification Commission for Acupuncture and Oriental Medicine (NCCAOM) makes no reference or recognition of fire therapy as a treatment modality.

---

[24] See www.pirasan.ro/en/therapies/tibetan_thermotherapy.html, accessed on June 5, 2011.

[25] Search for "acupuncture fire dragon" on YouTube for pictures of therapists scooping fire directly onto their clients. Search for "Yam Khang" for pictures of therapists applying the "hot foot massage."

[26] Now renamed the National Center for Complementary and Integrative Health. It is an agency within the National Institutes of Health.

* * * * *

As the class on physiology and deep tissue massage drew to a close, Sovine asked me if I had reconsidered about not becoming a professional therapist. We agreed that I needed the credentials if I were to share my unorthodox views on the therapeutic effects of massage with the healthcare profession or with society at large. She encouraged me to take the professional route because she felt I had hands to go with my brain. She rated my final practical exam with her as "a fantastic massage with perfect pressure," and my massage journal as "perfect"! With her encouragement, I was ready to enroll in the massage therapy program right away, but NOVA informed me that I had some more loops to jump through.

The full name of the massage program at NOVA is Massage Therapy Career Studies Certificate Program. It is a training program approved by the NCBTMB. Even though I was already admitted to the college, I had to provide evidence that I met the placement requirements. Unfortunately, as a foreign student who migrated to the U.S. many decades ago, I did not have the documents the community college wanted. I had the diplomas, but not the official transcripts. When I was at the Springfield campus, I went to the Student Services Center asking to meet with a counselor to discuss my situation, but the "gatekeeper" at the counter turned me away. The staff person at the Woodbridge campus gave me the same treatment. I might have earned a Ph.D. from Northwestern University, been a manager in U.S. Government Service and written a couple of books, but all that the staff person saw was an older "China man" wanting to be admitted to a NOVA program. I had to follow the rules.

I bit the bullet and took the COMPASS reading and writing placement tests to generate the paperwork NOVA needed to waive the English composition requirement. I met with Nancy Crippen, head of the Massage Therapy Program, to discuss the program requirements. She had already given me permission earlier to register as a regular student for the course on orthopedic massage and trigger point therapy and informed me that the courses I audited did not count toward certification requirements. I would have to repeat them!

What puzzled Crippen was my doing the program out of sequence. Other students met with her before they began anatomy and Swedish massage. I was ready to begin orthopedic massage and trigger point therapy when she first interviewed me. Other students completed their preadmission health history and physical exam before they began the program. I started without health clearance. When I asked my primary care physician to complete the two-page health history and physical form, she was surprised that I planned to start a new career at age 72. Admirable but insane, she probably thought!

Crippen reviewed the program requirements with me and confirmed with counselors in Student Services Center that I needed an official transcript from Northwestern to waive registering for the courses on Interpersonal Communication and Lifetime Fitness and Wellness. Those courses carry a total of four credits, one-fifth of the total credits for the massage therapy program. While waiting for Northwestern to send the transcripts, I registered for both courses and began doing the necessary homework and class assignments. They were not hard, just tedious, and the course on Lifetime Fitness and Wellness was even fun, at least for a while! However, I dropped them immediately after NOVA confirmed that my transcripts were in order. I did not believe in spending time doing what was not required. I did continue registering for orthopedic massage and trigger point therapy. Heidi Peña-Moog was the instructor.

Chapter 6

ORTHOPEDIC MASSAGE AND
TRIGGER POINT THERAPY

The course on orthopedic massage and trigger point therapy, listed as Therapeutic Massage III in the curriculum, met every Saturday. Lectures were held in a multi-use classroom and lab in the gymnasium. We had written tests before every lecture the old-fashioned way, using pen and paper and we had the usual requirements of class attendance, projects and massage exchanges with fellow students. We also had a weekly clinic for the public. Unfortunately, due to the gym's schedule, our clinic had to precede lecture every week, an arrangement that was far from ideal. Listening to a lecture after manual work and after lunch was a burden to the tired body and a challenge to both the instructor and the students.

The course had 18 students, the highest enrollment than any of the in-person classes I had at NOVA due probably to the timing of its offering. It was not available every semester. One-half of the class was made up of classmates from the physiology class I had just completed. The other half was from different massage classes in prior semesters. Most interestingly, both of my former classmates in anatomy and Swedish massage, Lisa and Sean, were also in this class. I tried to focus on scheduling my massage exchanges with new classmates for a different experience, but managed to trade with only three of them, Erika, Crystal and Kaz. Erika was a certified physical therapist assistant who encouraged me to go professional and helped me launch the posture assessment lab later in the semester. Crystal was an independent wellness consultant with a positive outlook on life and a fabulous touch. And Kaz was on the staff of a spa in Northern Virginia and a frequent study partner.

Posture Assessment Lab

The required textbooks for the class were *Orthopedic Assessment in Massage Therapy* (2006) by Whitney Lowe, *Graf's Anatomy and Graf's Physiology*, but Peña-Moog referred to *The Concise Book of Trigger Points* (2008) by Simeon Niel-Asher quite frequently. She often said to the class, "Everybody can rub-rub, but you need to know why you are doing what you are doing." She might have sounded tough and hardheaded ("*Do it my way or we will have issues*"), but she had a heart of gold. She was more than willing to go the extra mile if students took the initiative to get beyond her façade. From her weekly e-mails and her useful topical handouts, I knew she was a diligent teacher and she wanted her students to succeed. I did what I could to meet her expectations.

Due to my hearing problem, I tend to speak louder than I realize. That became a problem early in our weekly clinic. As I massaged, I usually checked in with my clients and explained to them what I was doing or about to do. That was fine for my practice at home or "trade" with my classmates. In the gym-turned-clinic setting, the tableside conversation was too loud for everybody and some of my classmates might have complained to Peña-Moog about the distraction. In order not to escalate an annoyance into disturbance, she set up a separate area in the women's locker room for me to do my practical (the same area where we took our practical exam for other massage classes). I had a practice room all to myself!

To take advantage of that unique accommodation, I suggested to her that we have the practice room double as a Posture Assessment Lab. Earlier in the semester, the class was introduced to posture assessment as a systematic way for observing the balance between body parts. We had learned that poor posture is a perpetuating factor for chronic pain and posture assessment can help therapists to identify what soft tissues we need to work on to alleviate pain. I wanted to have more hands-on practice on how to do posture assessment and I believed my classmates would benefit from mutual learning as well. Thus, I made the suggestion.

Peña-Moog liked the idea, discussed it with Crippen and asked me to draw up a weekly schedule for a classmate to work with me each Saturday. I used a homemade portable posture grid and a plumbing bob as assessment tools and mounted them in the women's locker room. I also developed a posture checklist with the help of Jeno. Shortly after I moved into "my practice room," we launched the posture assessment project. All the classmates were excited about it. Our clients were equally enthusiastic. For all of them, that was a new experience. My classmates and I worked as a team and I was glad to have another opportunity to learn from them indirectly. I usually leave it to them to do palpation assessment of pelvic symmetry because I had a tough time locating ASIS and PSIS. It was good to have another pair of eyes to assess whether the body parts were in alignment.

Trigger Point Therapy

Trigger Point Therapy, one of the primary foci in Massage III, was introduced to us early in the semester. The techniques included finding a trigger point, compressing it to keep blood from entering the muscles, stretching it to bring blood to the muscles and releasing it to promote blood flow, ending with muscle play to promote muscle flexibility, therapeutic stretch (muscle energy technique) to promote muscle strength and spray and stretch (ice massage) to soothe the strain of treatment. A key feature of the treatment was to have the client involved in deep breathing. In addition to class lectures and lab demos, we watched tapes of Dr. Janet Travell, a pioneer of the trigger-point techniques, doing actual treatment of patients with myofascial pain.

* * * * *

Volume I of the tapes is an "Introduction to Myofascial Pain Therapy." It provides an overview of MTrP (Myofascial trigger point) treatments for pains that are of myofascial origin and establishes the connection between MTrP and myofascial pain. According to Simeon Niel-Asher, Travell describes MTrP as "a highly irritable localized spot of exquisite tenderness in a nodule [within] a palpable taut band of (skeletal) muscle."[27] In the tape, Travell gave a slightly different description. To put it simply and simplistically, the way to treat myofascial pain is to get rid of the MTrPs.

The pain of MTrPs is expressed in twitching when the skin over them is touched, as the tape demonstrates. It is mostly associated with overused or strained postural muscles.[28] As massage therapists are primarily engaged in the treatment of skeletal muscles, knowing how to treat myofascial pain by getting rid of MTrPs gives us a useful tool to help our clients regain muscular homeostasis. Of special interest to therapists-in-training, the primary emphasis of myofascial treatment is on skilled and intelligent palpation. The healing begins with the therapist's touch! However, the tape is oriented towards the medical profession. Some of the prescriptions may not be within the scope of practice of general massage therapists.

Travell speaks of four phases of myofascial pain: Phase I as constant pain all the time; Phase II as no pain at rest, pain at motion – active MTrP; Phase III as no clinical complaint of pain – latent MTrP; and Phase IV as no MTrP at all. I think her use of "phases" might be misleading. It implied progression. A better description might be "expressions" or "facets" – how pain expresses itself. MTrP is one form of muscular pain, but not all muscular pains are amenable to MTrP treatment!

The tape's commentary on perpetuating factors for myofascial pain leads to Travell's demonstration on treating mechanical factors such as short upper arm, short hemi pelvis, short leg and seating. To appreciate the treatment process, you have to watch the tape. The demonstration on ergonomics is quite extensive and informative, and most of the recommendations can be implemented without undue expenditure. Travell exhorted us to listen to our muscles. It was sound advice from a veteran body worker.

While Travell was patient-centered in her examination and her "bedside manner" was gentle and attentive, her technique was almost entirely passive stretch with vapocoolant treatment. My sense is that, as a physician, she did not have time for shortened muscles to take their time for stretching. Once she identified the postural misalignment, she sprayed the muscles with vapocoolant and stretched the muscles passively to their full range of motion. It was almost "one size fits all"! While I do not know enough of the treatment to assess its efficacy, I

---

27   *The Concise Book of Trigger Points* (2008), p. 26.
28   *Human Anatomy & Physiology* (2007) by Elaine N. Marieb and Katja Hoehn.

cannot help but ask if the use of vapocoolant might have side effects. What are they? Have they been studied?

The coolant inhibits the pain receptors and enables the physician to apply passive stretch efficiently. Does the fast treatment deal only with the symptoms but not the cause of muscular pain? If muscular pain is developed over time, doesn't its elimination call for gradual muscular unwinding? How often does a patient return for treatment? As I am leaning in the direction of energy massage (focusing primarily on eliciting body energy to help the body heal itself and allowing time for thixotropy to work), I tend to believe the effect of vapocoolant treatment might be immediate but short-lived.

I believe working with injured sacromeres requires the transformation of connective tissue (fascia) from a gel state to a sol state through the use of energy – the therapist's touch on a client's skin. The gentle touch generates a "shearing force" within the soft tissue,"[29] causing the body tissues to "melt," and the leaked calcium to be flushed out. As actin and myosin are unhooked, the muscle tissues are relaxed. However, energy treatment is gradual. Massage therapists who follow Travell's style blindly might bruise instead of helping to heal their clients. For massage therapists to spray through a process is to argue against the alternate and complementary nature of massage therapy.

Finally, while I cannot pinpoint my uneasiness, I feel "true believers" of MTrP therapy might be guilty of over-claims. Reading derivative literature, one gets the impression that every muscular pain is MTrP-related. I don't think Travell would make that mistake. What I am trying to say is, while MTrP treatment has its role in treatment of myofascial pains, massage therapists do not have to give MTrP treatment in every massage for every one of our clients. Besides, the intensity of efforts required of a therapist doing MTrP treatment argues for selective and sparing use of the technique. Otherwise, the therapist will become the object of MTrP treatment due to muscle overuse and strain!

* * * * *

---

[29]   *Direct Release Myofascial Technique* (2004) by Michael Stanborough.

Dan's Presentation

One of the foremost practitioners of the Travell Protocol in the Northern Virginia area is Dan (not his real name), whose specialty is the treatment of myofascial pain through the release of trigger points. He gave a guest lecture to the class and wowed us with a demonstration of his techniques.

* * * * *

In his presentation, Dan focused his attention on perpetuating factors. He drew on many cases to explain them and demonstrated with several classmates on assessing and correcting postural distortion. He also demonstrated the short leg problem to show how different muscles and joints work to compensate for the problem. Dan was keenly attuned to the emphasis of Travell and Simon on perpetuating factors of chronic pain.

I believed Dan was effective because he was interested in treating the cause, as well as the symptoms, of muscle dysfunction. Whereas Travell was interested in chairs, Dan was preoccupied with shoes! Both had to do with proper posture alignment. Dan's gifts were in being able to explain and to suggest solutions for the causal factors for pain.

Following Dan's presentation, two of my classmate and I visited him to have the direct experience of a typical session at his treatment facility. The visit lasted almost two hours. The three of us formally filled out health history forms and shared with him our pain issues. However, only two of us had muscular pains. The third one was pain-free and was essentially an observer at the visit. Dan reviewed the health history forms with us and went on to talk about various perpetuating factors, similar to what he shared in class. That took up more than 45 minutes. I was able to hear much better because his office did not have background noises. At various points, he showed us how he rolled up a towel for lumbar support and how he stretched. He also observed and commented on how we walked.

I mentioned to him the pain on my right wrist and my left hallux. Just as he did with one of the classmates, he pointed out on a couple of wall charts some candidate sites of referred pain for my situation. However, he did not give me any manual treatment. Instead, he checked my hip height and my foot pattern and concluded that the pain on my left hallux could be due to the shoes I wear. That was a revelation to me. I never thought my shoes were a problem. He tried to fit me with toe pad but it could not fit in my shoes. Until I take care of the shoe problem, he had nothing to offer me in terms of treatment.

As for my wrist pain, he concluded it was due to the posture I probably used when I massaged clients, since I began to experience wrist pain midway through the course on physiology and deep tissue therapy. As it happened, I had with me pictures of my case study of a client with anterior pelvic tilt and I showed them to him. He observed that my massage table at home was probably too low and I might be overstretching as I massaged my clients. He showed me two sets of exercises (doorway stretch and wrist pull) I should do after each massage so that hand muscles can restore their balance. He also suggested I should do a hip check for my case study to confirm the client's uneven shoulders.

Dan shared with us his business practice. He is into social media and considers it a good source for promoting his business. People who surf the Internet for information on managing chronic pain are the ones who get in touch with him for treatment. He does not advertise his services and his operation is essentially a one-person office.

The disappointment I had about the visit was not seeing Dan demonstrate his manual technique. I was particularly interested in whether he made changes in his technique since I had just read that in the 1999 edition of Travell and Simons' *Manual* the pioneers of trigger point therapy had "abandoned the application of heavy ischemic compression upon MTrPs."[30] They found "deep digital pressure that produces additional ischemia is not beneficial" and "recommended applying gentle digital pressure to MTrPs to avoid exacerbating tissue hypoxia."[31]

I decided I would keep to the routine of my massage session instead of following Dan's model. In my practice, I tend to take care of clients' immediate massage needs first and talk to them about perpetuating factors after the massage. The post-massage talk is essentially advice on self-care. In Dan's case, people visited him not as a massage therapist but as a healer of last resort. He could therefore spend time to help them understand factors that perpetuated a condition instead of treating them right away.

---

[30]   *Myofascial Trigger Points: Pathophysiology and Evidence-Informed Diagnosis and Management* (2009) by Jan Dommerholt and Peter Huijbregts.
[31]   *Op. cit.*

Dan was not a massage therapist. Travell was not a massage therapist. Their "success" might not be directly relevant to massage therapy.

* * * * *

Treating Low Back Pain

To heed my own counsel, I continued my development as a therapist by treating Jo (not her real name), a client with low back pain, in my "old fashioned" way. She first came to me for a relaxation massage to help me fulfill one of my course requirements for Massage II, the same client for whom I wrote up a treatment plan (Chapter 5). Perhaps due to the relief she got, she agreed to be the subject of my case study for orthopedic massage. It was a time commitment in exchange for free massage and a chance to deal in-depth with her low back discomfort. Thus, the case study was continuation of what I started the semester before and I was able to complete 16 sessions with her. Jo traveled 60 miles round- trip for each treatment. Her time investment might be considered an indication that she found the treatment effective.

* * * * *

Jo was 53 year-old, Black and female. At the time she began her treatment, she was generally in good health, except for high blood pressure for which she took medication. When she first visited me for my Massage II class assignment, she was having a high amount of anxiety and irritability. She felt tension and stiffness in her lower back, legs and shoulders and she walked with depressed shoulders and bowed head. She appeared "heavy laden."

In Massage II, I treated Jo's lower back, leg and shoulder problems for six weeks. The treatment was directed at relaxing the hypertonic muscles by improving fluid circulation and reducing fascial restriction. At the end of the treatment period, Jo found relief in her muscle soreness and was in a more relaxed mood even though the treatment did not deal with the cause of hypertonicity of the muscles.

In Massage III, I decided to focus on one of the primary causes of muscular hypertonicity, a postural disorder known as anterior pelvic tilt (hyperlordosis).[32] Anterior pelvic tilt is marked by both innominates rotating in anterior direction, creating an exaggerated lumbar lordosis. "An anterior pelvic tilt will force the client to stand with her butt sticking way out behind" is how Graf described the condition.[33] The shortened hip flexors and lumbar muscles (postural muscles) inhibit the antagonist phasic muscles across from them, creating a postural distortion that affects directly the low back and pelvic muscles. This condition is visible to naked eyes. Posture assessment on Jo showed that her ASIS was lower than PSIS on both the right and left innominates. The proper treatment for her condition is to elongate the posture muscles and strengthen the phasic muscles.

In the first massage session for the case study, I focused on the gluts, quads, hamstrings and upper traps and I used compression, regional stretching, myofascial release, muscle play, MET, deep stripping and stretching. My objectives were to continue releasing fascial restrictions and hypertonicity, and to deactivate MTrPs. I asked Jo to continue the stretching exercises of arm and leg lift, abdominal curls and hip rotation she started in Massage II. The stretches were from Kit Laughlin's *Stretching and Flexibility* (1999).

In the second session, the techniques and objectives were essentially similar to those of the previous week, with emphasis on releasing TFL, ITT, and upper traps. I deactivated MTrPs in the pelvic area.

To strengthen the phasic muscles, especially the abdominals, I asked Jo to do the abdominal exercise that I designed. It involves a client lying in supine position to slowly effleurage the rectus abdominis, the oblique and the transverse abdominal muscles in a clockwise fashion.[34] Before each gliding stroke, the client is to inhale deeply. As the client begins gliding her hand over the abdomen, she is to exhale as she feels the pressure of the stroke. The gliding is to synchronize with breathing. When each stroke is completed, the client is to inhale and then exhale with the next stroke.

---

[32] For a more thorough discussion of anterior pelvic tilt, see *Clinical Massage Therapy* (2005) by Fiona Rattray and Linda Ludwig; *Orthopedic Massage: Theory and Technique* (2009) by Whitney W. Lowe; and *Orthopedic Assessment in Massage Therapy* (2006) by Whitney W. Lowe.

[33] *Graf's Physiology*, p. 117.

[34] This exercise is different from the one based on Yin Yang Touch that I later developed for strengthening abdominal muscles.

This abdominal exercise serves several functions. It allows in more oxygen to make metabolism more efficient. It strengthens the abdominal muscles and the visceral organs. It purges what is psychologically held up in the abdomen and it helps the client to stay focused on the exercise and to achieve "active relaxation."[35]

Active relaxation is tapping into the sympathetic branch of the nervous system to decelerate the release of ACh. It differs from passive relaxation in which the parasympathetic branch is engaged. However, this distinction is merely to clarify conceptualization rather than actual practice. I believe whenever one branch of the nervous system is engaged; the other branch is complementarily engaged, albeit with less intensity.

To get the full benefit of this exercise, Jo was to do it at home daily. The new exercise was a complement to the QL stretches Jo learned in Massage II. As Jo had missed her lunch that day, it gave me an opportune moment to discuss with her the role of malnutrition as a perpetuating factor in body malfunction. I also reminded her to drink adequate amount of water.

The treatment on the third session was focused on the QL, iliopsoas and the neck muscles (levator scapulae and scalenes, especially). Jo's QL and the upper aspects of gluteus maximus were extremely hypertonic. I deactivated MTrPs in the gluteus maximus and discussed with Jo the role of office environment as a perpetuating factor for low back pain. I asked her to fill out a workstation self-assessment checklist to raise awareness of ergonomic factors.

Treatments for the fourth and fifth sessions were similar to that of the third session. The sequence of massage was routinized. I focused on working on the quads, hamstrings, the gluteal muscles, the QL, the piriformis and the erector spinae groups. In the fifth session, Jo expressed pain for the first time as I applied elbow pressure on her gluteus maximus. Her abdomen was tighter than in previous sessions. I reminded her to do self-care for abdominal breathing and massage and to do QL and Iliopsoas stretches in the following two weeks when I had to interrupt the treatment process. The self-care routine was to improve ROM in the abdominal-lumbar region.

---

[35]   This is in the realm of psychosomatic medicine. It deals with the idea that we tend to hold everything psychologically in our stomach, hence, the expression, "I can't stomach it anymore." The deliberate breathing out is to let go of what is held back. It creates space – room to move about – and enables us to relax. All these are image education.

Treatments for the next four sessions continued to concentrate on the QL, gluts, quads and hamstrings. Fifteen minutes were set aside each session for stretching. I asked Jo to continue stretching and abdominal exercises for self-care. At the final session, I invited Jo to continue massage treatment regularly and to pay close attention to the role of perpetuating factors in chronic pain.

In Massage II, Jo and I had identified her work environment as a perpetuating factor for her low back pain. It was giving her stress, making her unable to deal with multiple and conflicting demands of her job and consequently she was in a positive feedback loop. Jo understood the dynamics, acted on them, and hired a lawyer to deal with job-related conflicts. I also alerted her to the impact of footwear on her leg muscles and the excessive pull of her leg muscles on the pelvic girdle, which in turn created low back pain. She "bought" my analysis, but she continued to wear high-heeled shoes. Massage therapists are no match for fashion designers!

Jo usually had a brief evaluation with me after each massage session at which time I shared my perspective on perpetuating factors reminding her what she already knew was good for her. She just needed encouragement and stimulation to do the right things.

At the end of the case study, Jo appeared to walk more erect. Her head was no longer tilting forward, but tended to tilt backward instead. Her gait seemed to be more assured. She sounded more cheerful. Her upper traps, rectus femoris and the superior aspects of her gluteal muscles were still hypertonic, but the muscles on her back, thighs and legs were practically isotonic. Her QL muscles were less tense.

Posture assessment pictures taken in the final session showed that Jo's right shoulder was still higher than her left, and her right hip higher than her left. Lateral views of Jo showed that her anterior pelvic tilt had adjusted posteriorly and she seemed to be more erect in her posture. The lumbar curvature did not appear excessive. If Jo continued to give her body a chance to restore itself, she should be able to maintain a more natural curvature of her lumbar spine and reduce the incidence and severity of low back pain.

In the ten-week treatment in Massage III, I found very few active MTrPs on Jo. That was contrary to my expectation. With her extensive and intensive involvement in almost all the common perpetuating factors for myofascial pains, I expected to find a lot of MTrPs on her. What was probably happening was that her high tolerance for pain had numbed the nociceptors and insulated the receptive nerve endings from pain sensation. Thus, I did not see local twitches on Jo even though palpation indicated the presence of a nodule in a muscle band. In the more sensitive regions of the body, such as the femoral triangle, Jo showed twitches as nodules were touched. It would be worthwhile for students of massage and bodywork to study the relationship between high tolerance for pain and manifestation of MTrPs and to track the evolution of active MTrPs into latent MTrPs.

The case study has underscored for me the importance of informed, case-specific treatment. As Jo had developed a high tolerance for pain, she preferred hard pressure for massage. However, I felt hard pressure was unlikely to elicit a fresh response from her muscles and decided to use a softer but sustained pressure as the primary mode of treatment. I explained my rationale to her and impressed upon her that "less is more." I even asked her to ease off whatever hard exercises she was doing to give the muscles a rest. I advocated doing softer exercises, with more emphasis on breathing and sustained movement. I wanted Jo to recapture her sensitivity to pain instead of burying it until the pain became unbearable, and I wanted her muscles to have fresh stimuli. The abdominal breathing I practiced with her was a model of "less is more." It is probably applicable to clients with similar temperament as Jo. Jo's anterior pelvic tilt will take more time to get re-balanced, but the progress thus far shows that massage is a viable treatment option.

* * * * *

I don't know how my classmates regarded the case study assignment. For me, it was an opportunity to integrate what I had learned from the classes on anatomy, physiology and massage techniques and what I had read about massage therapy. It was like a thesis or a dissertation, albeit in a much smaller scope.

* * * * *

Another Professional Massage

When I went to Healing Massage the second time to fulfill the course requirement of receiving a professional massage, I launched into a most enjoyable discussion on the business of massage with Cathy, the therapist I visited for the course on anatomy and Swedish massage. In addition to the actual massage and stretching, Cathy shared with me her experience in the profession and the dynamics of private practice. I told her about my case study on anterior pelvic tilt and we discussed pain threshold and the effect of habituation on pain perception.

I shared with Cathy my continuing problem with remembering muscle attachment sites and she assured me "once you are in practice, you don't have to do all that memorizing." She was down to earth about book learning, calling it "school stuff." In actual practice, she said, you rely on your intuition, provided you are not hurting your client. You are successful if you are able to help your client find relief from pain.

We discussed issues involved in working on gluteal muscles. Cathy, perhaps due to her gender, age and experience, stated that she simply told her female clients that she was going to work on their butt. "I will hike up your panties; tuck them in. It's hard to work around them. When you come next time, wear a thong." That's what she would say to her clients. I could not imagine myself saying any of that to a client! She added, "People do what they are comfortable with and you do what you are comfortable with."

After the massage ended, I was ready to pay for the session. Cathy surprised me by suggesting we have a massage trade instead. She wanted to experience the techniques that I talked about. That gesture was a sterling vote of confidence from a veteran therapist! I walked on clouds as I left her studio.

* * * * *

As I mentioned earlier, my classmates came from several Massage II classes. They tended to hang around with their own groups. I did not have an original group to attach to because Sean was a frequent absentee and Lisa was not a regular. I found myself linking up with all the groups and none of the groups. Dave, Jen, Meron and Erika helped me locate muscles, bones and ligaments. Tracy and Crystal helped me appreciate energy work. Susan, LaVerne, Meron and Kaz were my study partners. I felt close to them as we struggled over the course materials and traded massages. By mid-November, most of them had applied for graduation, but I had more courses to take. I knew I would have another set of new classmates when I retook Massage I: anatomy and Swedish massage in Spring 2012, this time for credit.

Chapter 7

ANATOMY FOR CREDIT

Even though I had passed the earlier class on anatomy in Summer 2010 as an auditor, I had forgotten most of what I learned with the lapse of six semesters. Sovine thought I should have an easy time with the musculoskeletal system, but I found it as familiar to me as an acquaintance I met at a cocktail party while I was half-drunk. However, I did remember my "old friends" Tricia Grafelman, Andrew Biel and Ben Benjamin. All I needed was to refresh what I underlined in their books, *Graf's Anatomy*, *Trail Guide to the Body* and *The Ethics of Touch*.

The class was a 16-week course, meeting every Friday. We were ten, more than one-half were people starting a second career. We had the usual lectures, lab sessions, quizzes, midterm and final, research paper on alternate therapy, exchanges with classmates, practice massages beyond the classroom and professional massage. As in her other class, Sovine had a detailed syllabus for the semester, with clear markers for each week. It was work, work and more work!

The outstanding feature of that class was using models for learning bones and muscles. It was one thing to talk about the femur as having femoral head and gluteal tuberosity. It was quite another to feel a model femur in your hand and to rub the femoral head or trace the gluteal tuberosity. The same distinction was true in the study of vertebrae. With the models, we learned how to identify atlas, axis, cervical bones, thoracic bones and lumbar bones. We learned origins and insertions of muscles. Before midterm, Sovine "fed" us bones; after midterm, we focused on the muscles (pun intended) of the course and I became more familiar with how they are attached to bones and to each other. I fell in love with fascia! That was also Sovine's favorite. However, she was more "multi-fide," equally in love with QL and a host of other muscles. Her patent enthusiasm was infectious, even though it was often short-lived.

Through her unique connections, Sovine arranged for the class to visit the cadaver lab of Howard University. We had the unique opportunity to have exposure to how muscles, bones and nerves were connected in a human body. We saw different organs submerged in preserving solutions and a number of wrapped bodies on different operating tables. Muscles of the two cadavers we examined were like slabs of turkey meat with freezer burn. I was especially intrigued by the bundle of nerves in the spinal column.

In addition to muscles and bones, the class also learned about pregnancy massage from Mercedes Olivieri (a doula) and sports massage from Jodi Scholes. I thought I would have no opportunity to use pregnancy massage, but I worked with several expectant and new mothers shortly after my certification. I knew I would put to good use what I learned about sports massage because I had enrolled concurrently in Coordinated Internship and one of its requirements was to give massage to athletes. Both Olivieri and Scholes were instructors in NOVA's Massage Therapy Program.

In addition to sports massage, Scholes also guest lectured on ethics, urging us to "leave [our] opinions at the door" when we worked with our clients. In other words, quit being judgmental! She challenged us to consider: "If money is not an issue, what would you do?" She was quite an expressive and energetic instructor.

In lab sessions, we learned palpation skill and Swedish massage technique. We saw demos on the use of hot and cold packs, paraffin and hot stone massage. We learned chair massage, PNF stretching and active isolated stretching.

For my professional massage, I arranged for Ket, one of my new classmates and an accomplished practitioner of Thai massage, to give me a massage. That was with Sovine's concurrence. Ket brought her massage mat to my house and laid it on the floor of my living room for the session. There was no undressing and no application of lubricant. It was much simpler to set up but much more demanding than a traditional Swedish massage.

* * * * *

Thai Massage

After I lay supine on the mat, Ket paused for a moment of obeisance before she began massage. She compressed and stretched my right foot, leg, and thigh slowly, with a moderate amount of pressure. The focus was on the hamstrings. She repeated the process on the left side of my lower body. She then asked me to lie in a prone position and repeated compression and stretching on my posterior legs and thighs, focusing on the quads. After that, she moved on to work on my shoulders, arms and neck. Just as I was comfortably settled, I had to return to the supine position for her to work on my anterior shoulders, pectorals, arms and head. In addition to using her hands, Ket used her forearms and feet to apply pressure and stretching. Compression, stretching and ischemic pressure appeared to be the dominant movements in her form of Thai massage. She made good use of her standing and kneeling positions to apply pressure on me.

After working on my upper anterior body, Ket had me sit as she pulled my hands over my head and behind me. She gently pushed me forward, rocking the body. She then did diagonal stretching and percussion on my back and ended the session with another moment of obeisance.

The massage was invigorating and I felt recharged. I believe Thai massage is an outstanding complement to Western massage. Many of its moves can be incorporated into deep tissue and orthopedic massages.

* * * * *

Chinese Tuina

For my report on alternate massage, I chose Chinese tuina, a modality I had tried when I visited Beijing many years ago. My sources were *The Science of Acupuncture and Tuina* (1988) by Wu Xu, in book. chaoxing.com, and "Tuina – Chinese Bodywork Massage Therapy," on tcm.health-info.org, both accessed on February 8, 2012.

* * * * *

Tuina – push and grasp – is one of the oldest self-help practices in traditional Chinese medicine. Tuina scholars believe that it originated from primitive people who found relief from massaging their wounds and bruises. Explicit references to tuina's application are in Chinese medical books more than 2,000 years old. As bodywork therapy, it was initially developed for treating diseases among children.

From the Qing Dynasty and through the period prior to 1949, for almost 300 years, the Chinese medical establishment practically discarded tuina as a therapeutic tool in the interest of "modernization" and catching up with Western medicine, even though common people continued to use it widely. Knowledge of this therapeutic practice continued to be passed on orally and through apprenticeship, from fathers to sons, from masters to disciples. In 1956, China established a formal Tuina School, affiliated with the Shanghai Hospital of Chinese Medicine. Two years later, China opened the first outpatient clinic for tuina. Today, there are more than ten subspecialties within Chinese tuina practice.

The goal of tuina is to restore and maintain optimal health through the free flow of qi (vital energy) through a network of passages, known as the meridians, in a human body. This network is a wrap (like fascia) around the body and the meridians connect the internal organs and the skin. Through clinical trials, tuina practitioners have discovered the therapeutic effect of warm hand(s) on skin, and that local stimulation is able to restore wholeness to body functions.

According to a master practitioner, tactile stimulation, as exemplified by tuina, is effective for regulating yin and yang, replenishing functional deficiency and purging congestion, improving blood circulation and dissolving stasis, opening the network of energy passages and making whole the musculoskeletal system.

At the risk of oversimplification, one might equate regulating yin and yang as maintaining homeostasis, achieving a pH balance at the tissue level. Yin is alkaline and yang is acidic. By stimulating the control (pressure) points along the passages, tuina can assist in releasing yin (alkaline) or yang (acid) from body organs for optimal chemical balance.

The practice of replenishing functional deficiency and purging congestion is similar to treating hypo-functions (deficiency) and hyper-functions (congestion), with the ultimate goal of achieving functional balance (homeostasis). Cross friction is similar to replenishing functional deficiency. It shortens a slacking muscle fiber. Stretching is similar to purging congestion. It elongates a tight muscle. To stimulate the pressure points on the meridians, with varying pressure and duration, is to activate the replenishing and purging functions.

Tuina's effect in improving blood circulation is similar to the general effect of Western massage, but tuina's role in dissolving stasis is a unique Chinese understanding about blood circulation. Stasis is sluggish blood (like a liquid bruise) that stagnates in the vascular system as the byproduct of imbalance in the pressure differential between arteries and veins. Tuina, through tactile manipulation, promotes blood circulation by breaking up the viscosity of stasis, increasing the diameter of the arterioles and restoring the pressure differential between arteries and veins.[36]

Tuina's emphasis on opening the network of energy passages is similar to the emphasis of deep tissue work in Western massage practices, especially myofascial work. When muscles contract to the point of spasm, they block the circulation of energy in the network and create local numbness or pain. A positive feedback loop is established. Tuina breaks the positive feedback loop by loosening the adhesion between layers of tissue. Muscles relax to allow freer flow of oxygenated blood into the interstitials and deoxygenated blood into the venous system. They gain needed nutrients and release metabolic wastes into the blood stream for removal from the body.

Tuina's emphasis on making whole the musculoskeletal system is beyond the scope of Western massage practice. It involves using external forces and structural manipulation to correct skeletal or postural misalignment. It is similar to chiropractic work.

Tuina is primarily handwork, the use of different hand techniques for therapeutic bodywork. Effective hand techniques are marked by sustained pressure over a target spot or area for an extended period of time, with sufficient strength to reach the target muscle layer according to a client's condition, evenness of pressure and rhythm, and gentle energy rather than brute force.[37] There are 13 hand

---

[36]   In the class assignment, I had focused on kinetic energy, which I believe is correct for describing the action of tuina. However, in my development as a massage therapist, I had broadened the understanding of tuina to include the transformation of kinetic energy into chemical and electrical energies.

[37]   However, in the practices I observed in China, most tuina practitioners

techniques for opening the meridians: pushing, rolling, rubbing, winding, grasping, pulling, stroking, twisting, striking, clapping (pounding), plucking, combing (as in combing hair) and ironing (as in warming up). Each technique has its own variations adapted to the treatment site. Like other serious therapeutic massages (in contrast to simple relaxation), tuina is interplay between theories and practices, a constant probe between what works and why it works. To achieve competency, a tuina practitioner has to learn under clinical supervision.

In summary, one might describe tuina as a therapeutic practice using external means to bring about internal healing. It elicits the body's own resources to restore wholeness and offers itself as an alternative to other forms of bodywork or traditional Western medical practices.

* * * * *

What I wrote about tuina in Spring 2012 was consistent with what I later learned in China in Winter 2013. My reading on acupressure showed that it is essentially a variation of tuina.

* * * * *

Acupressure

Acupressure is using fingers, hands, knuckles, elbows and even feet, with varying degrees of pressure, to stimulate pressure points on the meridians for therapeutic treatment. It is an ancient healing practice developed in Asia over 5,000 years ago, built on the foundation of folk medicine. The primary difference between acupressure and massage is the use of strokes. In acupressure, there is no stroking movement. It is entirely compression.

Like tuina, acupressure is based on an understanding of the relationship between qi (vital energy), homeostasis and meridians.[38] When qi flow is blocked due to stress, trauma or injury, cells at the congestion site harden into a micro mass and blood evolves into stasis, becoming more acidic. This mass puts pressure on the nervous

---

used force rather than gentle touch.

[38] http://en.wikipedia.org/wiki/Meridian_(Chinese medicine), accessed on 4/14/2012.

system to signal pain in the form of muscular tension. Acupressure is using physical energy to dissolve the micro mass, stimulate the metabolic process and create a wavelike movement of energy that in turn accelerates the flow of body fluid.[39] When the block is removed, pain ceases and the body returns to a state of wholeness. In other words, acupressure stimulates the body to heal itself.

The practice of acupressure is similar to, not exactly alike, the Western practice of trigger point treatment. In addition to popular Chinese form of acupressure, tuina, shiatsu and Thai massage are other expressions of acupressure treatment. You can watch an example of acupressure treatment on *YouTube* under the heading "How to eliminate back pain with acupressure points."

* * * * *

Thus, even before I went to China to study tuina, I had already begun immersing myself in learning about Chinese massage practices. Gradually, I have shifted my goal from getting to know some therapists for my own benefit to doing synthesis of Chinese and Western massage practices for more efficient and effective treatment of chronic conditions. I had no idea that a whole new world would open for me in the days ahead.

As hands-on practice was essential for developing massage skills and learning anatomy, Sovine's class required that my classmates and I pair up to work with each other in a lab session each week and exchange massages with each person at least once in the semester. I managed to trade with all my classmates and visited some of them at their homes. The massage "quota" for the semester was 32, but I completed 70 (!) with classmates, relatives and friends. With concurrent enrollment in the anatomy class and Coordinated Internship, I had no problem finding "clients" for my practice. I had exchanges with Alicia, Bahar, Cindy, Jonathan, Kaye, Ket, Mo, Tamie and Tiffany, some more than once in the semester. Most of us met in the college cafeteria for lunch and shared our learning experience.

<>

---

[39]   Zhiya (acupressure), http://baike.baidu.com/view/706271.html in Chinese, accessed on 4/14/2012.

In addition to anatomy and Swedish massage and Coordinated Internship, I had also enrolled in the Concepts of Disease class. The class on Coordinated Internship brought me into contact with yet another set of classmates and exposure to actual business practices in a wellness center. The class on Concepts of Disease brought me no new contacts but exposure to a host of disorders of the human body. Right before the beginning of the semester, I took a CPR class with the American Red Cross and joined Associated Bodywork and Massage Professionals (ABMP) for insurance coverage. Both CPR and insurance coverage were pre-requisites for the class on Coordinated Internship, which was essentially running a campus clinic and doing community outreach.

Chapter 8

CAMPUS CLINIC AND COMMUNITY OUTREACH

The class on campus clinic and community outreach ran on Saturdays. It had 14 students and the instructor was Maria Mercedes Olivieri, another ardent believer in timely communication. She sent a steady stream of weekly e-mails to us, giving us no excuse for missing opportunities to apply our massage knowledge on different client populations or overlooking some aspects of course requirements. The class was the most active class in the entire curriculum of massage therapy program.

We had no textbook for that class. Instead, Olivieri copied a number of articles on comfort touch, massage for the ill, mindful touching, boundaries and modesty, and cancer pain and anxiety for us to read, mostly to remind us of what we already knew or should have known.

We also had no written or oral test. Our grade was based on completion of all the class activities, with primary emphasis on attendance. Each of us started the semester with a 100-point credit. If we failed to show up at clinic or special events, 15 points per occurrence would be deducted from our credit. If we cancelled our attendance without the required 24-hour notice, 10 more points per occurrence would be deducted. If we cancelled our attendance with at least 24 hours' notice or if we were tardy, 1-5 points would be deducted for the first occurrence and 5-10 points deducted for each subsequent occurrence. It does not take many deductions for students to drop to a failing grade, making it necessary to repeat the class. The scoring system is harsh, but it reflects the real life requirements of customer service. Being present is the first rule of engagement in just about every occupation. The emphasis on presence is valuable for newcomers to the workforce and for veteran workers who have developed bad work habits.

Campus clinic and community outreach is the only class in the program that requires students to wear a uniform and to show proof that we have liability insurance and current certification for CPR. Again, this is a preview of what we might expect in an employment situation. When I was interviewed for a position with a spa in Northern Virginia after my certification, I had to provide similar documentation and wear an attire prescribed by the spa. To be treated as a professional, you need to dress like a professional!

As her class was made up of students from different streams, Olivieri asked us to introduce ourselves, tell our life stories and share our career goals. That was an excellent practice. I informed the group of my emerging interest in caring for caregivers and got to know a number of new classmates that included Robert, Laura, Christina and Erica, friends with whom I kept in contact after graduation. Robert is a retired Federal employee, almost like a godfather to the younger classmates. He started a website for classmates to communicate with each other and continued to keep it alive as of this writing. Laura is a yoga teacher and a consummate network builder. She introduced me to a veteran care organization when I explored doing a workshop on understanding PTSD later in my career. Christina is a generous spirit and a perceptive learner. She offered me the use of her massage table in the first session of campus clinic and provided me useful feedback on my massage techniques and my writing on massage. Erica shares my outlook on caring for caregivers. Even though she lived quite a distance from me, we had frequent trades and shared notes on what we discovered in our respective learning. I was fortunate to have a new group of friends and to build up a professional network of massage therapists.

Olivieri had a calm presence and a caring aura. Nothing could possibly ruffle her. She was attentive to students and clients and she made sure Chuck, her husband, was available to serve as a practice dummy for every clinic session. While she might appear low-key, she was observant of everything that went on during clinic and outreach events. She tracked the massage hours we accrued to inform us of our completion status. She gave us client feedback forms to inform us of our progress as professionals. Her end-of-semester feedback was constructive. Like me, she was formerly a Federal Government employee, but she became a massage therapist at a much younger age.

Just like the lab sessions in orthopedic massage, campus clinic converted the college gym into a massage clinic with screens, dimmed light and quiet music. We assigned a couple of classmates the role of traffic manager to channel clients to us. We reviewed client histories, confirmed what clients wanted us to work on, and led them to our individual stations. After our clients had settled on the massage tables, we worked. Each hands-on session lasted 50 minutes. We had five mandatory campus clinic sessions to give us opportunities to complete at least 12 units of table massage. For each massage, we had to prepare SOAP notes and to ask clients for written feedback. I made it my practice to meet with clients after the session for one-on-one verbal debriefing. I was not as interested in what clients thought of my massage skills as I was in how they felt about their condition after massage. Olivieri might disagree with me about post-massage interview but she did not penalize me for it. The interview was important to me (and possibly for the client) because it gave me the opportunity to educate clients about their conditions and self-care.

Despite my disinterest in clients' written feedbacks, I was elated by the comments of a young woman: *I thought the breathing exercise was a perfect way to make me relax initially. I also was pleasantly surprised when he didn't quickly attack my problem area (lower back) but gave me a thorough face, head, arm and hand massage. I think the hands are often neglected but not in this case! He had nice, warm hands and found tender points in my upper back I didn't realize existed. He spoke in a nice calm voice that added to the relaxing experience. He also did a unique shake up of my body that surprisingly stretched me out and gently woke me up. I thought it was a nice touch. What a wonderful massage and I would come back to him!*

The class had four community outreach events: two massage sessions at The Virginian, a senior living facility in Fairfax; and two sports massages, namely, the Irish Spring 10K race (Marine Corps Marathon) in Prince William County and the Rev 3 Run Rogue 5K race in Fairfax, Virginia. We also had a campus chair massage clinic on the last day of class. The off-campus events attracted many clients but the chair massage clinic drew only a handful of "customers."

Initially, Olivieri had also scheduled an outreach event at the Northern Virginia Training Center for us to work with a different client population. However, sometime into the semester, the Center threw in a new requirement for all to get TB tests before we were allowed to work with their residents. Even though we all had a physical before entering the Massage Therapy Program, they insisted on the TB test requirement. Since it was too late for us to comply, that outreach event was canceled.

The Virginian Stretch

In my first visit to The Virginian, I worked three hours non-stop on eight clients, including residents, staff and caregivers. Most of them complained of having neck, shoulder and lower back pain. I remember my frustration over the ineffectiveness of my treatment of low back pain of a CNA. I seated her just as I had seated other clients and applied compression, kneading and percussion on her back for 15 minutes (that was the time limit). While she felt less discomfort after the massage, her back muscles were as tight as when she began the session.

When a second staff member came to me with the same problem, I had already thought of a more effective way for pain relief. After I gave her ten to twelve minutes of chair massage, I asked her to stand, bend her knees slightly, and then bend her body forward as slow as she felt comfortable. As she bent forward, she was to breathe slowly and deeply. When she reached her end point, I asked her to raise herself from the lower back, again with deep breathing and slow motion. After she was fully erect, I had her bend herself and rise again. As she was bending and rising the second time, I tapped rapidly and lightly along the ES region of her upper back and the QL region of her lower back. When she bent and rose the third time, I patted the same areas gently with loose and empty fists. When she bent and rose the fourth and final time, I brushed her back laterally. After she resumed her upright position, I placed my hands on her anterior shoulders and asked her to pull them medially (inwardly) while she exhaled. On a count of three, I asked her to relax and stretched the shoulders laterally (outwardly). Then, holding the shoulders in the stretched position, I asked her to pull them medially again and I stretched them further. I repeated the process a third time and then tapped the shoulders firmly a few times to complete the session. I wish I had a camera to capture the look on that staff person's face after the stretches. She was beaming. "It worked!" She squealed with delight. That's how my Virginian Stretch was born, but most of my classmates were unaware of what I had done. They were busy with their massages and many received rave reviews from the residents. I have repeated the stretches on countless number of friends and clients, results were always positive.

Sports Massages

The Irish Sprint 10K race was a scaled down version of the October Marine Corps Marathon. We met before dawn at the campus to drive in carpools to the Prince William Forest National Park and set up the massage tables under a tent long before the event began. As the Marines had prepared the site professionally, we encountered no logistical problems. As expected, only a few runners drifted in for massage at the beginning, but a queue was formed outside the tent shortly after the race was over. All of us worked non-stop for two to three hours. It was tiring, especially hard on the feet and lower back. One of the runners I worked on had a foot problem, but she traveled all the way from North Carolina despite her physician's advice just to participate in the race. Incredible!

The Medical Director for the race visited us during our massage. Olivieri reported that he was impressed by the skills we demonstrated. *He made some important suggestions: first, to ensure that our post-race massages are slow rather than invigorating; second, that we help the athletes get off the table slowly in case their blood pressures have gone down; and third, that we have the athletes stomp their feet on the ground once they are off the table to stimulate circulation.*

<>

The Rev 3 Run Rogue 5K race was a family event held in Fairfax; young children and their parents were running together. Our massage station was off to a corner of the race "headquarters" at the Fairfax Corner Shopping Center. The race had fewer runners than the Marine Marathon; but everyone seemed to enjoy it. As the race was fairly informal, two of my classmates decided to run the race before massage and I became their cheerleader. I was at the starting line to see them off and at the finish line to cheer for them. After the race, they resumed their role as therapists and began working on their fellow runners -- perspiring people working on perspiring people! Actually, we could have excused them because we had more therapists than were needed at the event but they probably needed the credit. Some of us had set up our tables under the open sky because the organizers had provided us inadequate tent space, less than half of what the Marines provided. I was able to try out the Virginian Stretch on runners and classmates.

Wellness Center

Even before the class began, I had begun working as an extern at a wellness center in Northern Virginia through the introduction of a former classmate. From conversations with other classmates, I knew that working at an off-campus facility was an option for campus clinic and community outreach and I wanted to use that opportunity to explore what it was like to work in actual business before I became certified. I externed in the wellness center for two months, but I did not submit my experience for credit because I had earned enough credits from other activities. Two of my former classmates were my co-workers.

The center was a single-owner business in an office park. It had a spacious room for skin treatment, two less spacious rooms for massage on the ground floor and four rooms for massage on the first floor. The manager was the owner's daughter, a Korean-American woman. The center had a core of therapists working full-time and part-time, and they usually congregated in the staff lounge on the first floor to keep the ground floor free of congestion. Unless I was needed elsewhere, I stayed in the staff lounge to chat with the therapists about their experience and specialties. The therapists I met had Filipino, Iranian, Ethiopian, Thai, Hispanic, Black and White American backgrounds. There were several men among them.

A unique experience I had at the center was walking on the back and feet of a client receiving Thai massage. The manager arranged Thai massage as part of the in-service orientation for an "apprentice" and me. After showing us how she walked on her client (actually her husband), the therapist allowed the apprentice and me to try doing the same moves. The walk seemed simple and easy, but it wasn't. Trying to balance myself on a live body was precarious, regardless of the cooperation of a willing subject! That modality was more strenuous than it looked and too distorting for my body. Acrobatic moves require dexterity I don't have!

One of the staff persons also showed me how to prepare sugaring for skin care but I was not attentive. Esthetics was beyond my interest and my scope of practice. However, in an interesting twist of my massage career, my first public speaking as a massage therapist was at the International Congress of Esthetics and Spa held at Long Beach, California in 2014!

At the wellness center, I had massaged only one client in the entire time I was there and that was to assist one of the Thai therapists. Most of the time, I gave impromptu shoulder and hand massage to the therapists. I would have loved to give full body massage to the therapists for professional feedback on my techniques, but all of them were usually busy. I did not have a lot of hands-on massage practice, but I did learn a lot about the business of massage.

As an extern, I was involved in doing and folding laundry, refilling massage cream bottles, scrubbing hot stones, de-waxing the candle holders, answering the telephone (the most challenging chore), driving to Staples for office supplies, sweeping, mopping and vacuuming the floors, dusting the shelves, taking garbage to the dumpster and other menial chores. Not glamorous, but essential tasks for running a business.

The center gave me a taste of what it was like to work in a spa setting. I knew it was not a viable or desirable career choice for me. My interest had moved to massage research and I decided to conserve my energy to pursue it. The massages I gave to Heidi Peña-Moog to fulfill one of the course requirements affirmed my decision.

Ice Treatment

In addition to being an instructor of orthopedic massage at NOVA, Peña-Moog practices massage at The Virginian. She agreed to let me work with her to fulfill the course requirement of giving "at least 4 hours of table massage to a healthcare professional." I had to compile a "docket" of client history, feedback forms and SOAP notes for that requirement. I gave Peña-Moog four sessions of massage, each lasting 75-90 minutes.

In our initial interview, she stated her quads and hamstrings were extremely sore and she needed relief from muscle pain, but she was not interested in full body massage. After the first massage, she wrote that I was able to get to the root of her muscle problem and that I understood what techniques to use to address painful areas. In the second session, she continued to have tight and painful hamstrings and I used tapotement, passive and active stretching, friction and oscillation to release the tightness.

Before the third session, I thought of using ice to treat the tightness in her thighs, contrary to the usual application of heat treatment. I was drawing from what I learned in Massage II about how muscles tend to loosen themselves from perceived injury. Applying ice on the quads and hamstrings was to add stress to the highly stressed muscles to the point of "managed injury," and the overstress could induce them to give up the tightness. Peña-Moog was initially skeptical, but she agreed to have ice treatment on the thigh muscles. It worked! She "found [the ice treatment] to be more relaxing on her tight hamstrings," and the cool sports gel I applied on her made her "feel more relaxed and not as sore afterwards." I repeated the ice treatment in the final session.

Peña-Moog was very positive about her treatment and complimented me for thinking "outside the box." She continued to call on me to give her massage after my certification and was the first person to pay for my massage service. I was certain the thought process demanded in the course on Concepts of Disease that I had enrolled in the same semester had further conditioned me to analyze, make connections and explore treatment options. I felt fortunate to have "learning partners" willing to let me test out my techniques on them.

Chapter 9

ALL YOU WANT TO KNOW ABOUT DISEASES

The course Concepts of Disease was notorious for being difficult and the name Nancy Crippen was synonymous with toughness. "If you pass Dr. Crippen's course, you would have no problem with NCBTMB," was what a former student told me. Within the NOVA system, another instructor was teaching a similar course at the Springfield campus. I considered registering for it instead of Crippen's class, but my classmates advised against it. They felt her class was more relevant to massage therapy. I thought what they really wanted was for me to suffer as they did. It was a rite of passage I had to go through, but I did not look forward to another round of torture. The only saving grace of taking her class was that I did not have to attend class lecture.

The course was an online course designed to help us become familiar with conditions clients might report in their intake forms, make safe and appropriate practice decisions and recognize signs and symptoms of disease so clients can be referred to appropriate providers for evaluation. It was time sensitive, not self-paced. I had to follow its schedule strictly, neither early nor late. Not that I had any intention of submitting my assignments late, but the warning about losing one point for every day they were late was enough of an incentive to keep my nose to the grindstone. After all, each assignment was worth only five points. How many points could one afford to lose and still pass that course? As I thought about the course requirements, it dawned on me that Crippen was teaching something else in addition to pathology. She was teaching us to become professional therapists. Her meta-message was, to work as a therapist, you have to meet your appointment. If you are not on time or don't show up, you are useless to the client. You develop the habit of being on time by submitting your assignments on time. Other instructors had the same emphasis, perhaps with a little more latitude. Crippen's first email to the class stated clearly that she allowed no exceptions for due dates, hence, I nicknamed her "Dr. No Exception!"

Actually, the meta-messages of the course, intended or not, were as important as its content. One of the key features of Crippen's class was the requirement that you *"document the specific references used to answer each question including the name of the source and the page numbers and/or website section."* It was probably the toughest requirement since most students were not used to tracing ideas to their sources. However, her emphasis is exactly what professionals are required to do, either implicitly or explicitly. Tracing our ideas to their sources is one way for our audience and colleagues to gauge their plausibility. While I was able to cite most of the ideas in my answers, I had occasionally resorted to simply stating I heard them from Sovine's lectures.

Crippen probably recognized that it was difficult to study diseases. She made it easier for students to earn a passing grade by offering them the option of doing an article search related to the topic of the week. If we completed an article search and reported it on time, we gained bonus points toward our exam. That option was, in effect, training us to develop another set of habits for being a professional, the habit of reading current and relevant literature to stay abreast of our field. Most students had little or no time to read anything beyond the textbooks. The option gave us incentive to develop the habit of reading. It was a winning method. Except for the first exercise when I could not post the article search due to some administrative problems, I received full credit for all my subsequent submissions and the bonus points helped to boost my overall grade.

Show What You Have Learned

The textbook we used for the class was *Mosby's Pathology for Massage Therapists* by Susan Salvo (2009). If Crippen were teaching the class in person, she might have read the book aloud as her lectures. As it was, reading the textbook on our own became our lectures. Crippen divided the book into 12 lessons. For each lesson, she had a series of questions to guide us in our reading. Those questions were also the assignment for the week and our written answers had to show that we had learned something. That requirement reminded me of a fiasco in a different life in which I was learning theology. I had attended a class on Systematic Theology and I thought I learned it well. In the final exam the professor posed the question, "What is sin?" I answered it with what I learned in Sunday school about "falling short of the glory of God" rather than what I learned in his class. I wrote a one-sentence answer instead of a learned exposition of 4 or 5 pages of theological writing with citations from different sources down through the centuries. For my right-on-target, concise answer, I got a big F for my grade and had to repeat the course. Fifty years later, I have not forgotten the bitter lesson learned. I did not intend to repeat Concepts of Disease, so I pulled out everything I knew to show I learned something and I wrote my answers voluminously. Where the textbook did not provide the information, I did not hesitate to draw on other resources.

In Lesson 3, we had 8 questions. How I tackled them was typical of how I answered questions in the other lessons. For each of the answers below, Crippen posted the question at the beginning. The questions were open-ended for students to show what they knew.

* * * * *

1. *Describe the PPALM method of organizing the client interview.* PPALM stands for **P**urpose of session, **P**ain, **A**llergies and skin conditions, **L**ifestyle and vocation, and **M**edical and health information. It prompts the therapist to gather the essential information from the client's perspective for forming a preliminary treatment plan. Information gathered will guide the therapist in deciding if massage is contraindicated or indicated. The data will fit in the Subjective section of the SOAP notes. References: *Mosby's Pathology*, pp. 24-28.

2. *Describe methods of obtaining subjective and objective data on a client.* To obtain data on a client, regardless of their subjective or objective nature, the therapist has to ask a series of questions and listen or read the responses, using her ears, eyes and heart with undivided attention. Subjective data are information the client or the client's guardian or

representative provides, in written or oral forms. Besides the routine bio-data, the information includes various symptoms and how he feels. The data are what the client interprets as his conditions. Objective data are what the therapist gathers from observation and measuring devices. They include signs, referenced assessments and palpable evidence. The data are information other trained professional can verify. References: *Mosby's Pathology*, pp. 19-24.

3. *What is informed consent and why is it important?* To touch someone without his consent is to commit an act of battery liable for lawsuit, unless he is unconscious and in a life threatening condition. Massage (touching for therapeutic purpose) usually takes place in a "normal" situation. Thus, consent is required. Informed consent is giving permission after being told what the touch involves and the options a client has about the process of touching. It applies particularly to touching the more sensitive areas of the body such as upper and inner thigh, lower abdomen, or breast tissue in women, and the use of a technique that the client may feel strange or unusual or cause increased pain. The information is to temper his anxiety and stress. For example, massaging the gluteal muscles is essential for releasing tightness of the quadratus lumborum muscles in the treatment of lower back pain and flesh-to-flesh contact is more effective in the transformation of ground substance from gel to sol state. That's why we touch (massage) the glut muscles. It is important for the therapist to explain what and why she intends to do and for the client to agree to the treatment. Obtaining informed consent is another way to prepare the client for therapeutic massage and it should be done during the initial interview with a simple question such as "Is there any part of your body that you do not want me to touch?" References: *First Aid, CPR and AED*, 5th ed., p. 6 and *Tappan's Handbook*, p. 115.

4. *What is the purpose of post-massage communication?* I use post-massage communication (feedback) to find out how the client feels after the treatment, what she thinks work or does not work. I share what I observe from the massage about the client's condition and suggest self-care techniques, as needed. I also use the post-massage session to discuss perpetuating factors for pain and remind the client to apply what she already knows to maintain wellness. Post-massage communication is

education (for both the client and me) and empowerment (for the client). It also provides information for adjusting the treatment plan or techniques and for monitoring progress. References: *Mosby's Pathology*, p. 30.

5. *Why is documentation an important component of client care?* Documentation is writing down concisely what has been done to what part of client's body and why. It provides for the construction of a case history and yields information on patterns such as what worked and what didn't, and on progress and setback. It is essential for helping the therapist to remember the treatment performed and to build on the past for effective treatment. Also, documentation is essential for insurance billing and legal matter, to indicate massage is a medical necessity. However, from my perspective, a crucial role of documentation is its function as raw data (evidence) for research that is useful for improving the quality of overall (systemic) client care. For example, the SOAP notes and health history of clients attending the NVCC clinics are a source for assessing overall care provided to our clients and for developing expertise for treating common body pains. The analysis and subsequent refocus of teaching strategies might help educate massage therapists to become more effective and efficient practitioners. References: *Tappan's Handbook*, 5th ed. DVD Disk 1, "Clinical Applications: Documentation," "Documentation – SOAP notes, progress reports, narrative reports," Internet access on 1/23/2012 and "Massage Therapy Documentation and Software for a Successful Practice," Internet access on 1/23/2012.

6. *Distinguish between the client intake form, session charting and treatment plan.* An intake form is similar to a health history form in which the client provides her bio-data and medical history and the symptoms she feels. It is like a request for treatment. Session charting is a record of what happened in a specific session, usually in the SOAP form: **s**ubjective information provided by the client for a particular session (Why are you here?), **o**bjective information gathered by the practitioner in a specific session, **a**ssessment of both subjective and objective information and forming an action plan for the session (What needed to be done and did the practitioner reach the goal for the session?), and **p**lan (How does the client feel and what does he need to do for self-care and subsequent

sessions?). A treatment plan is a guiding document on what the massage involves—number of sessions, muscles to work on, treatment modes, self-care needed and milestones for progress. My definition of a treatment plan is different from Susan Salvo's. Hers is based on the PPALM structure and oriented to a specific session. Mine is a plan for treatment over a period of time. It is an "answer" to the request for treatment and spells out what I will do. References: *Mosby's Pathology*, pp. 28-30, *Tappan's Handbook*, 5th ed. DVD Disk 1, "Clinical Applications: Documentation," and Internet access cited in Question #5 above.

7. *What are guidelines for assessing pain levels prior to and during massage?* Pain is a subjective feeling, a sensation only known to the client. It varies from client to client. What appears to be painful to one client may not appear to be so to another client. Some clients seem to have developed a high tolerance for pain or become numb to pain. To assess pain levels, one has to ask the client but the client's reply must be tempered with the therapist's knowledge of pain manifestation. Before massage, the therapist might use the OPPQRST model to elicit information: Onset – When did the pain start? Provocative – What makes it worse? Palliative – What makes it better? Quality – How would you describe the pain? Radiation – Does the pain radiate to somewhere? Site – Where does it hurt? Timing – How often does it hurt? The therapist might use a descriptive or numeric pain intensity scale for the client to indicate the pain level. During massage, the therapist checks in with the client on the status and level of pain and the effect of massage on felt pain. In short, the primary guideline is to ask the client, but the therapist should lean on easing up on pressure rather than going with a client's professed ability to take pain. References: *Mosby's Pathology*, pp. 24-26.

8. *What aspects of a treatment plan should be considered in post-massage communication?* Recommendations for self-care such as stretches, self-massage, regular physical and breathing exercises (abdominal massage) and attention to the perpetuating factors for pain (including biomechanical stresses, nutritional inadequacies, metabolic and endocrine inadequacies and psychological factors) should be considered in post-massage communication. However, since the

massage therapy profession is healthcare and not medical, communication must be phrased in a recommendation mode rather than prescriptive or diagnostic. Treatment plan must be within our scope of practice. References: *Mosby's Pathology*, p. 26 and *Myofascial Pain and Dysfunction: The Trigger Point Manual*, Chapter 4 "Perpetuating Factors."

* * * * *

Case Study

In addition to lesson assignments, the course had five case studies which we had to provide answers. With all that I had learned up to that point, I decided to assume the role of a "trained therapist." I did not write just to fulfill class assignments. I wrote as though I were giving my professional opinion on the case. I wanted to feel good about what I wrote long after the completion of my class assignment. If my answers were wrong, they would be a matter of professional opinion and not factual or material mistakes. I could learn from why I was considered wrong and I did not try to guess what Crippen wanted for an answer. I did the best I could and trusted Crippen to give me at least the benefit of doubt even if she disagreed with my clinical reasoning. I tackled the case studies with gusto; the following was exceptional in that I would decline treating the client unless he followed my alternate mode of treatment! Crippen provided the health history and asked the opening questions.

* * * * *

Health history: The client is a 32-year old male, a former Navy Seal, and an avid body builder. He states that he has asthma but does not use an inhaler. He snores heavily, has a hiatal hernia, gastric reflux, genital herpes, jock itch, and TMJ. Last year he had surgery to reattach his right Achilles tendon which he ruptured playing rugby. He takes supplements to help him "max out" lifting weights.

1. *What therapeutic assessment questions pertinent to his specific condition(s) would the therapist ask in the pre-massage interview?* Pertinent questions that a therapist might ask would include: When did you retire from Navy Seal? What is your present occupation? What does it require physically? How often do

you do weight lifting and body building? When was your most recent physical exam? What did the physician recommend? What remedies are you taking for the hiatal hernia? Do you have fever? Do you have any body discomfort [as an indication of lymph swelling]? When did you eat before you came here? Was it a heavy meal? Do you have any problem with lying prone for massage? How do you cope with asthma? Do you have your inhaler with you? How widespread is your jock itch? Are you using any medication to treat it? What is your diet like? Do you drink alcohol, how much and how often? Do you smoke? How many cigarettes a day? Do you drink six to eight glasses of water each day? How well do you sleep? Does snoring interfere with your sleep? What brought you to this visit and what would you like to get from this visit? In addition to these questions, the therapist might do palpation, range-of-motion and resistive tests and special orthopedic tests to validate the subjective information. References: *Mosby's Pathology*, pp. 24-26, 41-42, *Orthopedic Assessment in Massage Therapy* by Whitney W. Lowe, 2006, pp. 20-22, and *Mosby's Pathology*, pp. 69-70, 126, 148, 291-301, 316, 343, 390-91.

2. *Is massage indicated and, if so, what adaptive measures should be employed?* There is no general contraindication for massage. However, since the client has (a) a history of genital herpes and jock itch which are contraindications for working on the glut muscles and medial thigh muscles; (b) a history of asthma and heavy snoring which signify chronic obstructive pulmonary disorder and makes massaging in prone position undesirable; and (c) a history of hiatal hernia which makes massaging the abdominals questionable, the client might be asked if he still wants to proceed with a modified form of massage. Given the hypertonicity of the client's muscles, he might also be asked to reconsider his request for a vigorous deep tissue massage. His muscles are so conditioned for pain and hard work that they need a different set of stimulations to release the hypertonicity. The therapist might use cryotherapy to contract the muscles for auto release and then re-tone the muscles to body temperature. If the client is willing to follow the alternate mode of treatment, the therapist could proceed with giving him a massage. Otherwise, the client should get his treatment from someone else. References:

Mosby's Pathology, pp. 69-70, 126, 148, 291-301, 316, 343, 390-91 and *Human Anatomy & Physiology*, 7th edition, p. 525.

3. *What observations and palpation should be made during the pre-massage interview and during the massage treatment?* If the client agrees with the modified form of massage, the therapist needs to pay attention to the reactions of various prior medical conditions. After the hypertonic muscles have been treated, the therapist can give him a Swedish massage to re-educate the client's body to a different touch sensation. During the massage treatment, the therapist might observe the client's movement and demeanor: How does he react to Swedish massage? Is he tense or relaxed during the massage? Is there any posture distortion? Is the body symmetrical? The therapist might also focus on the temperature, tone, tenderness and texture of client's muscles, and their reactions to the new stimuli. References: *Orthopedic Assessment*, pp. 21-31, and *Tappan's Handbook*, pp. 125-88.

4. *What massage techniques specific to his condition(s) should the therapist employ?* The therapist might use ice to over-contract the hypertonic muscles to induce the Golgi tendon reflexes to trick the muscles to relax. After that, give the client a full body Swedish massage to relax him and to focus on releasing overall tension. She might also take the client through muscle energy therapy to decrease the tonicity of the muscles and use the "Virginian Stretch" (Chapter 6) to open up the posterior deep muscles and reduce their hypertonicity. References: *Tappan's Handbook*, pp. 125-88 and *Human Anatomy & Physiology*, 7th edition, p. 525.

5. *What post massage instructions would the therapist be likely to give this client?* The therapist would likely suggest that the client alternate heavy body building activities with gentle aerobic and stretching exercises to give the muscles a more balanced development. The warm up movements of Taiji Quan (Taichi exercise) would be a good model to follow. Similarly, the client might work with a partner to practice the Virginian Stretch. Further along the treatment process, the therapist would likely recommend that her client review nutritional and lifestyle stresses that exacerbate his many medical conditions. The client might also be advised to get medical review of his use of supplements for bodybuilding. References: *Orthopedic Massage*, pp. 118-130. "Assessment," in *Mosby's Pathology*, p.

252, and *Taichi for health, Yang Long Form* with Terence Dunn, 2004, DVD.

* * * * *

After her review of my answers, Crippen posted extensive comments in my record, just as she did for the other four cases. She offered significant insights on how the case might be handled including sanitary precautions I needed to take and how I might deal with drug use. Even if the bulk of the written critique might be the same for all students, she still needed time to compose the critique in advance and to post it to the right cases with appropriate additional comments. In the class I enrolled, she had posted 17 comments on assignments and case studies, and 3 reports on exam results to *each* individual record. I believe teaching an online course is more labor intensive than teaching in person.

The course on diseases had three exams. We could take them at a test center of our choice. I chose the one at the Springfield campus. Each exam had questions requiring short answers, questions on contraindications and questions about matching. It also had a short essay question. The testing format and procedures were similar to the certification exam by NCBTMB. I was drilled well not only in exam content but also in exam procedures.

Salvo's textbook has a page of 20 questions of self-test for each chapter. It also includes "Evolve Student Resources" for more online study. They brought me back to my Human Biology days of doing as many of the exercises as I could. Thanks to bonus points I earned, I completed the course successfully.

<>

On the heel of that success, I wrote to Crippen asking for permission to do an independent study with Jodi Scholes instead of taking Scholes' regular class on Entrepreneurship for Massage Therapist, i.e., the Business of Massage. The emphasis of that class was on developing business plans, an activity I was engaged in during my prior careers with the U.S. Government. Going through similar materials would be of marginal value, especially since I was not planning to start or to be involved in a massage business. However, what made me ask for an alternative was my scheduled visit to China in the summer. That trip was planned many months before. I would have signed up for a similar class after the trip, but the Business of Massage would not be offered again until Winter 2013. If I had to wait until then, it would delay my completion of the program by at least six months and I might lose steam in the interim. Thus, I searched for an alternative. Scholes knew my interest was in research and not in business, and she was amenable to my doing an independent study, which was to be an analysis of the cases the campus clinic had handled in recent years. As Scholes was hired to do marketing for the Massage Therapy Program in addition to teaching the Business of Massage, she was very interested in knowing the demography of massage clients and the independent study would provide her the essential data. As I was focusing on becoming a research massage therapist, I was interested in knowing the discomforts that brought clients to the clinic so that I could better prepare myself to meet the challenge of the most prevalent problems. I believed I could glean the necessary information from intake forms and SOAP notes of the campus clinic. Crippen concurred with my request.

Besides the Business of Massage, I had to complete only one more course to fulfill the graduation requirement. That course was Therapeutic Massage II: physiology and deep tissue massage of which Sovine was the instructor. I had audited that class before (Chapter 5) and had completed all the assignments and tests, but I had to sign up for it again as a regular student in order to get the credit. I did not mind to repeat everything I had done, but I would miss at least four weeks of class and I needed Sovine's permission to be absent. On the other hand, if I could do an independent study in lieu of repetition, I could tackle it on my own schedule, but I still needed Sovine's permission. I had in mind expanding the case study on using massage to treat fibromyalgia with a client I worked with in the class on orthopedic massage and trigger point therapy (Massage III). I discussed with Sovine what I might do. Fortunately for me, she still had my record from the semester when I audited her course and she did not think it worthwhile for me to sit through her lectures again. She recognized the significance of the case study on fibromyalgia and was willing to discuss with Crippen about allowing me to do it as a substitute for attending her class. Upon completion of the case study, I was to receive credit for the coursework I completed previously.

Crippen concurred with Sovine's recommendation and I made the deadline for applying for graduation in August. "Dr. No Exception" was in fact exceptional! She might have to follow rules, but she was willing to work within the rules to move me expeditiously through the system.

Chapter 10

CLIENTS OF NOVA CLINIC

The Massage Therapy Program of NOVA runs a massage clinic on the Woodbridge campus on Saturday mornings. Students from the classes on campus clinic and community outreach and orthopedic massage and trigger point therapy provide free services to clients. The clinic has 453 files for the period between January 2006 and June 2012. Each file has intake form(s) that clients filled out in their first visit and/or updated in later years, and SOAP note(s) completed by students for every massage.

The primary focus of the independent study was on the clients themselves (who they were, where they came from, their medical history and why they came to the clinic), but the study also offered valuable information on how the operation of the campus clinic might be improved and what changes might be made to turn routine administrative and clinical data into research information.

Intake Form

The intake form is a primary treatment document for massage therapy. It is also known as a health history form. In our campus clinic, we included with it a consent and release statement which a client had to sign before receiving massage. The first intake form I used asked for the client's personal data such as name, address, age, sex, marital status, occupation, source of referral and medical history. It had 31 medical problems and 12 current medical conditions for the client to check off.

At first glance, compiling composite information on clients from data in intake forms seemed to be a simple and easy task, but it was made complicated by the clinic's use of several versions of the intake form in the period. When several intake forms are in file for a client, I used the oldest form to establish the profile and the newer forms to fill in information gaps. I also used SOAP notes for filling in missing information such as the client's gender and date of initial contact. I recreated as full a profile of each client as I could before I began data entry.

The lessons I learned from scanning the files are the importance of using consistent versions of intake form from year to year and the importance of ensuring that clients fill out the intake form completely and legibly. The first lesson, using consistent versions of intake form, is an administrative issue that Massage Therapy Program can and should decide *a priori*. If a newer version of intake form has to be used, it should ask for all the information the older version needed besides gathering new information for which a new version is designed, so that consistent data are available for longitudinal comparison.

The second lesson, ensuring that clients provide complete intake information, is the primary responsibility of the student therapist. Therapists should have reviewed and filled information gaps and clarified what is illegible in the initial interview before giving massage. In fact, the completeness of an intake form and the legibility of SOAP notes can be an unobtrusive measure of a student's potential effectiveness as a therapist. This unobtrusive measure is more useful than the feedback forms that clients fill out after a massage. The clinic can dispense with the feedback forms and use the post-massage time for client and student to assess the effectiveness of massage instead.

Data Elements

Before I analyzed the 453 cases, I had to select data elements relevant for the study, then code and organize them for data analysis. As my "mandate" was to do a descriptive study of the clients of campus clinic and I had no restriction on what I was to report on, I was free to select data elements that might yield a composite profile of clients. I decided to use a standard Microsoft Office software Excel® for analysis and organize the data elements accordingly.

From the plethora of information in the intake forms and SOAP notes, I chose client's name, home address (city, zip code), date of birth, age, sex, marital status, occupation, source of referral, prior massage status (Have you ever received massage therapy?), type of prior massage experience, type of massage preferred, current medication (Are you taking medication?), medical history, current medical conditions, date of initial visit, date of the most recent visit (as shown in SOAP notes), and number of SOAP notes to establish the profile of each client. To ensure privacy and confidentiality, I omitted street address and telephone numbers intentionally in the "raw" database.

In my preliminary visual inspection of the cases, I found that in the health history section, most clients checked off no more than three or four medical problems and reported one or two current medical conditions that warrant attention. So, I made room for four medical problems and two medical conditions in the raw database to make the study manageable.

After all the 453 records were entered into the worksheet, a data sort revealed eight cases had no intake forms and no date of initial visit. Without basic information, the cases were of no use to the study and were removed accordingly. After their removal, the working database had 445 files (clients). Each item of interest was then sorted and tabulated.

As to be expected from data not primarily collected for research, the database had gaps on age, marital status, address and medication, but missing information was not a systemic problem. However, since some versions of the intake form did not ask about the client's occupation, we did not have occupational data for many clients. That was a systemic problem. Also, many intake forms had no information on client's prior massage experience and types of massages a client preferred and we had to exclude these items of interest from the final report.

The issue of missing data underscores the necessity not only for closer attention to the initial interview before massage but also a preview of the importance of the intake form and SOAP charts. Students would benefit from a group discussion of the significance of each item in the intake form for them to understand why a specific piece of information is collected. They need to appreciate that intake forms and SOAP charts are not just case-specific, but source data for understanding the relationship between individual traits and group phenomena. For instance, one might ask, why does the clinic collect information on addresses? Individually, we want to be able to contact the client for follow-up services. As a group, we want to know of the geographic reach of our service and how we might use this information to develop our program. From a research perspective, we are more interested in patterns than personal data.

Composite Profile

Of the 445 clients in the working database, 316 (71%) had their initial clinic visit in the more recent two and a half years (2010-2012) and 129 (29%) had first visited the clinic before 2010. According to the number of SOAP notes, a total of 265 clients (60%) were "one-timers" who had visited the clinic only once, but 63 were "regular visitors" who had visited the clinic four or more times. Among the regular visitors, 16 had visited the clinic 20 or more times. The top one made 84 visits! Some clients had begun their association with the clinic as early as January 2005, and some stated they had received treatment from Sovine, Olivieri and Peña-Moog, three of the present faculty members of the Massage Therapy Program while they were students at NOVA.

As expected, most of the clients (93%) were from Northern Virginia, with 170 from Woodbridge and Dale City, 107 from Stafford, Manassas, Dumfries, and Fredericksburg, and 135 from other Northern Virginia cities. Interestingly, the clinic had also drawn clients from Virginia Beach and Newport, Virginia; Maryland, Washington, DC, and other states such as South Carolina, Ohio, New Jersey, California, West Virginia and Guam.

A majority of the clients were from the younger generations, with 116 (26%) under 30 years old, 84 (19%) from the 30-39 age group, 74 (17%) from the 40-49 age group, 82 (18%) from the 50-59 age group and 52 (12%) 60 years or older. There were 37 clients (8%) who did not provide information on age.

There were more women than men visiting the clinic, 65% female, 35% male and more married people than single people among the clients: 194 (43.6%) married; 169 (38.0%) single and 21 (4.7%) divorced, separated or widowed. There were 61 clients (13.7%) who did not provide information on marital status.

A majority of the clients, 297 (67%) of them, had prior massage experience while 131 (29%) were newcomers.

While most of the clients 266 (60%) were not on medication, 317 (72%) had some health problems. Indeed, 64 (14%), had five or more problems. Among the more prominent health problems were low back and mid back pain, neck pain, headaches, disk problems, joint aches, sprains, high blood pressure, decreased range of motion, arthritis and allergies. These are probably the ones the Massage Therapy Program should concentrate on instead of a general survey of diseases.

The most common health conditions from which clients sought relief were problems related to soft tissues, stress, headaches, extreme tiredness and numbness. They were the conditions that my classmates and I learned to treat directly or indirectly in the NOVA massage therapy. One might say the clients had come to the right place!

Getting Bigger Bang for the Buck

As the intake forms and SOAP notes are case-specific clinical documents, student therapists and instructors may not be aware of their potential utility as research documents. Besides, students and instructors are usually focused on clients as individuals and not clients as a treatment population. However, with the massage profession putting more emphasis on research literacy, it is worthwhile to point out that, with minor administrative adjustment and major attitudinal change, intake forms and SOAP charts can become useful sources for research. What the change requires is thinking ahead to what data are needed and how data will be used. I believe a streamlined intake form might include biographical information such as a client's name, date of birth, address, phone number, email address, occupation, source of referral and emergency contact. These are basic markers for each client.

Beyond the bio data, the streamlined intake form might have an open-ended question on the general health status of the client followed by a question on current medications instead of lists of past and current medical conditions pre-printed on the form. Student therapists can have a list of more common disorders on hand to use as a prompter as necessary. This list might include salient conditions that have direct impact on massage therapy. For instance, I would certainly include asking if clients have neck problems because I usually work with a client's neck in my massage. Clients who are forthcoming will provide information about their past and current medical conditions. Those who are reticent will withhold information initially but, as we work with them and "discover" new information from our observations, they will confirm or clarify what we have found. In any case, despite what we learn in Concepts of Disease, we are unlikely to follow up on clients' medical disorders other than issues related to soft tissues and clients with unusual disorders are unlikely to come to us for massage. Thus, asking clients to review a list of medical conditions on the intake form is a waste of time. We probably get more accurate information on clients' current medical conditions from their answers regarding current medication(s). What therapists need to be familiar with is not so much a list of disorders, but a list of popular drugs. If the Massage Therapy Program at NOVA is revamped in the future, it might include Introduction to Pharmacology as an option.

The intake form can further be streamlined by including questions on clients' pain and stress levels and how well they slept the night before their visit. These three simple questions will establish the baseline for measuring effectiveness of massage. The form can also include questions on headache, recent surgery, previous injury, whether the client has received massage therapy before, whether the client exercises regularly, smokes or drinks. It should include question on why the client is seeking massage therapy but restrict the answers to the options of relaxation, stress reduction, headache reduction and treatment of specific conditions. Such restriction provides a clearer focus for therapy.

The SOAP chart should be structured to show a client's overall stress and pain levels before and after massage, how well he/she slept the night before, whether he/she had headache the day before and/or has headache now, what other symptoms he/she has, which parts of the body are most uncomfortable and in need of treatment and what manual techniques were used. Most of these are quantifiable data that can later be extrapolated for research. The chart should also include what the practitioner observes about the client before and during the massage, about the overall presentation of the client after massage and an assessment of whether the techniques worked as expected. It should also provide room for a treatment plan for the next session and a recommended self-care routine for the client.

Before the massage, student therapists and clients should have one-on-one interviews to review the information on the intake form and fill any information gaps. Therapists should ask the questions on stress and pain level before and after massage for every session with a client. Immediately after the student therapists have submitted their SOAP charts, instructors should scan through them for clarity and completeness and ask for additional information as needed. The complete intake forms and SOAP charts will provide data on not only the relative effectiveness of massage for a medical condition in one session but over time. They become better source documents for future research with no extra effort by the clients or the therapists. They are arguably simpler to use and clearer for follow-up. Subsequent therapists could build on the efforts of their predecessors to continue treatment for the client or to design new treatment plans.

The use of extant SOAP notes for research is notionally possible. However, the quality of extant SOAP notes is uneven. Most student therapists are not physicians but they tend to scribble their notes like physicians -- in a frenzy. Many SOAP notes are illegible, case-limited, open-ended and unfocused. Using SOAP notes as research documents will require therapists to be clear about their purpose and be more focused in recording the relationship between a health condition and a treatment modality. It is purposive. It calls for very little additional effort but yields potentially big rewards!

One of the recurring themes in extant SOAP notes is "insufficient time" for a full massage. To deal with that problem, the clinic schedule on Saturday might be restructured to allow more hands-on time for clients and more recording time for therapists. Instead of consecutive appointments for each student, an interval might be inserted between sessions to ensure each massage will have at least one hour of "table time" and one hour of writing and rest time. The emphasis of a clinic session should be on developing students' appreciation of massage therapy as a profession as well as developing them as skilled professionals.

With revision of the intake form, focused data gathering, and having more time for pre- and post-massage interviews and disciplined recording, therapists can transform the case files from case-specific clinical documents into research documents. The case files, as a whole, can become a valuable data source for assessing the effectiveness of massage therapy and contribute to the advancement of massage therapy as an evidence-based profession.

In the independent study, I had limited the analysis to the most basic level of tabulation, to account for how many cases fell in each category within an item of interest. If the study was more than a class project and resources were available, I could have run some cross tabulations to show the relationship between and among the variables. For instance, one might wish to know whether younger men use massage more than younger women or whether there are differences between men and women in why they use massage, and why these questions are important for the profession and the business of massage. However, in order for intake forms and SOAP charts to attain the status of research tools, massage practitioners need to develop a series of questions for which we want answers, and do so in advance of data collection. We need to be selective and focused in data gathering. Until we have the right data, we will not be able to satisfy our professional demands.

<>

I submitted the independent study to Scholes and shared it also with Sovine. I have no feedback on what they did with the report, but I did notice changes in clinic schedule when I worked with some students on their case studies of fibromyalgia (Chapter 25). The Massage Therapy Program had apparently adopted some of my not-so-bashful recommendations. From the report on clients of NOVA clinic, one might conclude I had discovered another area of interest. That's not exactly true. I have always been interested in research, ever since I first enrolled in Sovine's class on physiology and deep tissue massage. I had always asked questions about the connection between theory and practice, even though I had no idea of the source of my curiosity. As I progressed in my development as a massage therapist, I found I was constantly navigating less-charted waters. I was no longer satisfied with knowing the routine of massage. I wanted to know more and I was evolving into a research massage therapist.

Chapter 11

USING MASSAGE TO TREAT FIBROMYALGIA

When I visited the parents of my niece Angela (not her real name) in November 2011, she told me she had fibromyalgia (FM).[40] I was then enrolled in orthopedic massage in which the topic of FM was raised and massage mentioned as a treatment option. I told Angela of what I learned of the possible healing effect of massage on FM and asked her to consider using it to treat her condition. At that time, she was under the care of a physical therapist and we agreed she should defer the option until after completion of her physical therapy. Several weeks after she completed her PT routine, she came to me for her first massage in January 2012. At that time, hers was merely one of the massages I had to do for the class on anatomy and Swedish massage (Chapter 7).

Who is Angela?

Angela was 43 years old, 5'2" in height, and weighed 118 lbs. Her BMI was 21.6, which was within the normal range. She was neither overweight nor underweight. She was in fairly good health, except

---

[40]   Case information used with permission of the client.

for soft tissue and joint problems. In July 2010, she noticed a pattern of lack of sleep, getting tired easily and getting dizzy frequently, and initiated a regimen of self-care to cope with the problems. After a year of coping, she finally went to see a doctor.

After a complete physical examination in July 2011, the doctor noted that Angela had "mild tender points in the trapezius muscles, throughout the scapular and back and [in] various areas above and below the waist [but] no specific swelling of joints" and concluded that since she had those symptoms for over a year, her "chronic muscle aches [were] from FM."[41] The prescription was to start a graduated exercise program at home, to undergo physical therapy and to take medication.

What is Fibromyalgia?

The American College of Rheumatology defines FM as a condition of widespread pain in both sides of the body, above and below the waist, in the axial skeleton, and pain in 11 of 18 tender points on digital palpation.[42] According to professionals, this pain condition has a myriad of causes such as "hyper excitement of the central neuron," allergy/chemical sensitivity, abnormal production of cytokines, depression, dysregulation of brain function, fatigue, hypermobility of connective tissues, hyperventilation, bacterial and viral infection, irritable bowel syndrome, sleep disorders, thyroid dysfunction, and trauma.[43] It elicits a variety of treatment options. However, none of the causes is definitive and some of them are conditions associated with FM rather than causal factors. Most of the prescribed treatments are designed to help the patient learn to live with FM pain, either through medication or psychosocial behavior modification but most drugs have potentially negative side effects. They deal with symptoms rather than root causes.

Most discussions of FM put an undue emphasis on muscle pain even though tender points of FM are made up of skin, fascia and muscle, all of which are connective tissues or tissues wrapped

---

[41] Medical information provided by the client and used with permission.

[42] The American College of Rheumatology 1990 Criteria for the Classification of Fibromyalgia. Report of the Multicenter Criteria Committee. *Arthritis & Rheumatology*, February 1990; 33 (2): pp. 160-172.

[43] *Fibromyalgia Syndrome: A Practitioner's Guide to Treatment* (2009) by Leon Chaitow.

and held together by connective tissues. In my initial thinking, I visualized tender points as adhesions in the interweaving of skin, fascia and muscles. Sovine suggested that since connective tissues are fasciae innervated with nerves with free nerve endings,[44] a more plausible explanation of the development of tender points is the entanglement of free nerve endings. This became the focus of our explanatory model. Muscle pains associated with FM are pains in the fasciae where free nerve endings become entangled with each other, leading to fasciae pulling on each other and on the organs around which they wrap. The mutual pulling of free nerve endings, which are embedded with pain receptors, creates friction in multiple sites and causes widespread pain.[45]

Free nerve endings are microscopic filaments of nerve embedded in fascia. Under normal condition, they glide in the ground substance. However, when viscosity of ground substance increases, it slows the flow of lubrication through the fasciae and hinders the movement of free nerve endings, and some of the microfilaments touch and entangle with each other and begin pulling on each other inadvertently. The mutual pulling excites the pain receptors in the fascia to signal the central nervous system (CNS) that something is out of balance. As the entanglement is gradual, internal, gentle and non-threatening (the case of weak stimuli), the signal for intervention does not reach the threshold for action and CNS treats it as a non-event. However, the entanglement does stimulate fibroblasts in ground substance to secrete collagen fibers into the extra cellular space to repair damage that might be present. The fibers released into the ground substance make it more viscous. When ground substance is more viscous, the gliding of free nerve endings has less space to move about, and more of the microfilaments get stuck to each other. Thus, the relationship between viscosity of ground substance and entanglement of free nerve endings is a vicious cycle: Initial entanglement leads to fiber secretion leads to more viscous ground substance leads to more entanglement.

---

[44] Sovine's idea is supported in "Fascial plasticity – a new neurobiological explanation: Parts 1 & 2" by Robert Schleip in *Journal of Bodywork and Movement Therapies*, 2003; *Job's Body* (2003), and *Human Anatomy & Physiology* (2007).

[45] The explanatory model was first formulated in "Using Massage to Treat Fibromyalgia: Report of a Case Study," by Samuel Wong and Jennifer Sovine, in a poster-presentation at the International Massage Therapy Research Conference, in Boston, Massachusetts, 2013.

The entanglement process is similar to scar formation with notable exceptions. Upon tissue injury, inflammatory chemicals are rushed to the injured area to construct a clot or scab. Fibroblasts then begin to produce collagen fibers to repair the damage and fibrous tissues grow beneath the clot to generate an area of scar tissue.[46] However, the entanglements of free nerve endings are different from scars. Entanglements are non-traumatic accidents in the ebbs and flows of ground substance, non-inflammatory and formed with innate collagen cells. On the other hand, scars are reactions to acute trauma, inflammatory and formed with new collagen fibers.

Nonetheless, collagen fibers developed from entanglements of free nerve endings or from scars have the same dynamics of overproduction, overprotection and random linkages, resulting in increased friction. Gradually, other entanglements develop, still not reaching the level to trigger action by CNS, and the process of collagen release is repeated and multiple tender points are developed. When the number of entanglements reaches what CNS considers significant, the pain has become chronic. Moreover, entanglement of free nerve endings creates dehydration of tissues and "dehydration of the tissue, with the accompanying development of cross-links at the modal points, can put enormous and excessive pressure on pain-sensitive structures and limit the fascial system's ability to glide,"[47] and put further pressure on the entanglement. Thus, another positive feedback loop is established.

As free nerve endings become entangled with each other, some of them become strangled due to lack of nutrients, lubrication and movement. This form of unscripted, cellular suicide is different from normal apoptosis and it leaves debris at entrapment sites, usually myotendon junctions. The dead microfilaments decay and stagnate to become toxic waste. The toxins irritate the points of friction caused by entanglement (like adding sand to an under-lubricated engine), making the tender points hypersensitive to pain. The more prominent of these entrapment sites are the 18 tender points identified by the American College of Rheumatology as indicators of fibromyalgia.

Tender points do not develop in response to stress. They are antecedent to stress. The causal loop is entanglement leads to stress, chemical reactions, over-stimulation of collagen growth, increase in viscosity of ground substance, and entanglement, sequentially. The initial accidental entanglement of free nerve endings is due either

---

[46]   *Human Anatomy & Physiology* (2007).
[47]   "Inner Journey," by John F. Barnes in *Massage & Bodywork*, 2012.

to the questing of these microfilaments for molecular stability or to their reaching out for the same nutrient (which might be vitamin, hormone or trace mineral), but subsequent entanglements are the results of prior reactions. The very substance (ground substance!) that lubricates the fasciae is, in fact, the agent that contributes to the entanglement. For conceptual clarity, we speak of two free nerve endings trying to reach for the same electron or same nutrient and getting entangled in the process. In actuality, multiple sets of free nerve endings are engaged concurrently. Other free nerve endings are not entangled because they are able to glide over each other in the adequately lubricated ground substance.[48]

Ground substance, a key component of the connective tissue fascia, is an intercellular, unstructured material composed of interstitial fluid, cell adhesion proteins, and proteoglycans. Proteoglycans are the attachment sites of glycosaminoglycans (GAGs), which are the substance that can change from a viscous state to a watery state. They are also lubricants of the ground substance.[49, 50]

Thus, the logical treatment option for FM is to activate ground substance so that the interstitial fluid and GAGs can detangle the free nerve endings and flush away the toxins at the entrapment sites. The treatment entails transforming GAGs from gel to sol with heat and movement from manual massage and complemented by the client doing abdominal breathing during the massage session. The transformation of ground substance is maintained through the client's doing abdominal breathing, abdominal massage and joint movement daily before bedtime, and through the use of natural ingredients such as raw ginger root and sea salt.[51] When heat and movement are applied to connective tissues, they not only transform ground substance, they also soften fasciae and stretch (loosen) free nerve endings. GAGs in sol form are then able to permeate the entanglements of free nerve endings, soften their mutual pulls

---

[48]   As an aside, one might postulate that pharmaceutical treatment of chronic pain would be more effective *after* the free nerve endings are detangled and drugs are able to hook on to the target receptors in the nerve endings.

[49]   *Biochemistry* 7th ed. (2012), by Jeremy M. Berg, John L. Tymoczko, and Lubert Stryer.

[50]   *Job's Body* (2003).

[51]   The use of ginger root to keep the ground substance in the sol state was not in the initial treatment plan. It was tried in reaction to the client's condition.

and allow them to detangle themselves. It enables the fasciae and the free nerve endings to regain the capability of gliding over one another. It flushes away toxic waste around the tender points to reduce or eliminate irritation. It reduces and eliminates chronic and widespread pain associated with FM.

I explained to Angela the transformation of ground substance in terms of changing gravy into soup and the freeing of entangled free nerve endings as seepage of soup into the crevices of the skin, fascia and muscle. I also proposed using sustained gliding, rhythmic compression and deep breathing as the primary "tools" for detangling the entangled free nerve endings. I accepted the medical definition of FM and my work with Angela was based on the understanding that entanglement of free nerve endings is the probable cause of FM. We explored ways to reduce pain in the 18 tender points and ways to contain widespread pain. Based on the insights of Grafelman and Juhan,[52] I believed massage in the forms of sustained gliding and rhythmic compression could generate sufficient heat to transform gel to sol and the body could repair itself when body fluid could circulate to detangle the free nerve endings. I envisioned this form of massage as a process of energy transfusion (that for ease of communication was later referred to simply as the "NOVA-S Method").[53] Angela agreed to give massage a try.

Treatment Process

Angela and I decided on the criteria for success in advance of treatment. We agreed that massage could be deemed effective if, after a treatment period, she did not feel pain when normal pressure was applied to the 18 tender points or if she did not feel any widespread pain. In other words, we were looking for a reduction of the number of painful tender points and localization of pain. She

[52]   *Graf's Physiology* (2001) and *Job's Body* (2003).
[53]   Reading Barnes' "Inner Journey" made me feel like I was using his method of myofascial release even though I had no formal training in his modality. I was strictly applying the massage techniques I had learned in Northern Virginia Community College (NOVA). In the process, I identified the coupling of sustained gliding, rhythmic compression and deep breathing as the NOVA-S Method so that I did not have to repeat the three components ad nauseam in oral or written presentation. The NOVA-S Method stands for a method Sam Wong developed while he was a student at NOVA.

might still have tension and aches in other parts of her body, but the pain configuration would no longer be that of FM. She would have graduated from it and could utilize different modalities to treat other emerging pathological conditions. A "systemic disorder" would be resolved into diseases about which causal factors are known and cures are available.[54]

For seven months in 2012, Angela had 21 treatment sessions. Each session typically began with a conversation between us about her pain status, sleep pattern and what specific body areas she needed work on. I then shared with her the session's treatment plan, explained the rationale for different techniques on various tender points, alerted her to my need to work near sensitive areas and asked for her reaction and permission before I proceeded. Angela occasionally would ask for adjustments. After the massage, she provided feedback on whether the techniques and variations worked and I alerted her to what might be done in the next session. Each session usually lasted between 75 to 120 minutes; a typical session took 90 minutes. Angela drank water before and after massage in all the sessions.

The treatment sessions evolved into four phases. Each phase involved either an addition or subtraction of some new treatment element. In the initial intake interview, I told Angela that since the development of FM was gradual, the treatment process would have to be gradual. We needed to be patient and not feel discouraged when there was no positive result immediately. I impressed on her that the body needs time to respond to new stimuli and to heal.

Phase I, consisting of three sessions, was essentially for Angela and me to get a feel for each other. In the first session, she came to me with depressed shoulders and bowed head. It was as though she was carrying a burden and was resigned to the pains in her body. She complained of being unable to sleep; her shoulders, lower back and hips were aching. Posture assessment pictures taken in that session showed her left shoulder higher than her right, and her anterior upper body tended to lean forward. On palpation, I found hypertonicity in her upper trapezius, quadratus lumborum, quads and hamstrings. There were trigger points along the upper trapezius and the supraspinatus.

In Phase I, I used effleurage, compression, cross fiber friction and longitudinal stripping, with deliberately lighter-than-normal

---

[54]   A complementary perspective on using massage to treat fibromyalgia is in an article "Myofascial Release for Fibromyalgia" by Richard Harty, PT, in *Massage Magazine*, April 2012.

pressure, to give Angela a full body relaxation massage in each of the three sessions. I refrained from deep tissue massage and stretching in this phase but I deactivated trigger points whenever I found them. My primary interest was to sensitize Angela's body to my touch, in preparation for energy transfusion in later sessions.

In Phase 1, Session 2, I completed palpation of the 18 tender points and found 14 points tender to the touch and some points had "shooting pain." I was quite amazed to find some of the tender points were sweating as I worked on them. Due probably to the activation of dormant nerves, Angela felt her back was sorer after massage. I encouraged her to continue her self-care routine of walking and stretching, and to begin doing the abdominal exercise (the same routine that I suggested to Jo – Chapter 6).

In the next session, Angela told me the abdominal exercise had helped her to establish more regular bowel movements. "The 'lazy' stomach is not lazy anymore." Thus, serendipitously, abdominal exercise takes care of Irritable Bowel Syndrome, a condition that is often associated with FM.

Phase II of the treatment, consisting of sessions four through seven, was primarily focused on energy transfusion. The process required that I began with warming my bare hands (by rubbing them together) and laying them on Angela's tender points. After I made contact, I asked Angela to synchronize her breathing with mine by exhaling when she felt the pressure of my hands. I then applied gentle pressure on the tender points as I exhaled. When I inhaled, I eased off pressure on them. This rhythmic process set off an energy flow similar to diffusion, heat moving from my warm hands to Angela's cold tender points. The heat set off a thixotropic reaction to transform ground substance from gel to sol and release tension in the fasciae. After a round of rhythmic compression, I applied sustained gliding on the same tender points. When my hands glided over them, both Angela and I exhaled. When my hands were off the tender points, both of us inhaled. After energy transfusion, I gave her a relaxation massage.

In Phase II, Session 4, I applied moist heat to L4, L5 and S1 to relax the nerves that innervate the upper trapezius and scapulae and I put an ice pack on the hips to cool off those tender points. The hot and cold treatments were "mixed signals" to CNS; they told the nerve endings in the upper traps to take it easy and those in the hips to "cool it," contradictory signals to induce the CNS not to overreact to the sensory data. I repeated the hot and cold treatments in the next four sessions.

In Phase II, Session 5, I stretched Angela's arms and shoulders gently and passively. During the hot and cold treatments, she had profuse perspiration, which might be a sign of toxins being removed from the body.

In Phase II, Session 6, I discovered rashes on Angela's back. The breakout might also indicate that toxins were being expelled from the body.

In Phase II, Session 7, I focused treating her scalenes to unglue the tender points in upper traps and between the scapulae.

The self-care routine for these four sessions included the Virginian Stretch (Chapter 6), ice treatment on the hip joints and a foot rub with a blended essential oils[55] before going to bed. Angela reported that the ice treatment on the hip joints and Virginian Stretch were effective, but she did not find the essential oils helpful.

The week between Phases II and III was a difficult week for Angela. She had to skip a scheduled treatment session because of her lack of sleep the night before. Through the week, she did not sleep well, usually less than five hours each night. "Just could not sleep," was her repeated complaint. Sleep deprivation was emerging as a primary covariance of FM.

Angela also had an allergic reaction and pains in upper traps and lower back that week. Her energy level was low. Besides missing the massage session, she also had to miss work and a dental appointment. She was highly stressed.

In Phase III, consisting of the next ten sessions, I introduced ginger root and sea salt into the treatment process and I tilted the massage table to let gravity work for Angela's condition. In these sessions, Angela listed lack of sleep, high stress, low energy level, pain in the shoulders (especially in the acromion area), upper traps and lower back, thighs and legs and occasional lack of appetite as continuing problems. In addition to techniques used in previous sessions, I used light tapping over the head to treat the tender points

---

[55] The essential oil was a commercial product blended with tangerine (*Citrus nobilis*), orange (*Citrus aurantium*), ylang ylang (*Cananga odorata*), patchouli (*Pogostemon cablin*) and blue tansy (*Tanacetum annuum*). According to the producer, the oil can be a wonderful prelude to a peaceful night's rest when it is massaged on the bottoms of the feet. This is aromatherapy. As Angela was questing for a restful and sufficient amount of sleep, I recommended it for her to try.

in the occipital region and applied a compress of ground ginger root and sea salt to heat up the tender points and to promote chemical reactions in the ground substance. The intent was to dilute the intercellular fluid and soften the fasciae so that seepage of lubricant could occur to unglue the entanglement.

Ginger root as complementary medicine has been used for various ailments for centuries.[56] It is pungent in flavor and it generates heat on contact. "The major active ingredients in ginger are terpenes (quite similar to the chemical action of turpentine) and an oleo-resin called ginger oil. These two, and other active ingredients in ginger, provide antiseptic, lymph-cleansing, circulation-stimulating and mild constipation relief qualities along with a potent perspiration-inducing action that is quite effective in cleansing the system of toxins." However, most uses are internal. In this case study, fresh ginger root was for external use, focusing on its capacity for heat generation.

Salt as a healing substance has also been used for centuries. It "dissolves, sanitizes and cleanses toxic wastes from our system." It is "the cleanser of bodily fluids." Sea salt is effective in speeding the healing of skin disorders, promoting cell health and easing the pains of aching joints and muscles.[57] If entanglement of free nerve endings produces toxins, sea salt would be an effective, natural cleansing agent to neutralize or remove them. Thus, I introduced the use of sea salt for FM treatment.[58]

In Phase III, Session 8, I recommended to Angela to incorporate abdominal exercise in her pre-sleep routine and added to it a similar arm exercise. The arm exercise requires the client to lie in supine position, lift (extend) her arms slowly from hip to overhead as she exhales and keep her arms still (suspended) as she inhales. It is to synchronize with deep breathing. After the arms have reached overhead, the client is to reverse the process, lift (flex) them from

---

[56] For a discussion on the use of ginger root, see "Ginger" in www.umm. edu/altmed/articles/ginger-000246.htm and "Ginger Root" in www. herbwisdom.com/herb-ginger-root.html. The reference about the property of ginger is from "Ginger Root."

[57] For a discussion on the use of salt and sea salt, see "The Healing Properties of Sea Salt" in www.livestrong.com/article/262946-the-healing-properties-of-sea-salt and "Everything you Ever Wanted to Know about Salt" in altmedangle.com/salt.htm.

[58] I discussed the use of ginger root and sea salt with Sovine before I actually used them.

the overhead position back to the hip area. The abdominal and arm exercises were meant to help tire and yet relax Angela and induce her to fall asleep and stay asleep. I also recommended to her a book, *Sleep to Save Your Life* (2005) by Gerard T. Lombardo, for tips on more restful sleep.

In Phase III, Session 9, I used the analgesic Tiger Oil (made by the producer of Tiger Balm) as a warming agent to treat some tender points and the QL, but Angela did not feel any significant improvement.

Starting in Phase III, Session 11, I used a compress of ground ginger root and sea salt to heat up the tender points and to draw toxins out of them. After ice treatment, I applied moist heat to hasten the return of normal temperature to the body.

In the same session, I began using normal pressure and gentle stretching in massage and tilted the massage table as a treatment option. I tilted the massage table slightly (less than 15°) so that the head was lower than the foot. The tilt was meant to promote an increased flow of body fluids (not just ground substance) superiorly to "flood" the upper traps, where several tender points were located. It was also to create a different sensation for the nervous system to divert its reaction. Starting with Phase III, Session 15, and in all subsequent sessions, the tilt was increased to 30°. Angela did not have any adverse reaction to the tilt.

After Phase III, Session 11, Angela had a medical check-up with her doctor. The doctor confirmed that her FM condition did not get worse and concurred that massage was good for FM. He also recommended yoga and meditation for her. Angela was to take Tylenol or Advil for pain.

In Phase III, Session 12, I recommended Angela to soak in Epsom salt for relaxation after work and before going to sleep. She told me she was comfortable with the use of the ginger root compress because it made her body feel less cold. During this session, Angela fell asleep for the first time in her massage experience.

In Phase III, Session 13, I gave Angela passive cross-body stretch, posterior muscle strumming, skin rolling and abdomen rocking.

In Phase III, Session 14, Erica, a former classmate in campus clinic and community outreach, assisted me in giving Angela a four-hand massage. I was interested to assess how the tender points would react to unfamiliar touch. They were not as sensitive to pressure as before.

In Phase III, Session 17, I repeated palpation of the 18 tender points and found 11 points still sensitive to pressure even though they did not seem to react as negatively as before. I used effleurage, petrissage, sustained gliding, rhythmic compression and stretching, while omitting ice, ginger root and sea salt from the routine. I also used moist heat to wipe off massage oil and to further warm up the body. Angela had begun working to relax her elevated shoulders and she felt her neck, upper traps and shoulders continued to give her pain.

As Angela and I reviewed the progress, it was apparent that sleep deprivation had a vicious effect on FM and she was in a vicious cycle of sleep deprivation leading to tiredness and fatigue, pain all over the body and sleep deprivation, sequentially. Breaking the cycle would be a prudent treatment strategy. As Angela is my niece, my wife and I visited her at her home to check up on her pre-sleep routine after Phase III, Session 16, and I gave her a relaxation massage. We visited her again the following week for another massage.

The consecutive home visits were primarily to reinforce the regimens that I wanted Angela to follow when I was on a four-week trip overseas. When I returned from Asia, she was on vacation. Thus, the treatment for FM was interrupted for seven weeks. Interestingly, the interruption was apparently beneficial, as Angela appeared to be more energetic when I next saw her. She had begun biking for exercise.

Phase IV had four treatment sessions. Angela told me she had some restful and some restless nights in that period. She continued to have shoulder pain, mid and lower back pain and pain in the gluteal area. I decided to begin each session with seated massage to focus on treating shoulder pain and stretching the neck. After the seated massage, I gave her ginger root/sea salt/tilted table treatment along with energy transfusion.

In Phase IV, Session 20, Angela did not feel pain in any of the 18 tender points as I applied pressure on them. I deactivated trigger points in her upper traps.

In Phase IV, Session 21, the focus of treatment was on her neck, shoulders, and gluteal muscles. I used cross-fiber-friction, stretching, sustained gliding and rhythmic compression for overall treatment and light feather touch as a finishing stroke to give the muscles a different sensation. Angela felt stretching was painful but not unbearable, and she felt good after massage. I suggested to her to stretch her hamstrings and quads in self-care.

What's in the Future?

FM is idiopathic. What Sovine and I postulate as the probable cause is yet to be confirmed by laboratory science. I used various modalities to treat Angela's FM condition because I felt they were capable of de-stressing her to give her a better quality of life. The healing process is complicated and explanation is not always comprehensible. The challenge is, do we wait for a thorough understanding of the causal links of a problem before we tackle it, or do we tackle the problem with what we know or feel plausible, and through practice learn to develop optimal treatment? If FM has no known cure, why not try something that might work? Energy transfusion is simple and relatively easy. It is inexpensive and without negative side effects. Ginger root and sea salt are readily available and inexpensive. And tilting the massage table incurs no extra cost. All these might be unconventional, but they seemed to contribute to Angela's graduation from FM.

In pure research, one would focus on the working of one variable in random samples, but this class project is not pure research. It is clinical research on what works and its primary focus is to help a client regain a relatively pain-free life. It is committed to trying whatever might work, doing no harm and within reason, of course. Now that we discover these "add-ons" are effective for Angela, we need more cases to confirm their effectiveness for other FM clients.

The class project did not claim to define the etiology of FM conclusively but it postulated a plausible connection between collagen production and the entanglement of free nerve endings. Collagen production and entanglement of free nerve endings are basic sciences. To explore them is to engage in theoretical and laboratory research that is beyond the scope of the class project and certainly beyond my competence or that of Sovine, my mentor-partner. We put our postulation on record so that competent scientists who have greater resources can test its plausibility more rigorously.

<>

Results from the case study seem to support the claim that massage is effective in treating FM. By the time I wrapped up the case study as a class project, Angela was walking more erect. She appeared to have more energy and sounded more cheerful. She did not sigh in resignation as she used to do. The 18 tender points appeared to be less sensitive to touch. Her upper traps and the superior aspects of her gluteal muscles were still hypertonic, but they were open to normal treatment.

After the class project, I continued to give massage to Angela, sometimes twice a week, to test whether increasing the frequency of massage would diminish the sensation of pain faster. However, a few weeks later, Angela felt that she had graduated from FM and she did not need regular treatment anymore. The case study had ended.

What Did Angela Think?

Before I submitted the report of the class project, I asked Angela for her impression of the treatment. She sent me an extensive account.[59]

> Everyone wants to be healthy including myself so when I was diagnosed of FM, I was stunned. I thought that the body aches that I had been feeling were just results of the physical demands of my work. The diagnosis gave me emotional stress for days after I learned about my condition. The first thing that worried me was my obligations like, "if I get sick who will pay the mortgage, who will take care of my parents, etc.," but at the same time the thought of it snapped me out of my shock. "I can't get sick!" As soon as I told this to myself, I started researching about FM, its causes and the possible cure. I also found the courage to tell my sisters, my mom and my closest friend about my condition. I was overwhelmed with their support and it gave me the determination to seek help to lessen if not take away all the symptoms of FM.
>
> First, I worked with my primary doctor and rheumatologist for a possible "treatment." I was prescribed Neurontin to relieve nerve pain and Flexeril for muscle relaxation. However, my body reacted strongly to both medications. I experienced fatigue, dizziness, shaking and drowsiness, so I stopped taking them. Then I underwent physical therapy, which helped lessen the pain. I did stretching and stationary biking. Heat therapy was also applied, especially on my shoulders and lower back.
>
> As I was concluding my PT sessions, I learned that [my uncle] was taking a course on Massage Therapy. When he heard about my condition, we discussed the possibility of

---

[59]   Used with permission.

him making me as his case study. At that point, my attitude
was to find every possible way to relieve my pains so I could
function normally – work without stress, sleep well and enjoy
the people and things that I love. I embarked on my massage
sessions with the total trust that I would get well. I literally
surrendered my complete healing to the therapist. I committed
three hours each Sundays, which included my commute to my
massage session.

What I liked during my sessions were the conversations
that I had with the therapist when I got to tell him my
experiences during the week. This practice had some kind of
therapeutic effect on me -- to have someone listen and know
that he could do something about what I felt. It also helped
that I knew exactly what to expect during my sessions when
he explained to me the procedure that he would undertake.

During the first few months, I was in so much pain
because all my tender points were being triggered. At times, it
was so painful that I alerted my therapist and he discontinued
the massage on the specific area of pain. Sometimes the pain
made me nauseate. A slight touch or even the soft blow of the
wind would make me scream of pain. Sleep was so difficult to
come because the physical pain would prevent me from doing
so. The most difficult part of this was that I could not stop
doing the things I needed to do. I still had to go to work even
if I did not sleep the whole night or even if my whole body
was in pain. My tolerance was affected so that I got moody
and impatient. Yet, I thrived on because I really wanted to get
well. It helped that my therapist was so patient with me that
if some techniques did not work, he always found another
way. The treatment plan was always based on my condition
during the week and the goal for the next.

The combination of intense massage when the therapist
applied pressure and relaxation massages when needed
helped loosen my tight muscles. The breathing exercises
during the massages helped me relax and endure the pain
when the tender points were touched. Heat from the massage
table, temperature of the room, ginger root application and
the therapist's hands definitely brought an enormous amount
of pain relief. Following his advice of soaking my body in
Epson salt also did wonders in lessening my body aches and

helped me to sleep well. But the one thing that I observed was that I was very sensitive to cold.

As sessions progress, I could sense a great deal of improvement. I noticed that physical touch even on my tender points did not bring me so much pain anymore. Sometimes, it was not even painful at all. My mood improved and I had more energy to go to work. I had also developed a more positive outlook in life. I did not stress with small stuff anymore, which I believed strengthened my faith that everything would be taken cared of. It also paved the way to get back to my recreational activities like biking. I believed having an active lifestyle complemented my massages.

I can honestly say that I have come a long way from the first time I came for my first massage. I desperately wanted all my aches to go away and this great expectation was achieved through my therapist's unflinching commitment and hard work. I feel much, much better than seven months ago though I know that there is so much more work to be done. There are still nights when I cannot sleep. I still have shoulder and back pains and lately my sciatic nerve has been bothering me. But I do not worry now like the day of my [initial] diagnosis. I know within my heart that I will get completely healed. I am in good hands. At the same time, I know that another goal is for me to be able to be independent, that at some point I should wean from my therapist and manage my FM symptoms on my own. Should I dread that time? No, I should not and will not because I know that when that time comes, my therapist has prepared me well.

Numerous researches and published readings on FM state that there is no cure but just relief to the widespread pain and effects of FM. Experts claim that a combination of medication, physical therapy, diet and exercise will help in the treatment of the symptoms. I believe that each case is different depending on what works well. I tried each one; medication and diet did not complement me. What helped me were the following: physical and massage therapies, having an active lifestyle, imbibing a positive outlook, having the loving support of family and friends and getting the professional help from a committed and sympathetic therapist. Based on my experience, [I believe] a combination of medical treatment with one's determination to get well and the psychological

*and emotional support from significant others can greatly
assist in the healing process of a person with FM just like me.*

<>

With submission of the report on July 26, 2012, I had reached
another major milestone in my massage career. I was eligible for
graduation from the Massage Therapy Program. On August 8, 2012,
NOVA awarded me a Career Studies Certificate in Massage Therapy,
summa cum laude.

Chapter 12

NATIONAL EXAMINATION AND
STATE CERTIFICATION

To become a massage therapist, I needed to be certified by a national certification board and a state board after completing formal training. In Virginia, registration for certification is quite simple. The Board of Nursing is the certifying authority and the requirements for certification stipulate that an applicant should be at least 18 years old; have successfully completed a minimum of 500 hours of training from a [recognized] massage therapy program; have passed the national certification exam for therapeutic massage and bodywork; and have not committed any acts or omissions that would be grounds for disciplinary action or denial of certification [essentially, fraud or deceit, and unprofessional conduct]. Once I filed an application for certification in Virginia, I could begin to practice massage therapy for a maximum of 90 days between completion of the education program and receipt of the results of my first qualifying examination.

Registering for the national certification examination was also quite simple. I went to the website of the NCBTMB and found a checklist of 11 items for applying for the test. I downloaded the 48-page Candidate Handbook which told me everything I wanted or needed to know about the examination process, including eligibility requirements, how to apply for the examinations, fees, test centers and dates, results and score reports. The tests were "designed to measure the knowledge and skills that massage and/or bodywork practitioners have identified as important for safe and competent practice *at the entry level* (emphasis added)." I had the option of taking the NCTMB route (with a few questions on Asian bodywork) or NCTM route (with no questions on Asian bodywork). I decided to take NCTMB even though NOVA did not cover much of Asian bodywork in its curriculum. I had been reading about Asian bodywork on my own and felt comfortable to test what I knew. I chose the closer test center in Alexandria and the test date October 18, 2012, exactly ten weeks after I graduated from NOVA. I used the interim to prepare for the exam.

Performing under pressure had never been my forte. I could not handle massive data and my ability to recall isolated facts was average. Despite passing (and sometimes failing) countless exams, I usually froze before an exam. The more I reread a test item, the more confused I became. Nonetheless, organizing everything I had learned about massage therapy and responding to questions within a fixed timeframe were the final hurdles I had to overcome to become a massage therapist. I knew the exam would ask about the body systems, anatomy, physiology and kinesiology, pathology, therapeutic massage and bodywork assessment and application, and professional standards, ethics, business and legal practices. I had learned most of these at NOVA. I just needed a system to match my knowledge with the exam questions. Learning from hindsight, I should have organized all the tests I had taken at NOVA and memorized the answers. That would have put me in excellent shape for the test.

The NCBTMB exam was a computer-based test. I had quite a bit of practice in using a computer for testing at NOVA and I had no problem using that technology for the national exam. The exam had 160 multiple-choice questions for 160 minutes. That meant I had, at most, one minute for each question. My testing strategy was, "If I know the answer, check it. If not, look over the choices, eliminate the obviously incorrect one(s) and check the best guess. No second-guessing! And, most importantly, read the question carefully."

To help with my test review, I bought three study tools: *NCETMB Secrets*[60] published by Mometrix Media, *Mosby's Massage Therapy Review* (2010) by Sandy Fritz, and NCBTMB Exam Prep, an online course

---

[60]   NCETMB is the acronym for National Certification Examination for Therapeutic Massage and Bodywork.

offered by NCBTMB. Of these, I found Fritz's book most helpful for understanding why the correct answers were correct. She made it clear I had to learn "factual recall" to ensure I remembered what I learned at NOVA. That meant revisiting Benjamin, Grafelman, Biel, Lowe and Salvo and reviewing my class notes in addition to Fritz's book. I used the NCBTMB's online exam prep to condition my brain for short-term memory.

I was in my own boot camp. Except for time set aside for rewriting the fibromyalgia report (Chapter 11), I was glued to my books and review tools. I had logged on to the NCBTMB exam prep website at least 67 times and answered questions 3,319 times in the ten weeks of preparation. I filled every page of a 60-page notebook with notes such as "brachialis does not cross the glenohumeral joint," "spasticity is a condition due to upper motor neuron lesions," "damage to cerebellum results in loss of balance and coordination," "right arm does not empty into the thoracic duct," and hundreds of other tidbits. If I ever have to make up test questions, I have a wealth of samples I can draw from. I doubt many practitioners remember more than one-quarter of the tidbits they were exposed to in their training. They remember what they know through actual practices. When I become an active therapist, I will know what I need to know. That was how I consoled myself. My immediate task was to memorize enough to pass the certification test.

The check-in process at the professional test center was similar to what I had to do for my online courses at NOVA, with one crucial difference. At both the professional and NOVA test centers, I had to establish my ID with a driver's license, but the NCBTMB test required that I be fingerprinted and photographed. After I put my personal items in a locker, I went with a staff person to a computer station and she showed me how the system worked. When I informed her I was ready, the staff person left me alone to face the computer screen for the entire period. Some questions I answered automatically; others I thought about before I gave an answer. I timed myself, neither tarrying nor hurrying. I arrived a candidate for certification at 8:00 a.m. I left a CMT, certified massage therapist, before 11:00 a.m.

As the certification exam results were sent electronically to the Board of Nursing, all I had to do next was to complete a simple two-page form to apply for state certification. I did that the afternoon of my NCBTMB certification exam. A Notary Public countersigned my application. I was issued my state certificate on October 25, 2012, within a week of my application. My first professional job as a CMT was doing chair massage at a dentists' convention in Tysons Corner, Virginia on October 19. Robert (from campus clinic and community outreach) found the opportunity, issued a call for assistance through Facebook, and I responded. I thoroughly enjoyed myself and felt good that clients I worked on were pleased with the relief. I had reached my goal of becoming a massage therapist.

The following weekend, I volunteered to give massage to the runners of the Marine Corps Marathon in Rosslyn, Virginia. Solace Clinical Massage was a sponsor of the event and many of my former classmates at NOVA were also volunteers. Jonathan, one of the classmates, kidded with Sovine about inviting me to speak to their class on fibromyalgia. I offered to speak on Yin Yang Touch instead. That was how the Massage III class in winter semester 2013 became the first practitioners of Yin Yang Touch. It was exciting to share my discovery with a receptive audience.

Even before my career took off, I decided to focus on research. I still want to care for caregivers, but I felt I could make better use of the remaining days of my life exploring what massage could do for some specific conditions and what insights I could find and share in traditional Chinese massage, than working as a massage practitioner in a spa or wellness center. Sovine fanned the spark of my research interest until it became a flickering flame. She first offered me a professional base at Solace Clinical Massage and then agreed to partner with me to turn the class assignment on fibromyalgia into a case study report. We submitted it to the Massage Therapy Foundation, which advised us to make it a poster presentation at the International Massage Therapy Research Conference held in April 2013 in Boston, Massachusetts. The three months before the conference, I was in China learning tuina.

Interlude

Chapter 13

SEARCHING FOR A CHINESE MASSAGE SCHOOL

When I was in Massage I for the second time (Chapter 7), I reported on tuina (Chinese massage) as an alternative modality in massage. It was a topic some of my classmates were interested in and asked me about. They thought I might know it since I am of Chinese lineage. However, I knew it only by name and was aware that it was a form of chiropractic practice in traditional Chinese *external* medicine (*dieda*), often associated with Chinese martial arts. It was not a relaxation massage as practiced in the West but a manual technique for fixing muscular-skeletal problems. Every Chinese writer on that subject stated tuina had a long history and proven record in China, but I did not come across any Western writings about it until after I began to study massage. The Western writings made me realize what a heritage I had missed and that I should learn more about it and integrate it into my massage practice.

I decided to go to China to have tuina training instead of getting it in the U.S. because I did not find a school offering tuina in Northern Virginia. If I had to go out of state to study, I might as well go to China, the land of its origin, where tuina is a common practice among Chinese TCM practitioners. Besides, I could learn it at a much lower tuition cost. I would also have more opportunities to observe and practice it in real life situations. Of course, the teaching would be entirely in Chinese, but since I am fluent in Putonghua (Mandarin) and Cantonese, I expected no problem with the language requirement.

I made inquiries about training opportunities at the Henan Chinese Medical College, located in the same town where my brother Robert was working; at the Guangzhou University of Chinese Medicine and the Guangzhou Medical College in Guangzhou (the city) where I worked in before my retirement. Both the colleges in Henan and Guangzhou offered the same curriculum and had similar admission requirements, which led me to believe that China has established a national standard for massage training. However, the Guangzhou University of Chinese Medicine had a different emphasis in its program. I decided to enroll in the Guangzhou Medical College because in Guangzhou I would be in a familiar setting and could concentrate on my studies. In Henan, my brother would be busy with his extensive travel and I would have to divert my attention to coping with an unfamiliar environment.

I verified the enrollment information on the Internet with Doris Zhang, a Guangzhou resident who was my former colleague in the U.S. Agricultural Trade Office. I mentioned to her that I wanted to study the massage aspect of traditional Chinese medicine (TCM) so that I might build the foundation for doing cross-cultural study between Chinese and Western massages. I was interested in TCM, but I had no time for training as a TCM practitioner. Doris gave me a thoughtful analysis on the two schools in Guangzhou.

The program at the Guangzhou University of Chinese Medicine focuses on health and self-care. It is a two-month program consisting entirely of lectures and in-class demonstration and practice among students. Teachers from the University are the lecturers. Classes are offered three times a week in the evenings, from 7:00 p.m. to 9:30 p.m., Monday, Wednesday and Friday; and whole day, Saturday. Program materials are from the university curriculum. If a student has the need to repeat the program for a better understanding of the subject, he can do so without additional payment and without time limitation. Enrollment is open year-round. There are no specific admission requirements and no restriction on nationality or age. When enrollment reaches the target number, a new class is launched. Generally, each class has no more than 30 students. In practice, a new class is formed every three months. Upon program completion, no testing is required. The tuition cost was RMB 3,500 *yuan* (*Yuan* is a Chinese currency, which in 2013 was approximately USD 556).

Guangzhou Medical College also offers a two-month program. Its focus is on preparing graduates to find jobs in massage. The first month is dedicated to lectures on Chinese medical theories and demonstration on Chinese massage practices, and the second month to practical training. Lecturers trained in TCM are hired to teach the theory and demonstration classes, and massage practitioners are available to supervise students in actual practices in two working clinics with which the school is associated. Classes are held five days a week; from 9:00 a.m. to 6:00 p.m.[61] Practical training (internship) is available in one of two clinics. The school develops its own program materials according to the guidelines of the Bureau of Labor. If a student needs to repeat the program for a better understanding of the subject, he can do so without additional payment, but he can repeat only for a maximum of six terms. Enrollment is open year-round. There are no specific admission requirements, and no restriction on nationality or age. A new class, with no more than 20 students, is launched every month. Upon program completion, written and practical tests are required. The tuition cost was RMB 4,000 *yuan* (USD 635 in 2013).

Doris felt the university program was more educational-theoretical and the college program more commercial-practical. Given what she knew of my academic background, she thought I would choose the former. However, I felt I could get book information from reading. What I needed most was actual hands-on tuina practices and I liked the idea of doing an internship in a Chinese clinic. The Medical College's program was a better choice for me.

When I was in China during summer 2012, I visited the tuina program at the Guangzhou Medical College and confirmed the admission procedure with Li *laoshi*. I attended a class lecture and was pleased I could follow most of what the lecturer said even though I had to guess about the technical vocabulary. The tuina program is one of 16 offerings in the Center of Continuing Education of the Medical College. It is apparently under contract with Dr. Yuan Jianqiang, an expert in spinal tuina and co-author of a textbook on that subject. Yuan is also the owner of the clinics where students have their practical training.

---

[61] Students can also elect to attend class on Saturdays only and complete the program in six months.

The tuina classes are held in a classroom on the thirteenth floor of a building on the main campus of the Guangzhou Medical College, located along one of the main roads of Guangzhou, with easy access to public transportation. The tuina classroom has 12 massage tables and an assortment of chairs and stools. That means it has room for 24 students. Along the back wall of the classroom is a row of chairs for auditors and observers. On the classroom walls are posters about spinal tuina and human anatomy. In the front area of the classroom are a one-person study desk, a makeshift stand for a projector and a non-descript chair. That's the area from which teachers lecture and show slides or video clips. A couple of table-top skeletal and muscle models lean in a corner of the room and a pile of pillows and blankets is stacked on a massage table along the right front wall of the classroom.

The tuina program has eight different modules, with four on anmo (Chinese massage) techniques and one each on foot wellness, acupuncture, spinal adjustment and spinal tuina. The anmo modules are divided into beginner, intermediate, advanced and comprehensive. The people I talked to in China did not make a distinction between anmo and tuina even though the classes were so differentiated. In my subsequent exploration, I concluded anmo (press and touch) is what we might label as relaxation massage and tuina (push and grasp) is therapeutic massage, but this distinction is true only in practice, but not in history. The two terms are interchangeable in Chinese literature on massage. In the textbook, *Foundation of Chinese Massage*, the editorial committee differentiates between wellness massage and therapeutic massage, but it uses the term anmo for both types.[62]

The spinal tuina module, with its focus on treating the vertebrae, was especially appealing to me. It promised to offer information for comparative study with spinal reflex therapy, a modality in which Sovine and some of my former classmates were deeply involved. I decided I would enroll for the module on spinal tuina, but before doing so I had to arrange for lodging.

Upon hearing that I might return to Guangzhou to study tuina, several friends invited my wife and me to stay with them. Mimi Kuang, a former student of my wife, invited us to stay with her or her parents. We decided to stay with her parents whose apartment was

---

[62]   *Foundation of Chinese Massage* (n.d., Chinese). The original title is *Therapist for Wellness Massage – Basic Knowledge*. I rename it to better reflect its role in the training program.

conveniently located. I could take the bus or subway to school. The "forces" were aligned for me to take the plunge!

After I was certified by NCBTMB, I applied for admission into the spinal tuina program and began to immerse myself in learning Chinese vocabulary of anatomy, physiology, meridians and pressure points in the four months before I left for China. The book on tuina that Doris bought me for overview was most helpful. It gave me a feel for the challenge ahead and allowed me to prepare in advance. From what I read about yin and yang (shadow and light), I developed a preliminary framework for studying tuina.

Chapter 14

YIN YANG TOUCH

Yin and Yang

Yin and yang[63] are key concepts in Chinese medicine and bodywork. Their effects on health have been much discussed, as far back as the 2,200-year-old *Huangdi Neijing*, (*Yellow Emperor's Canon of Internal Medicine*). Yin and yang are often described in terms of the contrasting concepts they represent:[64] yin is quiet, shady, feminine, midnight, cold, interior, lethargic and winter; yang is loud, bright, masculine, midday, hot, exterior, energetic and summer. But yin and yang are more than contrasts; they are also complements, and each is present within the other, as seen in the yin-yang symbol. Yin and yang are two ends of a continuum, opposites blending gradually into one another. The concept of yin is essentially "more yin than yang," and the concept of yang is essentially "more yang than yin."

---

[63] This Chapter is an expanded version of "East Meets West: Yin Yang Touch" in *Massage and Bodywork, March/April, 2014*. Used with permission of *American Bodywork and Massage Professionals*.

[64] *The Handbook of Chinese Massage: Tuina Techniques to Awaken Body and Mind* (1997) by Maria Mercati.

The expression yin-yang is actually a simplification. In Chinese medicine, it is more accurate to speak of yin-qi and yang-qi, two aspects of the vital energy (qi) that permeates the human body and is crucial to health. When qi does not flow freely, due to imbalance of yin-qi and yang-qi or blockage of the channels through which it flows, ill health is the result. The dynamic tension between yin-qi and yang-qi is needed to maintain qi balance – without the pull of yin qi, yang qi would not flow, and without the reciprocal pull of yang qi, yin qi would lose the force to continue pulling. The correct balance is continually aligning and realigning itself according to the needs of the body.

Qi and Meridians

Qi flows in the human body in a web of meridians: 12 pairs of regular meridians, which are divided into two groups according to whether they are linked to yin or yang organs. The regular meridians are connected in two identical series of continuous, ascending and descending loops of varying length, on the left and right halves of the body. There are also eight extra meridians and a number of secondary and tertiary meridians. On the meridians are 361 regular pressure points and 48 extra points.

Yin meridians are linked to and named after the yin organs: the lungs, spleen, heart, kidneys, pericardium and liver. Yang meridians are linked to and named after the yang organs: the large intestine, stomach, small intestine, bladder, sanjiao (triple burners)[65] and gall bladder. Along each meridian are qi-points (pressure points) that propel the ascending or descending movement of yin-qi and yang-qi.

The Chinese textbook *Tuina*[66] depicts the flow of qi through the regular meridians as follows: qi flows from lung (yin) into large intestine (yang), stomach (yang), spleen (yin), heart (yin), small intestine (yang), bladder (yang), kidney (yin), pericardium (yin), sanjiao/triple burners (yang), gall bladder (yang) and liver (yin),

---

[65]   According to *The Web that Has No Weaver: Understanding Chinese Medicine* (2000) by Ted J. Kaptchuk, sanjiao, also referred to as triple burners, may best be understood as the functional relationship between the lungs, spleen, kidney, small intestine and bladder, organs that regulate the water element of the body.

[66]   See *Tuina* (2011) by Yan Juantao, Wang Daoquan and Fang Min

sequentially. From liver, qi flows into lung (yin) and starts the whole cycle anew.

Among the extra meridians, Du and Ren have distinctive, significant qi points. The other six extra meridians generally share the qi points of regular meridians, but some of them also have extra qi points, of which *yintang* (EX-HN3) and *taiyang* (EX-HN5) are most prominent. The secondary and tertiary meridians do not have qi points.

The Du meridian begins in the pelvic cavity.[67] An internal branch descends to emerge at the perineum, passes across the anus to the tip of the coccyx, ascends over the spinal processes, crosses the top of head (midway between the ears – at the qi point *baihui* [GV20]) and penetrates into the brain. The main branch continues over the top of the head and descends across the forehead and nose to terminate inside the mouth at the junction of the gum and upper lip, the last qi point *yinjiao* (GV28). The first qi point of the Du meridian, *changqiang* (GV1), is midway between the anus and the tip of the coccyx.

The Ren meridian also begins in the pelvic cavity. It emerges at the perineum, runs anteriorly across the pubic region, ascends along the midline of the anterior trunk, crosses the navel, the xiphoid process and the throat to the lower jaw, where it penetrates internally to encircle the lips and sends a branch to the eyes. The first qi point of the Ren meridian is *huiyin* (CV1), located at the perineum. The last qi point is *chengjiang* (CV24), midline below the lower lip.

The Du and Ren meridians regulate qi flow through all of the body's yang and yin meridians, respectively. On the Du meridian, the qi point *baihui* (GV20), at the apex of the body, is the focal point toward which all yang-qi surges. *Baihui* (GV20) is the most yang area of the body and serves as an escape valve for excess yang-qi. On the Ren meridian, the qi point *huiyin* (CV1) is the focal point toward which all yin-qi converges. *Huiyin* (CV1) is the most yin area of the body and serves as an escape valve for excess yin-qi.

Yin and Yang Aspects of the Body

Yin Yang Touch is a massage method that applies the principle of yin and yang to enhance traditional Western massage techniques. To use Yin Yang Touch, it is necessary to know which areas of the body

---

[67]   The description on Du and Ren meridians is based on *The Web that Has No Weaver* (2000).

are yin and which are yang. In a massage setting, two sets of qi are interacting: those within the therapist and those within the client. The essence of the Yin Yang Touch modality is making informed use of these interactions.

In combination, the meridians might be seen as an electromagnetic field through which electrical energy of qi flows. As the electropositive and electronegative energies (yang and yin energies, respectively), move through the Du and Ren meridians, a positive charge accumulates in the body's posterior-superior aspects, and a negative charge accumulates in the anterior-inferior aspects.[68] Therefore, we can assign yin and yang aspects to different regions of the body – an important concept in the Yin Yang Touch massage method.

Yin: Anterior trunk, anterior sacrum, posterior and medial thigh, posterior leg, plantar side of the foot, anterior and medial arm and forearm, and palmar side of the hand. Movement toward the hip is yin.

Yang: Head, face, posterior and lateral trunk, posterior sacrum, anterior and lateral thigh and leg, dorsal side of the foot, posterior and lateral arm and forearm, and dorsal side of hand. Movement toward the head is yang.

Based on the principle of "opposites attract and likes repel," when yang aspects of the therapist come into contact with yang aspects of the client, or yin aspects of the therapist come into contact with yin aspects of the client, the result is stimulation of the muscles at the point of contact, as qi forces at the deep level move away from each other. An example would be the therapist using the back of her hand (a yang area) to massage the client's posterior trunk (a yang area).

In contrast, when yang aspects of the therapist come into contact with yin aspects of the client, or vice versa, the result is relaxation, as the forces at the deep level are joined and move in harmony with each other. An example would be the therapist using her palm (a yin area) to massage the client's posterior trunk (a yang area).

---

[68]   *Chinese Medical Qigong Therapy, Volume I: Energetic Anatomy and Physiology* (2005) by Jerry Alan Johnson, pp. 123-5.

Yin Yang Touch and Western Massage

Yin Yang Touch fits perfectly with the primary function of Western massage, which is to relax or stimulate soft tissues (Pictures 9-20).[69] If addressing a condition requires stimulation (such as treating hypotonic muscles in scoliosis) or if a client wants an invigorating massage, the therapist should opt for the yang-on-yang touch or the yin-on-yin touch. However, if a condition requires muscle relaxation (such as treatment of hypertonic muscles in anterior pelvic tilt) or if a client wants a relaxing massage, the therapist should opt for the yang-on-yin touch or yin-on-yang touch. As with any modality, individual clients may react differently than expected, so the choice of touch should always be tailored to the individual.

Of the various categories of Western massage techniques, effleurage, petrissage, friction, tapotement and vibration are most adaptable to Yin Yang Touch. Effleurage (sliding or gliding) is the cardinal stroke in Western massage. In traditional effleurage, therapists are likely to use their palms. However, therapists using Yin Yang Touch with effleurage would use her palms over the yang areas of the client's body and the back of the hand over yin areas, if the session's objective is relaxation. This would be reversed if the session's objective is stimulation.

Petrissage normally involves using the fingers to lift, wring, or squeeze soft tissues in a kneading motion. It primarily uses the yin aspects of the hand. Applying Yin Yang Touch to petrissage, therapists can first stimulate the tissues with yang-on-yang touch or yin-on-yin touch. After the tissues are warmed up, the therapists can relax them with yang-on-yin touch or yin-on-yang touch.

In yang-on-yang touch, therapist kneads with the back of her hand (yang) in a rolling motion over the client's posterior trunk, anterior thigh and leg. In yin-on-yin touch, she kneads with her palms and fingers (yin) over the client's anterior trunk, posterior thigh and leg. In yin-on-yang touch, the therapist kneads with the palm and fingers (yin) over the client's posterior trunk, anterior thigh and leg. In yang-on-yin touch, she uses the back of the hand or

---

[69]   Generally, Western massage uses the palms (yin) and anterior forearms (yin) for most of the techniques. However, Yin Yang Touch uses both the palms (yin) and dorsal hands (yang) and the anterior (yin) and posterior (yang) forearms. The pictures are predominantly "yang on yin" because I want to highlight this less common mode of massage.

posterior forearm (yang) over the client's anterior trunk, posterior thigh and leg.

Kneading with the back of the hand in a rolling fashion is exactly what Maria Mercati, in *The Handbook of Chinese Massage*, introduces as one of the techniques of Chinese bodywork and what she has further improvised. Her technique is affirmed in the Chinese textbook *Tuina*. However, neither Mercati nor the editors of the textbook applies the yin yang distinction to the rolling technique.

Friction, in Western massage, is usually accomplished with palmar action. Applying Yin Yang Touch with friction, the therapist can follow the same routine as outlined for petrissage: first stimulate the soft tissues and then relax them, using yang-on-yang or yin-on-yin touch initially, and finishing with yang-on-yin touch and yin-on-yang.

Tapotement, which includes hacking, rapping, cupping,[70] clapping, slapping, tapping, and pinching, is essentially a variety of yang touches. However, within each of these percussive movements one can introduce the yin-yang gradation. Hacking can be either light or heavy, rapping can be either soft or hard, and cupping can be full or empty. Some of these movements cannot be done with the back of the hand or forearm, but other back-of-the-hand movements (such as pummeling or double cupping) can be devised or refined for percussion work.

Vibration, which involves oscillating, quivering or trembling motions, moves a body area gently back and forth or up and down. It is yin touch, but can be performed with yang vigor. The back of the hand is as effective in creating vibration as the palm. Moreover, Yin Yang Touch can be integrated into vibration through variation in pressure and amplitude.

The therapist can increase the desired effect by performing her strokes or techniques either toward the head or hip. She might use her palm (yin) to glide over client's trapezius or latissimus dorsi (yang) toward the head for relaxation strokes and toward the hip for stimulation strokes. I have found alternate strokes of relaxation and stimulation are effective in addressing scoliosis.

The therapist might also increase the strength of qi by combining multiple examples of the type of qi required. For example, using the palm (yin) to massage loosely (yin) and moving inferiorly (yin) aligns three different dimensions of the yin aspect, while using the back

---

[70]   Cupping in tapotement is about how the hand is shaped for percussion. It is different from cupping technique in TCM discussed later in Chapter 18.

of the hand (yang) to massage firmly (yang) and moving superiorly (yang) aligns three different dimensions of the yang aspect. The variations are practically limitless.

Performing Yin Yang Touch

Applying Yin Yang Touch for a relaxation massage might include the following routine (with the client doing intentional deep breathing, exhaling as pressure is felt and inhaling as pressure is eased):

- Place the client in a supine position.
- Align your body current with that of the client. Cradle client's head in your palm, applying touch without movement, for 1-2 minutes.
- Apply palmar effleurage lightly and slowly to client's facial muscles, neck muscles, and upper trapezius.
- Use the back of the hand or posterior forearm to effleurage client's right shoulder, pectoral muscles, anterior arm and forearm.
- Use palmar effleurage on client's posterior arm and forearm.
- Repeat Steps 4-5 on client's left side.
- Use the back of the hand to effleurage or vibrate over client's abdomen muscles and pelvic muscles.
- Apply palmar effleurage or petrissage to client's right anterior and lateral thigh.
- Use the back of the hand to effleurage or to roll over client's right medial thigh.
- Apply palmar effleurage on client's right anterior and lateral leg and dorsal side of the right foot.
- Repeat Steps 8-10 on the client's left side.
- Use the back of the hand to slide over the drape along client's anterior midline, from the jugular notch to the hypogastric region for several light strokes.
- Use back-of-the-hand touch, without movement, over the midpoint of the sternum for 30 seconds.
- Place the client in a prone position.
- Use the back of the hand or posterior forearm to effleurage or roll over the plantar side of client's right foot, right posterior and medial leg and right posterior thigh.

- Use the back of the hand or posterior forearm to effleurage or roll over client's right gluteal muscles.
- Repeat Steps 15-16 on client's left side.
- Apply palmar effleurage, petrissage, friction, vibration and tapotement over client's trapezius and latissimus dorsi.
- Apply palmar friction over client's upper trapezius.
- Use palm to slide over client's posterior midline from L5 to C7 for several light strokes.
- Apply palmar touch, without movement, over client's posterior epicranius for 1-2 minutes to conclude the massage.

Yin Yang Touch is safe and simple to use and it does not require therapists to make an extra investment, other than greater awareness of the primary purpose of a massage session and a conscious use of their hands and forearms. Other benefits of using Yin Yang Touch include:

- The therapist reduces the risk of repetitive strain, as all sides of her hands and forearms are used.
- The client feels more secure and the strokes are less invasive when the therapist uses the back of her hand or posterior forearm over sensitive areas such as the anterior neck, pectoral region, abdomen, medial thigh and inguinal region.
- The therapist recovers faster from the rigors of manual work because she is actually engaged in internal massage of her own while treating her client.
- The client can also practice Yin Yang Touch for self-care between sessions.

The self-care routine[71] of Yin Yang Touch outlined below requires all gliding movements be slow and firm and that each step be done five to six times. It also requires the therapists or clients to be aware of empty and firm hands according to the yin and yang principle.

- Lie supine, exhale as pressure is applied and inhale as pressure is eased off.
- Press forehead and top head with both palms.
- Press side head (cheeks) with both palms.
- Glide palm from *yintang* (GV29) to *baihui* (GV20).

---

[71]   This self-care routine was developed after the article was accepted for publication.

- Glide palm from *taiyang* (EX-HN5) to *baihui* (GV20).
- Glide palm from above *yintang* (GV29) to *taiyang* (EX-HN5).
- Glide side neck, superiorly, with palm.
- Glide pectoral muscles, medially & inferiorly, with backhand.
- Glide from jugular notch to the area below navel with backhand.
- Glide over abdomen clockwise with backhand.
- Press below navel, *guanyuan* (CV4), with palmar hands, hand on hand.
- Glide palm over quads, superiorly, with knees bent.
- Glide palm over front leg, superiorly, with leg over thigh.
- Glide backhand over mid-thigh, medially, with leg over thigh.
- Glide palm over dorsal foot, from toes to heel, with leg over thigh.
- Glide hand over plantar foot, from heel to toes, with leg over thigh.
- Press edges of each toe, with leg over thigh.
- Press *yongquan* (KI1), with thumb or fingers.
- Squeeze upper trap muscles, with palm across chest and on shoulder.
- Glide hamstring and back leg with backhands, superiorly; curl thigh to chest.
- Glide palm over posterior forearm and arm, superiorly.
- Glide backhand over anterior arm and forearm, inferiorly.
- Rub hands with backhand in palm.
- Press *hegu* (LI4), with thumb.
- Lie on one side with the opposite arm overhead, glide palm over side trunk & back muscles, superiorly.
- Seated, press *yongquan* (KI1), *hegu* (LI4) and *laogong* (PC8) as well as *taiyang* (GV29), *baihui* (GV20) and *yintang* (GV29), with thumb or fingers.

<>

Thus, I prepared for study in China. I was ready and eager to engage my new teachers in discussing the application of yin and yang to massage.

Part II

TRAINING IN CHINA

Chapter 15

TUINA CURRICULUM IN CHINA

When I reported for class in Guangzhou in early January 2013, Li *laoshi* gave me a package consisting of three textbooks on massage, a book on spinal tuina, a notebook, ballpoint pen, plastic file holder, a white uniform, a set of sample test questions for the beginner level and a one-page class schedule (syllabus). Everything was included in the tuition cost, which, incidentally, had increased to RMB 4,200 *yuan* (USD 667 in 2013). From the instructions I received, it was clear that the program was oriented to preparing students for the external examination, for which I had applied while I was still in the U.S. That was quite a process. Li told me to work on the sample questions before January 26, the test date, and to prepare for attending a review session a week before that.

The class started with a core of ten students -- six men and four women. Other visitors joined this core at various times after the beginner sessions. One of the visitors I met had already passed the advanced level, but she came to class for refresher training and was quite interested in Western massage. Even though I noted on my application letter my former employment in Guangzhou and my recent graduation from the massage therapy program at NOVA, Li and the staff treated me as though I were just another beginner student. That was fortunate. I did not have to deal with unusual expectations. The new learning environment was more challenging than I expected and my relative anonymity had saved me from embarrassment. In class, I heard partially what was said and understood most of it. What I missed I asked my newfound friends and tried to fill in the gaps from reading the textbooks and other books.

The Textbooks

Contrary to what I read on the school's website, the textbooks (Picture 22) were not developed by the school. Instead, a national vocational group edited them. The first book in that series is *Foundation of Chinese Massage.*[72] It includes the ethics of massage, the basics of massage business, human anatomy, TCM, meridians and pressure points, theories and functions of massage, massage media and tools, laws and regulations, and psychology. It has 165 pages, jam-packed with information, dense and obtuse.

The second book is the *Training Manual*, what therapists at different levels of training need to know in actual practice. It is organized into three sections: beginner, intermediate and advanced. Each section has three chapters. The beginner section has chapters dealing with reception and consultation, massage in supine position and massage in prone position. The intermediate section is organized exactly as the beginner section. The advanced section deals with reception and consultation, full body massage and esthetic massage. It has 134 pages.

The third book is the *Handbook for Practitioner*. It deals with reception and consultation, wellness massage, common diseases, sports massage, physical therapy (different from the Western form), training and supervision. It has 72 pages.

Materials in the first book are like the lectures at NOVA. They are theoretical and foundational. Those in the second book are like lab notes, guidance for practices, similar to *Tappan's Handbook*. And those in the third book are similar to courses in continuing education, what Western therapists might elect to meet requirements for recertification.

---

[72]   The original titles of the three books are alike, simply *Therapist for Wellness Massage*. The subtitle of the second book is "*beginner, intermediate and advanced*" and that of the third book is "*technician*." I rename these books according to their contents.

I thought the class I signed up for was entirely focused on spinal tuina. As it turned out, that topic was only an add-on to the regular curriculum of massage training. I had to go through the entire curriculum of massage training in order to learn spinal tuina. The misunderstanding was fortuitous because it gave me the opportunity to learn Chinese massage and to have a better appreciation of what I learned in NOVA.

The Syllabus

The class syllabus was organized into lecture and demonstration sessions from 9:00 a.m. to 11:45 a.m. and 2:00 p.m. to 4:00 p.m. -- two sessions each weekday. The beginner section spanned 14 sessions (seven days). Its theoretical aspects covered the overview of tuina, axial and appendicular skeletons, limbs, joints, muscles, yin yang, *wu xing, zangfu,* qi, *xue,* and *jinye.* Its practical aspects covered the techniques of friction, compression, swaying, percussion, vibration and joint mobilization, and massage in supine and prone positions.

Both the intermediate and advanced sections required 13 sessions (six-and-a-half days) each. The theoretical aspects of the intermediate section covered digestive, respiratory, urinary, reproductive, vascular and nervous systems; regular and extra meridians and pressure points; foot reflexology and diagnostics in Chinese medicine. The practical aspects of the intermediate section covered massage in prone and supine positions and foot reflexology. The advanced section included theoretical discussion and treatment of 15 malaises and 15 pathologies and the theory and practice of lymphatic drainage, *guasha,* cupping and acupuncture. Spinal tuina was offered in two late afternoon/early evening sessions. Thus, the training was actually a 20-day program, highly intensive but relatively short. If Massage I (my first time) at NOVA was information overload, training at the Guangzhou Medical College gave me acute constipation. I had severe digestion problems, but my classmates seemed agreeable with the feeding process. That was a cultural shock for me! Due to an emergency visit to a city hospital and the field visit to the clinic where I had my internship, I missed the lectures on acupuncture and on some of the pathologies.

Students were scheduled for classroom practices from 4:30 p.m. to 5:30 p.m., but in the first couple of weeks, everyone left the school as soon as lecture or demonstration was over. I did likewise, since I wanted to avoid the rush hour traffic. In the third and fourth weeks, some classmates stayed for massage exchanges, but I did not join them. My massage exchanges were confined to in-class practices.

Each weekday between sessions, we had two-and-a-quarter hours of midday break for lunch and rest. One of the habits I acquired in the four weeks of attendance was following my classmates' practice of having a nap in the classroom after lunch, and I made good use of the travel blanket that my NOVA classmates gave me for my China trip. It kept me comfortably warm for my midday nap and every morning I did not leave for class without it. Lunch was a good time for me to get to know my new classmates. I usually joined them for lunch in the college cafeteria or in a neighborhood restaurant that served fast food (similar to Chinese buffet in the U.S.). I had more interaction with men than women, except for Jaymee Li, a Chinese-German female classmate. She was born and raised in Guangzhou and married to a German. She and her young daughters were visiting her parents in Guangzhou and she had decided to learn tuina for self-care. As both of us were "foreign" students, Jaymee and I bonded well. Two of the classmates were already practitioners of traditional Chinese external medicine, assistants to veteran *dieda* masters. Their enrollment in the tuina class was to get the credentials so that they could dispense tuina treatment legally. The treatment they dispense may or may not be what is taught in the class.

Three Instructors

Three women instructors taught the class. I do not know their backgrounds. They were probably TCM practitioners, all of them in their late 20s. Two of them wore white physicians' garb when teaching; one wore street clothing. The garbed instructors, Ma and Lin (not their real names), were usually seated as they lectured and augmented their lectures with PowerPoint presentation and video clips. I believe much of their lectures were a verbatim reproduction of what they learned in their university classes (an echo of the textbook *Tuina* I read before I left for China). They seemed to have forgotten that we were not enrolled in a four-year course on TCM and the materials they shared were too much and too complicated. They would have been more effective if they had focused on explaining what was in the three textbooks and what was to be done in actual massage. Instead, both of them seemed to read from the same sources and they relied on their thumb drives for visual presentation! They were so identical in their teaching styles that they were practically interchangeable. Their delivery was fast, monotonous and boring. Instead of making a statement, they liked to ask rhetorical questions such as "the function of (blank) is what?" and the blank could be any subject. This teaching mode might be all right if the lecture session were a review of what we learned before, but it is ineffective for teaching new materials. Perhaps rhetorical teaching is the mark of a mediocre teacher! Their style of teaching is definitely not a variation on the Socratic method!

In contrast, the other instructor, who joined the teaching team in the second half of the training program, was much better. She introduced herself to the class as Chen Shuo and wrote her email address and telephone number on the blackboard before her first lecture. What struck me about Chen was her more relaxed demeanor. Unlike Ma and Lin, she moved about in the classroom during her lectures and made sure students located the pressure points she was talking about. She did not hesitate to deviate from the textbook and she responded to students' questions from her clinical experience. Chen could become an outstanding teacher if she used more visual cues (such as writing on the blackboard) instead of relying entirely on oral communication. I did not mind missing what Ma or Lin said, but I wanted to understand better what Chen shared with the class. She was far more engaging in her presentation than her peers.

Unlike my NOVA teachers, the instructors did not bother to check if I followed what they taught. They just kept on talking. In addition to the unique vocabulary of Chinese anatomy, physiology, meridians and pressure points, I had to cope with listening to lectures in *Putonghua*. While I am fluent in it, my hearing was not fast enough for academic discourse. Following the printed syllabus, I was able to read as much of the materials as I could the evening before the lecture, and I had a general sense of what was being taught. When the instructors deviated from the syllabus, I was lost.

Chapter 16

TUINA AND TRADITIONAL CHINESE MEDICINE

Introduction to Learning Tuina

The first lecture on tuina was listed in the syllabus as an overview of tuina. Following the textbooks, I expected it to focus on business ethics and values, the essentials for tuina practices, and the therapist's professional conduct. The foundation book's discussion of business ethics is similar to that in Western massage, but with a heavy dose of socialist morality (*A person's greatness is determined by his willingness to contribute to society*). The essentials for tuina practices are similar to the scope of practice in Western massage, and the basic Do's and Don'ts about professional conduct are similar to what NOVA instructors hand out in their class syllabi, but the Chinese locus is business setting and not the classroom (*Wash and protect your hands because you use them most frequently to touch other people and things in your everyday life*). The training manual and the handbook provide information on how to receive a client and make him aware of the scope of practice, menu of services and schedule of fee, but nothing about completing an intake form or SOAP notes, or securing a client's consent.

In addition, the training manual has an interesting section on culture and customs of Chinese minority and special groups to help students understand their clients better. We are told, for instance, the custom of hand washing among Uygur people before a meal (*only three people at a time, hands are not immersed in a wash basin but rinsed with water pouring from a pitcher*) and why Chinese people in Hong Kong use a different expression than what mainlanders use to greet each other at the beginning of a new year (*Hong Kong Chinese greet each other with "kung hei fat choy" [May you strike rich] instead of the mainlanders' "xin nian kuai le" [Happy New Year] because the Cantonese expression for "happiness" has "fast falling" as its homonym, thus it is not a propitious salutation at the beginning of a new year*). However, even though these topics were included in the certification exam (as I found out later from the sample test and actual test), they were not covered in the overview or in any subsequent lectures.

The class lecture began with Ma providing a survey of tuina as a therapeutic practice in China through the ages, from its origin in the pre-*Qin* era; through its development in *Tang, Song, Yuan, Ming* and *Qing* dynasties; to its evolvement in Modern China. Before leaving for China, I had scanned through the history of tuina from the book that Doris gave me; what Ma mumbled was familiar. Even though the historical account is academic and might seem irrelevant to everyday tuina practice, it is critical for students to have the background so that they can understand the root of their prospective profession, just as I started learning Western massage with reading about Pehr Henrik Ling, Johann Mezger and Mary McMillan. Listening to the lecture on the history of tuina and reading about its development, I was excited that finally I could study it in depth. Tuina's evolvement from folk medicine to complementary and alternative medicine (CAM) has stood the test of time, and whatever results not yet verifiable from laboratory science is the problem of science, not of tuina. With its continuing practice down through the centuries, tuina is probably more reliable for restoring wellness from chronic pain than laboratory and pharmaceutical medicine. I also felt that tuina's initial development as treatment for children would argue for a gentle touch as its proper modality and that subsequent emphasis on "no pain, no gain" is a deviation from its root. The emphasis on developing manual strength for tuina treatment might be all right for chiropractic, but not for massage. What is widely practiced and accepted is not necessarily the right way!

After the historical overview, we learned contraindications and indications for tuina, similar to what's in *Tappan's Handbook*. Unfortunately, these topics were not found in any of the three Chinese textbooks. According to Ma, tuina is indicated for chronic straining of muscles and ligaments, peripheral nervous diseases, closed soft tissue injuries and diseases associated with internal medicine, pediatrics, gynecology, sense organs, esthetics and wellness maintenance. It is contraindicated for skin problems, infectious diseases, critical and severe illnesses, circulatory injuries, blood problems and patients who are physically feeble, extremely strained, drunk or extremely hungry and people with unclear diagnoses, especially those associated with acute spinal injuries.

The next topic was the "eight processes of tuina," again, a topic not found in any of the textbooks. According to Ma, the eight processes of manual work are warming, nourishing, unclogging, purging, sweating, harmonizing, dispersing and cleansing. While Ma did not cite her source for these processes, they were standard treatments in TCM.[73] In other words, the therapeutic effects of massage are achieved through one or more of these processes. Among these processes, nourishing and purging are most important. Hand techniques that follow the flow of qi in the meridians, move toward the heart and clockwise and have light stimulation and low frequency are nourishing techniques. Reverse actions are those of purging techniques. They resonate with what I wrote about Yin Yang Touch (Chapter 14), offering more seminal ideas for exploration.

Within the context of TCM, Ma then discussed principles and functions of tuina, essentially repeating the materials in the foundation book. Like Western massage, tuina is capable of promoting circulation of qi and blood, opening the meridians, adjusting visceral functions, lubricating joints and increasing immune functions. She further talked about the pathology of acute and chronic muscle injuries and how tuina might help to reduce pain and swelling, restore alignment and unglue adhesion, the same claims made by Western massage.

The first session ended with Ma reciting a ten-word rhymed formula (what Chinese call *kouque*) on the essence of tuina's hand techniques: "*you li, chi jiu, jun yun, rou he and shen tou.*" She spoke at length about each of the emphases. *You li* means using strength at an optimal level, ready to adapt to a client's needs; *chi jiu* means sustaining and continuous over time; *jun yun* means rhythmic, steady and resilient; *rou he* means light but not superficial, anchored but not stagnant; and *shen tou* means deep and penetrating, blending of soft

[73] *Fundamentals of Chinese Medicine* (2012) edited by Gao Sihua, Wang Jian, *et al.*

and hard, hands move with the heart and techniques flow from the hands. These are simple yet profound concepts for life-long reflection and refinement. The ten-word formula is probably an oral tradition that every Chinese practitioner is familiar with, but none of the school's textbooks list it.

Foundation of Chinese Medicine

Lectures on the Foundation of Chinese Medicine were divided into three sessions, for a total of nine hours. They were unbelievably dense and condensed. If my first exposure to Human Biology or the Concepts of Disease at NOVA was bewildering, absorbing and digesting the richness of TCM as expressed in yin and yang, *wu xing* (five elements), *zangfu, jing,* qi, *xue, jinye* and *shen* in that short span of time was insanely impossible. Nonetheless, the lectures were delivered according to the syllabus and on schedule, without a murmur of protest from anyone.

Both the textbook and lectures emphasized the holistic nature of the human body. By holistic, they mean the unity and integrity of the human body and its harmony with nature. The internal human body is linked to its own external; it is capable of self-regulation and self-adjustment. Its organic wholeness is shown in the composition and location of its internal organs and cavities, structurally inseparable, functionally interdependent.

Most of my classmates know the theories of yin and yang and *wu xing,* which are fundamental to TCM. I was familiar with yin and yang, a subject I read and wrote about before going to China. I was aware of *wu xing,* as any educated Chinese of the older generations would be but not familiar with it. The textbook and lectures emphasized the mutuality and reciprocity of yin and yang and stated categorically that, without yang, yin cannot be formed, and without yin, yang cannot be transformed. I had stated the same in my paper Yin Yang Touch. However, the *wu xing* (five-element) theory is much more complicated.

The five elements in the *wu xing* theory are wood, fire, earth, metal and water. These elements are linked to several body organs: wood to liver and gall bladder, fire to heart and small intestines, earth to spleen and stomach, metal to lung and large intestines, and water to kidney and bladder. The *wu xing* theory has the pivotal concepts of birthing (as giving birth, *sheng*) and checking (as holding in check, *ke*) to show how these elements interact with each other. To me, the elements are indicators of the gradation of yin and yang present in each body organ; birthing and checking are the pulling of yin-qi and yang-qi.

As I learned later, TCM differentiates between hand and foot meridians, and yang and yin meridians are classified in degrees: *yangming* as first degree, *taiyang* as second degree, and *shaoyang* as third degree for yang meridians; and *taiyin* as first degree, *shaoyin* as second degree, and *jueyin* as third degree for yin meridians. If I rank-order the five elements according to the yin-yang designation of body organs, scoring hand meridian as 0.5 point, *yangming* meridian as 3 points; *taiyang* meridian as 2 points; and *shaoyang* meridian as 1 point; I would have metal (3.5 points), earth (3 points), fire (2.5 points), water (2 points), and wood (1 point) in the yang order. The reverse sequence is the yin order. These orders would tell me how I might extend Yin Yang Touch to Chinese massage, but they are not the established order in TCM. To me, *wu xing* is an expression of yin and yang, not an independent system and the use of any one of these elements is approximation with no exact measurement. It is a simple way to diagnose a body condition, indicating the relative balance of yin-qi and yang-qi, similar to the Western concepts of hypertonicity, hypotonicity and homeostasis. Most TCM practitioners would find this interpretation preposterous because down through the ages they have been taught a complicated theoretical scheme that connects the five elements to the natural world and the human body, even though the connection is by assertion, not explanation.

In Guangzhou, I learned yin yang theory and *wu xing* theory as two separate systems. I expected both of them would be put aside in actual wellness anmo or therapeutic tuina, just as most Western massage practitioners would put aside the basic theories such as fasciae and thixotropy in their massage practice. Most of us are body workers, not brainworkers.

Zangfu, Jing, Qi, Xue, Jinye, and Shen

The lecture on *zangfu* was about visceral organs. In Chinese anatomy, visceral organs are divided into three groups, the *zang* organs consisting of liver, heart, spleen, lung and kidney; the ordinary *fu* organs consisting of gallbladder, small intestines, stomach, large intestines and bladder; and the extraordinary *fu* organs consisting of brain, marrow, bone, arteries and veins, gallbladder and uterus. No mistake here – the gallbladder is an ordinary *fu* organ and extraordinary *fu* organ. I have searched for an explanation and found no rationale for it. Generally, scant attention is paid to the extraordinary *fu* organs.

In the meridian scheme (next section), *zang* organs plus pericardium are yin organs and *fu* organs plus sanjiao are yang organs, but, due to its theoretical straitjacket, the *wu xing* theory treats pericardium, sanjiao and the extraordinary fu organs as though they are non-existent. This glaring omission and the contradiction between five elements and two sets of six organs are what made me question the adequacy of *wu xing* theory despite its time-honored position in TCM.

Ma talked about the functions of *zang* and *fu* organs and sanjiao, stressing the storing functions of *zang* – firm and not full, and the transforming functions of *fu* – full and not firm. While *zangfu* organs have names similar to Western anatomy, they represent ideas more abstract than just biological organs. The following description of the anatomy and functions of gallbladder, which I translated loosely from the foundation textbook, with my comments in parenthesis, is illustrative of what I mean.

The gallbladder is first among the six ordinary *fu* organs. [Why is it first among *fu* organs? Is it because gallbladder is on a foot-shaoyang meridian?] It is also an extraordinary *fu* organ. [Why is that?] It is located under the right ribs [seems precise but not really] and connected to the liver, nestling in latter's short lobes [It might be clearer to indicate that it is in the visceral surface of the liver]. The gallbladder is a storage sac for bile [Bingo! This is common to both Chinese physiology and Western physiology]. Its primary functions are to store and secrete bile [The repetition on storage is in the Chinese version] and to help a person make decisions [How does a body organ help a person make decision? Through the bile that the gallbladder secretes?] Both the gallbladder and liver are connected through the gallbladder (yang) meridian and liver (yin) meridian in the foot [another unique insight in Chinese physiology] and anatomically linked [True – an emphasis I did not catch in my study of human physiology]. They act mutually as the outer and inner expressions of each other [another unique insight in Chinese physiology].

After Ma had belabored over the 11 visceral organs and sanjiao in her lecture with a plethora of four-word or six-word phrases about their functions, Lin followed her monologue with the unique concepts of *jing*, qi, *xue, jinye* and *shen* (essence, energy, blood, body fluids and spirit) in her lecture. Even though I label each of these Chinese concepts with an English approximation, there really are no exact words to describe them. In popular Chinese idioms, *jingshen*, *xueqi* and *jinye* are usually linked together to express three aspects of life and each aspect has two sides. In academic circles, these are dismembered and treated as distinctive entities.

Lin and the textbook assert *jing*, qi, *xue* and *jinye* are the basic substances that form the human body and sustain its activities. Their formation and transformation are dependent on the normal working of visceral organs and meridians and the normal working of visceral organs and meridians are dependent on the free flowing of these basic substances which Xiaolan Zhao describes as "treasures" in her book *Ancient Healing for Modern Women* (2006). Zhao's description signifies the richness of the concepts of *jing*, qi and *shen*, which defy succinct translation. Jinye, for instance, might include genes, semen, mucus, saliva, lymph, cellular fluid and extracellular fluid.

Shen, both Lin and the textbook pontificate, is the master of a body's activities. It is the totality of a body's expression. They further elaborate on each of the "treasures," claiming *jing* is a kind of essence blended from the life substance (matter) of our parents and from the nutrients we ingest. It is the source of life, the fundamental substance for forming the body and sustaining life – a reiteration of what they asserted earlier. According to them, *jing* is stored in *zangfu* as a body fluid, which circulates among the *zangfu* [So *jing* is a form of *jinye*, body fluid?]. I did not ask the instructors for clarification because I did not have the vocabulary to ask an intelligent question. Besides, I did not want to appear stranger than what I already was in that class.

Qi is of special interest to me. I wrote about it and I was eager for more insights. I paid close attention to the exposition of its function as a powerful continuing life force. Chinese physiology considers qi as a "micro matter," one of the basic building blocks of the human body. Its continuous motion promotes and regulates the metabolic process and maintains life's process. When qi ceases to move, we are dead (Qi as brainwaves?). Qi comes from three sources, primordial qi transformed from life substance (what we inherit from our parents [genes?]), qi of micronutrients of food and qi of the natural environment. It is the joint product of spleen, kidney and lung. More assertions, but no new insights! I know I will need to learn more about the functions of spleen, kidney and lung to take my study of yin and yang to a higher level.

As I plowed through the obtuse textbook and listened to the droning of Ma and Lin, I could not help but feel that I was learning theology, not physiology, and that the basic epistemological problem of Chinese medicine might be similar to that in Western theology. Western theology is based on the Bible, a book with many authors and perspectives. Thus, we have a variety of theologies and lots of assertions. Chinese medicine is based on *Huangdi Neijing* (Picture 21), which is also a work of many authors and diverse understanding of life force. It has many "schools" and lots of assertions. Both Western theology and Chinese medicine have to deal with the problem of orthodoxy. Western theology maintains its orthodoxy by burning the heretics. Chinese medicine maintains its orthodoxy by including everyone. This inclusive stance makes it difficult to harmonize the diverse perspectives. Instead of fashioning one grand theory, compilers of *Huangdi Neijing* offered the diverse perspectives as unique expressions of the whole system, with each of them valid in its own right but seemingly unrelated to each other. Heresy in Chinese medicine is to imagine that different perspectives are essentially describing the same reality, which is exactly what I am saying about Yin Yang and *wu xing*, and about *jing*, qi, *xue*, *jinye* and *shen*. Since I am just a tuina practitioner and not a TCM practitioner, my heresy is of no consequence to the medical profession, but it helps me to make better sense of the "treasures" and might help other practitioners to develop a better synthesis in the future.

Meridians and Pressure Points

Lectures on meridians and pressure points were divided into five sessions, a total of 15 hours. The first session was an overview of the pressure points on the 12 regular meridians and eight extra meridians and the "*a shi xue*" (literally, 'Ah, yes!' points, which are defined by where the client feels pain). It also covered the flow of qi through the meridians in synchronization with the circadian cycle. The lectures emphasized that upper and lower limbs and the head are significant highways for meridians.

Lin further mentioned the correlation between five "specific points" on the four limbs -- *jing*, *xing*, *shu*, *jing* and *he* – with the five elements of wood, fire, earth, metal and water and the significance of these "specific points" for TCM. She talked of the presence of nine groups of pressure points (*yuan xue, luo xue, xi xue, bei yu xue, mu xue, ba hui xue, ba mai jiao hui xue, xia he xue,* and *jiao hui xue*), which are essentially ways to highlight and classify functions of the 361 pressure points. The lecture was evidently meant for TCM students based on the university textbook *Meridians and Pressure Points* (2012) edited by Shen Xueyong. However, none of the instructors seemed to feel the need to cite their sources. They probably taught from the assumption that intellectual property in a socialist society is the common property of everyone and that TCM's long history makes it practically impossible to trace original ownership. Whatever is new, like the musings I have in these notes, is probably heretical, not to be considered seriously. The class galloped from pressure points to pressure points, and I wrote down under what category they were to be listed. Lin threw out names of more than 30 pressure points but she did not show us where they were on the body.

In the next lecture, Ma picked up where Lin left off. We focused on the meridians of spleen, heart and small intestines. She gave us 20 more names of pressure points and mentioned the functions of some of them. For instance, *sanyinjiao* (SP6), coupled with *taichong* (LR3), is effective for treating insomnia; *yinbai* (SP1), coupled with *sanyinjiao* (SP6), *xuehai* (SP10) and *qihai* (CV6), is effective for treating menstrual problems. The notion of using several pressure points to treat a condition confirmed my suspicion that the lectures were not developed specifically for teaching tuina; they were lectures on acupuncture. However, I envisioned involving clients actively in their treatment (similar to active stretching), or using cupping to achieve the same result of concurrent treatment on multiple pressure points. Since returning from China, I have done some cupping but have not pursued the research on coupling pressure points. More work ahead!

In the subsequent lecture, Chen Shuo talked and walked us through the bladder and spleen meridians. We covered 40 more pressure points, but the learning process did not seem as onerous as the earlier classes.

The next set of lectures was about pressure points on the pericardium, lung, sanjiao and gallbladder meridians and extra meridians. Ma followed a pattern of describing the location of a pressure point, explaining its functions and the primary diseases it deals with and connecting it to clinical work. After her droning, she showed video clips of the meridian. We learned the names of another 40 pressure points. In her lecture, Chen added a new dimension to Ma's teaching pattern. In addition to citing the traditional location of each pressure point, she pointed out its anatomical position. She mentioned, for instance, the beginning point of *changqiang* (GV1) is located below the coccyx, midpoint on the line that connects the tip of the coccyx and anus. It is beneath the skin, the subcutaneous tissue and anal ligaments. The main nerves in the superficial layer are branches of the coccygeal nerves, and in the deep layer are branches of the femoral nerves, arteries and veins. *Changqiang* (GV1) is effective for treating hemorrhoid, anal prolapse, diarrhea and constipation. The cross reference to anatomy is especially useful for therapists who are more familiar with human biology. It enables cross-cultural study. Chen went through the major points on both the Du (governing) and Ren (conception) meridians and highlighted some popular extra points such as *sishencong (EX-HN1)*, *yintang (EX-HN3)* and *taiyang (EX-HN5)*. Much of what she elaborated on was not in the textbook, but in *Meridians and Pressure Points*.

Among Chinese practitioners and the books I have scanned through on the nomenclature of pressure points, I had not found when or why Chinese names for pressure points were presented in alphanumeric codes. As a Chinese reader, I find most of the names so colorful and associative that their substitutions in codes have rendered them lifeless. The Chinese names are associated with heavenly bodies, mountains and rivers, hills and dales, strategic transportation hubs, animals and plants, buildings and lodging, everyday tools, human activities, anatomy and physiology, and functions of pressure points.[74] Indeed, a classmate pointed out a large number of points using entrance (*men, hu, guan* in Chinese) in their names. The Chinese names provide an intuitive grasp of the functions of various points. For instance, *baihui* on the Du meridian is designated as GV20, with no notion that it is a point where "a hundred [streams] meet." However, the alphanumeric code does make it easier to identify and memorize the relative position of a pressure point on a specific meridian, especially for non-Chinese speakers.

My continuing search for answers finally led me to the web where I should have started. I struck gold! I discovered that the alphanumeric code was first developed by a World Health Organization's Scientific Group in 1984 to meet "the pressing need for a uniform, standardized nomenclature for acupuncture." The colorless terms, like the coordinates of latitude and longitude, are to facilitate precise communication. One trades off the richness of a medium for the richness of intercultural communication. The

---

[74]   *Meridians and Pressure Points* (in Chinese, 2012) by Shen Xueyong.

report issued by the Scientific Group agrees with me about the nature of the Chinese names. It states, *"The Han character is widely used in oriental medicine in China and Japan, in Hong Kong and Singapore, and by Koreans. It confers philosophical concepts on meridians and acupuncture points which often defy translation, and should therefore be an essential element of the standard nomenclature."*[75] In terms of tuina practice, I am not sure if it is worthwhile to study pressure points in depth since tuina deals essentially with macro-anatomy whereas pressure points are microanatomy. The focus of our learning and practice should be on meridians and their primary functions, not pressure points. If necessary, we might select a number of critical pressure points to complement our practice. As a smart practitioner, I would concentrate on the Du, Ren and bladder meridians.

Diagnostics in Chinese Medicine

TCM diagnostics uses a therapist's sensory organs (eye, ear, nose, finger tips and mouth) to gather data for diagnosis. It involves questioning (*wen*[4]), observing (*wang*), "receiving" (*wen*[2]) and touching (*qie*). Questioning is the subjective part of SOAP note-taking; observing, "receiving," and touching are the objective parts of SOAP. Data gathered from these processes are for assessment of the problem and formulation of treatment plan – the A and P parts of the SOAP chart. Despite the critical nature of diagnostic process, the foundation book has exactly one paragraph on it under the heading of "differential diagnostics." The instructor (I don't remember which one) drew on her TCM training and elaborated on each of the processes,[76] but made no comments on the importance of record keeping. As I discovered later in my practical training, the tuina practitioners I knew did not maintain written files on their clients. They relied on the client's memory and their own recollection.

Observing has several elements. It involves using the naked eye to look at a client wholly and locally, and to look at (examine) his tongue and excretions such as phlegm, nasal mucus, saliva and vomit. Looking at a client wholly involves observing how the client expresses his spirit, color, form and appearance. You pay attention to the vitality

---

[75]   *A Proposed Standard International Acupuncture Nomenclature: Report of a WHO Scientific Group*, 1991.

[76]   Which is discussed in detail in *Diagnostics of Chinese Medicine* (2012) edited by Li Xiandong and Wu Chengyu.

of his eyes, the color and brightness of his face, the naturalness of his look and the steadiness of his posture. You notice whether the color of his skin leans more to green, red, yellow, white or black. You pay attention to the strength and weakness and the weight of his physical body, as seen from his hair and skin, muscles, arteries and veins, ligaments and bones; and how he sits, stands and walks and whether he shows abnormal movements and gestures of fatigue.

Looking at a client locally involves observing the shape, size and posture of his head, the luster of his hair and the nature of his hair loss, the shape and color of his face; the shape and expression of his five sensory organs (eye, ear, mouth, nose and tongue); the shape and movement of his neck; the symmetry of his chest and abdomen, the shape of his spinal column; the shape and movement of the upper and lower limbs; the condition of his urinary and reproductive organs; and the color and texture of his skin.

Tongue examination is unique to TCM. Thus, the instructor spent considerable time on the subject, beginning with reviewing the structure and functions of the tongue. She lectured that, through the meridians, the tongue is connected to the visceral organs. The connection enables the tongue to show the relative health status of the visceral organs. In classical Chinese medicine, the tongue is divided into three sections, which are associated with the visceral organs: the tip of the tongue is associated with the heart and lungs, the mid-portion of the tongue is associated with spleen and stomach, and the root of the tongue is associated with kidney. In addition, the lateral edges of the tongue are associated with liver and gallbladder.

We were introduced to lively tongue and parched tongue, old tongue and young tongue, fat tongue and thin tongue, spotted tongue, cracked tongue and tongue with bite marks; flaccid tongue, stiff tongue, slanting tongue, shaking tongue, protruding tongue and arrested tongue. We learned about tongue color, whether it is pink, pale white, red, purple red or purple, and what the different colors signify. We also learned about the quality and color of the coating on the tongue, and the meridians underneath the tongue.

Under "observing," examining a child requires a slightly different approach than examining an adult. To examine a child, TCM practitioners are to examine his/her fingerprints of the index finger and they have a 20-word ditty for this examination: *fu chen fen biao li*, (floating-sinking divide surface-depth), *hong zi bian han re*, (red-purple separate cold-hot), *dan zhi ding xu shi*, (light-heavy define empty-firm), *san guan ce qing zhong*, (three joints probe mild-severe).

Translated, the ditty says, if the fingerprints appear as though they were floating, the disease is on the surface (external). If they appear sinking, the disease is beneath the surface (internal). If the fingerprints appear red, the disease is due to external coldness. If they appear purple, the disease is due to internal hotness (fever and dehydration). If fingerprints appear light and fine, they indicate energy deficiency. If they appear heavy and coarse, they indicate energy stagnation. If the meridians are prominent at the base of the finger, the disease is mild. If they are at the mid-section of the finger, the disease is moderately serious. If they are at the tip section of the finger, the disease is severe.

The concept I translate as "receiving" is what TCM calls wen^2, normally associated with smelling, a nasal function. However, wen^2 is also associated with hearing, an auricular function. The common denominator between the two is their reception of external stimuli, thus, I use "receiving" to include both the nasal and auricular functions.

Receiving involves listening to a patient's voice: How does he vocalize it? Is the sound clear or dull, coarse or mute? Is it shrill? How does he speak: delirious, repetitive, speaking to himself, babbling, raving or stammering? How does he breathe as he speaks: gasping, wheezing, short of breath, lack of breath or snoring? Does he cough, vomit, hiccup, belch, sigh or sneeze? Does his stomach growl? It also involves smelling the odors of the patient's mouth, perspiration, phlegm and nasal mucus, vomit, excrements and menstrual secretion and the odors of the confinement room.

As far as the patient is concerned, observing and "receiving" are passive activities, what the practitioner does. Questioning (wen^4), however, is entirely dependent on the patient or his caregivers. They need to provide answers to what the practitioner asks. The questions for which answers are sought include biographical information, medical history and daily habits of the client, family history, primary complaints, status of body temperature (much more complicated than simply taking temperature with a thermometer), perspiration, location of aches and pains, symptoms of discomfort in the head, chest and abdomen, the condition of eyes and ears, sleep status, appetite and taste, urination, defecation and menstruation.

Touching (qie) is using one's hand to feel, touch or press a body area to ascertain its health status. It is divided into pulse palpation and digital palpation. Pulse palpation is central to TCM diagnostics. It uses three fingers to probe the status of pulse and enlists it under one of the 12 types of pulses or their counter-pulses. In addition to these pulses, Chinese practitioners also identify seven strange pulses that indicate terminal conditions. Digital palpation uses not only the fingers, but also the palm and hand to press, push, knead and rap the chest muscles, ribs, abdomen, muscles, limbs and pressure points.

Data gathered from these processes are analyzed in the matrix of eight principles consisting of surface and depth, cold and hot, empty and firm, and yin and yang. The configuration is mindboggling. Some variations in the diagnostic process are beyond the scope of Chinese tuina practices and some are definitely not applicable to Western massage. It seems to me that the benefit of learning Chinese diagnostics is that, while we are not TCM practitioners, we can use the knowledge to help us become more aware of the health status of our clients and more sensitive to latent or manifest health problems. At the very least, we have the tools to assess whether our client is contraindicated for tuina therapy.

What surprised me in these lectures was the omission of the cardinal dictum of Chinese medicine, $tong^4$ ze bu $tong^1$, $tong^1$ jiu bu $tong^4$ (Pain means no free flowing; free flowing means no pain), and the lack of explicit discussion on the goal of Chinese medical treatment, which is focused on facilitating $tong^1$. Free flowing in TCM is the unimpeded movement and optimal balance of yin-qi and yang-qi in the meridians. Luo Dalun, a nationally known TCM practitioner in China, stated convincingly in his book, *Moderate Yin Yang for Health* (2012), that when yin and yang are in balance, good health is assured. His book is another tool for my continuing study of yin and yang.

Chapter 17

ANATOMY, CHINESE STYLE

Axial Skeleton

The first lecture on human anatomy was on the axial skeleton. It was one of six sessions on human anatomy, for a total of 18 class hours. Anyone familiar with the subject of human anatomy would recognize the impossibility of learning even the barest basics in that short period. For Chinese tuina, the barest (no pun intended) anatomy materials are summarized in Chapter 3 of the foundation book and that chapter is the longest in the whole book, with 44 pages of text and illustrations. Having studied human anatomy and physiology at NOVA, I had no problem reading the materials and I found the illustrations useful, but I had to learn a new set of Chinese names for anatomical positions and terminology, planes of the body, tissues and the "locomotor system" consisting of bones, joints and muscles. I wrote next to the many terms their English equivalents. Some of my classmates watched me taking notes and thought it strange that I interspersed Chinese characters with English scribbling. The textbook stressed that the locomotor system is closely linked to the practice of wellness tuina, but Ma and Lin, unlike Grafelman, did not point out how human anatomy is applicable to massage therapy.

The Chinese text was so compact that I had to read and re-read each paragraph several times and I had to rely on a Chinese-English dictionary to help with some of the new words. The terse prose of the textbook can perhaps be illustrated with its coverage of tissues. Whereas most English textbooks would have several pages on epithelial tissue, connective tissue, nervous tissue and muscle tissue, the foundation book devoted less than one page to them.

At the outset, I had to translate constantly, not only words, but also concepts. For instance, what Ma identifies as "locomotor system" is simply the muscular and skeletal systems in Western terminology. Ma did not mention organ systems in her lecture, but the textbook recognizes nine organ systems, not the 11 groupings that I learned in Human Biology at NOVA. In addition to combining the muscular and skeletal systems into one locomotor system, the textbook also combines lymphatic and cardiovascular systems into what it calls the "vascular system." It includes skin, eye and ear as a sensory organ system, different from the Western groupings of integumentary system and special senses. As a massage therapist, I like the explicit recognition of skin as a sensory organ.

In the lecture, Ma focused on the locomotor system. She followed the textbook with an overview of bone composition, and delved into structure of bone and classification of bones (skull bones, axial bones and appendicular bones). As the syllabus listed, our time was mainly spent on learning axial bones. We mentioned skull bones only in passing, noting they have eight cranial bones and 15 facial bones.

Under axial bones, Ma recited the unique features of thoracic vertebrae, sacrum, coccyx, sternum, first, second, sixth, and twelfth ribs, skull, clavicles, scapula, humerus, radius, ulna, hand bones, hipbone, femur, patella, tibia, fibula and foot bones. She used the drawings in the textbook and video clips to reinforce her recitation. Occasionally, she made reference to the table-sized anatomical model. The old names of spinous process, transverse process, vertebral foramen, atlas, axis, superior and inferior articular facets, xiphoid process and a host of other skeletal terms popped up in their Chinese identity. The anatomical terms are rendered in Chinese, not Latin or Greek. Thus, vertebrae are simply *zhui gu* – spinal bones, and cervical vertebrae are *jing gu* – neck bones. *Gu* is the Chinese word for bone. However, numerical labeling of vertebrae follows the universal convention of C1-C7, T1-T12, and L1-L5, and C1, C2 and C7 were singled out for special mention. In Western terms, C7 has the awesome name of vertebra prominens. The Chinese call it *long zhui* – bulging vertebra. Two words, much simpler! We also talked about true ribs, false ribs and floating ribs.

Anyone familiar with human anatomy would agree that many of these bone structures require at least 15 to 20 minutes of elucidation each. To cover all of them in one lecture is no better than just going through the motion of teaching. My classmates might be at home with that kind of teaching and learning. I had grown out of it. Unlike the classes at the Woodbridge campus, we did not handle any models of bone (I don't think the school has a set of bone models). I was back to the dark ages of rote learning a vast number of isolated names. But for the prior exposure at NOVA, I would have been totally lost and my time in China wasted. The academic jargons, the monotonous delivery and the constant noise of street traffic conspired to make it difficult for me to learn. Fortuitously, I found a couple of study partners in Chen Jianhua and Guo Jin, two classmates steeped in TCM. They clarified what Ma mummified.

Appendicular Skeleton

The lecture on appendicular bones covered bones of upper limbs and lower limbs. In both the textbook and classroom presentation, each set of the bones of the limb is divided into girdle bones and free bones. The girdle bones of upper limbs (pectoral girdle) are the clavicle and scapula, and the free bones of upper limbs are the humerus, radius, ulna and hand bones (carpus, metacarpus and phalanges). The girdle bones of lower limbs (pelvic girdle) are the pelvic bones and the free bones of lower limbs are the femur, patella, tibia, fibula and foot bones (tarsus, metatarsus and phalanges). This is a clearer scheme than what I learned in NOVA. We learned about the shape and substance of each bone from the text, the illustrations and video clips. I wished I had brought Biel's *Trail Guide* with me to China for faster and clearer reference and comparison, but I hadn't. While Ma made no comments on bones as attachment sites for muscles, she alluded to learning anatomy for finding acupressure points.

Joints

The lecture on joints was about how bones are connected to each other. It began with a discussion of two types of joining, direct and indirect. Direct joining of two bones is accomplished with fibrous tissues or cartilage. Indirect joining of two bones is accomplished with joint surfaces, joint capsule and joint cavity. This schema is different from what I learned at NOVA. Grafelman has joint classifications by form or function. In the Chinese scheme, direct joining (amphiarthrodial and synarthrodial joints such as pubic symphysis and bones of the skull) would restrict or eliminate joint activity, and indirect joining (diarthrodial joints such as elbow and knee) would allow free joint activity. Joints indirectly connected are simply synovial joints!

The movement of synovial joints was one of the first lessons I learned in massage, in Biel's *Trail Guide to the Body* (2005), and it took me several days of review to appreciate what's what. Based on their movement, joints are usually classified into six types: pivot, hinge, saddle, condyloid, plane, and ball and socket.[77] However, the Chinese have no special names for different types of synovial joints. They classify joint movements into four types, flexion and extension along the sagittal plane, abduction and adduction along the frontal plane, rotation along the horizontal plane and circumduction with little movement at the proximal end of a limb but a great deal of movement at the distal end. I cannot decide if the Chinese scheme is better than its Western counterpart, or vice versa.

The lecture on axial bones and appendicular bones was about how they are connected. The instructor recited about their connections and showed video clips on joints of the spinal column, chest, shoulder, arm, wrist and hand, pelvis, hip, thigh, leg and foot. The video clips were excellent, but the densely labeled illustrations in the foundation book are not easy for one to grasp.

Muscles

The lecture on muscles began with typing according to tissues, thus, smooth muscles, cardiac muscles and skeletal muscles. The focus of the course is on skeletal muscles, which are dealt with in four groups: trunk muscles, head and neck muscles, upper and lower limb muscles. I like the Chinese nomenclature for muscles; they are so simple. Instead of trapezius, they say *xiefangji* (slanting, square muscle). Instead of latissimus dorsi, they say *beihuoji* (back, broad muscle). Instead of erector spinae, they say *shujiji* (erect, spine muscle). *Ji*[1] is the Chinese primary word for muscle. Most of the

---

[77]   *Graf's Anatomy* (1998).

names do not require learning a foreign language. None of the Latin or Greek stuff! Of course, I had to learn a different vocabulary, but that's a different challenge. More translation!

Trunk muscles are muscles of the back, chest, stomach, diaphragm and perineum; head and neck muscles are muscles of head and neck; upper limb muscles are muscles of shoulder, arm, forearm and hand; and lower limb muscles are muscles of pelvis, thigh, leg and foot. Quite straightforward, just like what I learned at NOVA. We heard description and saw pictures of muscles with two heads (biceps), muscles in triangular shape (deltoid), muscles of upper fossa (supraspinatus) and muscles of the whole body. We must have seen video clips of at least a hundred muscles. We heard and read about their functions, their origins and insertion points; unfortunately, what I heard and read had no staying power, they were transient: into the left ear and out from the right ear! To mouth off all that information in three hours was just insane, but none of my classmates uttered a word of discomfort or showed signs of indigestion. They probably had dismissed them as unimportant. The level of my inattention is reflected in the blank spaces in my notebook. I have only a listing of muscles, some in Chinese and some in English. Despite good intentions and determination, I just could not concentrate. I decided to give my brain temporary respite!

Organ Systems

The lectures on organ systems covered digestive, respiratory, urinary, reproductive, vascular (consisting of cardio vascular and lymphatic) and nervous systems; the first five systems were covered in one lecture. After mentioning the various organs that made up the digestive tube and those that secrete glandular fluids, Ma listed ingestion, digestion and absorption of food as the primary functions of the digestive system. Under digestive glands, she differentiated between major glands that are independent, glands such as salivary gland, liver and pancreas; and minor glands that permeate the whole digestive tube, glands of the lips, cheeks, alimentary canal, stomach and intestines. After the lecture, we saw video clips from the site www. sciencep.com.

The lecture on the nervous system was presented by itself. It has two sub-systems, the central nervous system (CNS) and the peripheral nervous system (PNS). The former is made up of the brain (cerebrum, cerebellum, diencephalon and brain stem) and spinal cord (with 31 pairs of spinal nerves); the latter is made up of 12 pairs of cranial nerves, 31 pairs of spinal nerves and a host of somatic and visceral motor nerves. The spinal cord is connected to both CNS and PNS.

What Chinese physiology called somatic and visceral motor nerves were what I learned at NOVA as somatic nervous system and automatic nervous system. Unlike my exposure at NOVA, somatic and visceral systems in Chinese were discussed in parallel and the division made sense. Similarly, sympathetic nerves and parasympathetic nerves of the visceral system were discussed in parallel and the contrast was better than what I learned at NOVA. Ma augmented the dense materials in the foundation book with information on reflex arc and nerve plexus. Interestingly, Chinese physiology, as taught in the tuina training program, does not discuss the form and functions of neuron and neurophysiology. While I applauded the selectivity, I felt the compilers missed an opportunity to connect the nervous system with meridians and pressure points.

Chapter 18

EXTRAS IN THE TUINA CURRICULUM

In the tuina curriculum, there are a number of extras that are similar to the courses that Western practitioners take for their continuing education. Perhaps due to their elective nature, only a few of the extras were included in our class. They were foot reflexology, *guasha* and cupping, lymphatic drainage, spinal tuina and acupuncture.

Foot Reflexology

Foot reflexology is part of the curriculum for the intermediate level. Instead of linking it with what was taught before by focusing on the 30-some pressure points on each foot, the lecture on foot reflexology shifted the emphasis to the correlation between body organs and zones, with no reconciliation between the 12 organs in TCM and the 60-some organs reflected in the foot.

We learned about imagining both feet together as a microcosm of the whole body. The midline (sagittal line) that divides the body into two halves is the same imaginary line diving the feet into left foot and right foot, the medial aspects of both feet reflect the spine and the big toes reflect the head. However, the reflections for the head are crossed, the left big toe is related to the right side of the head, and the right big toe to the left side of the head. Each foot, in turn, can be divided into three sections: the front reflecting the chest (and the heart is reflected only in the left foot); the middle reflecting the abdomen (and the gallbladder is reflected only in the right foot); and the back (or base) reflecting the pelvic cavity. Along the lateral aspects of the feet are reflections of shoulders, elbows, buttocks and knees.

We also learned about hand techniques for foot reflexology. They included using the thumb singly, thumb and index finger together, or both hands, to push, press, knead, rap, pluck, pinch and scrape. We saw demonstrations on doing foot reflexology and we practiced what we saw. We went through locating the zones for many of the body organs, reviewing the effects of massaging those zones and trying out hand techniques. We were reminded to keep our nails trimmed and to wash our hands with warm water after foot massage. We should also ensure that clients are not exposed to chill during foot massage.

What I got out of the lecture, textbook and demonstration is an appreciation of the versatility of bodywork, that I am able to facilitate healing in a condition by working at a remote site of the body. Instead of working directly on sensitive areas and organs beyond our reach (such as the various glands, plexuses, internal organs, breast and diaphragm, eyes and nose) we can work on the reflexive zones to achieve curative effects. I can incorporate foot massage into my practice without fanfare.

Guasha

The modalities of *guasha* and cupping are closely associated with tuina. They were the substances of a lecture for the advanced level of tuina training. One might call them "tuina plus." *Guasha* literally means the scraping of sands, a common practice in Chinese folk medicine. It uses a scraping tool to scrape the skin to promote the release of toxins from the body. After a client is treated, her skin usually appears in different shades of red and sometimes it shows tiny red spots (petechiae) like sands, hence the name *sha*. The traditional scraping tool is made with buffalo horn or bone. It is still available in China, but much more expensive than the hard plastic tools in use these days. Actually, in folk practice, any tool with a smooth edge can be used for scraping. When I was a teenager, I saw friends of my aunt using ceramic spoons to scrape her shoulders. The most common areas amenable to *guasha* are the back and the lateral sides of the neck. However, other body areas such as the abdomen, chest, knee pit and elbow pit can also be treated. The popular pressure points used in *guasha* are *zusanli (ST36), tianzhu (BL10), quci (LI11)* and those on the meridians in the back (especially the Du meridian and the bladder meridian).

Guasha technique is relatively simple. Before treatment, ensure that the room is warm. To begin, clean the treatment area with warm water, lubricate the edge of the scraping medium, hold it in an angle between 30° and 60° and scrape the skin of the treatment area gently but firmly. Scrape inferiorly or laterally, in one direction only, for 20 times or until the skin shows dark red streaks or spots. Lubricate the skin continually. Upon completion, pat the treatment area several times with salt water.

Guasha is contraindicated for people who are too thin or whose skin lacks resiliency, people with heart diseases or edema, hemophilia, skin disease or contagious disease. It is also contraindicated for children and older people who are feeble. People who receive *guasha* treatment should wait for at least 8 hours before bathing in cold water. They should drink warm water to help flush out toxins.

In Guangzhou, we had a *guasha* demonstration in class, but we did not break out to practice in groups. After a brief break, we continued with the lecture on cupping.

Cupping

Cupping is also a common practice in Chinese folk medicine. Known colloquially as "pulling [the] fire can" (*ba huo guan*), it uses the principle of negative air pressure to extract toxins from a treatment area. The "can" can be any non-combustible bamboo, ceramic or glass container. A set of "cans" usually has 12-16 cups of four sizes (large, medium, small and smaller), all of them look like Chinese teacups. After you have found the hypertonic muscles and lubricated the area, you swirl a cotton ball of fire in a cup for a second or two to create negative air pressure, and place the cup over the treatment area. You can leave it on the treatment area for ten to fifteen minutes, glide it over the treatment area, or put it on and off the treatment area in rapid succession. After cupping, a client's skin usually shows circles of bruises whose color may vary from light to dark red. A dark bruise indicates a high concentration of toxins in that area of the body. The bruises usually fade away within five to seven days.

Due to the risk of fire and burns, some practitioners use vacuum cups instead of fire "cans." The vacuum cups are made of hard plastic. A set of vacuum cups usually comes with a hand suction pump. The version that I use has a built in pointed nipple in each cup to facilitate direct contact with pressure point. They are tools for acupressure treatment. You locate and lubricate the treatment area, place a vacuum cup over it and withdraw the air with the suction pump. As you squeeze the pump, the skin area under the cup rises to counteract the negative pressure. Adjust pressure according to the client's reaction. You can do stationary or gliding cupping with vacuum cups.

Cupping is contraindicated for people with sensitive skin, ulcer, edema, high fever and twitching. It should not be put over the heart and the primary blood vessels. For pregnant woman, cups should not be put on the abdomen, lumbar and sacral areas.

Lin demonstrated cupping with fire "cans" and some classmates practiced fire cupping on a couple of "volunteers." I observed. Even though I would never use the fire technique in the U.S. due to prohibitive insurance costs and fire risks, I could adapt the technique for vacuum cupping and incorporate it in my bodywork.

Lymphatic Drainage

Lymphatic draining is also part of the advanced level of tuina training. Lin had a cursory introduction of the lymphatic system with recitation on lymph formation, lymphatic vessels and ducts, and distribution of lymph nodes. She also mentioned the inflammatory response of lymphoid cells. However, despite the crucial role of the spleen in TCM and in the lymphatic system, nothing was said about the interplay between traditional understanding of the spleen and modern understanding of its physiological functions. Lin cited three sources of lymph movement: (1) propulsion of new lymph; (2) peristalsis of smooth muscles; and (3) compression of skeletal muscles and pointed out the rate of lymph movement is affected by liquid pressure (osmosis) and motor activities. She recognized massage can hasten lymph movement and cautioned that as lymphatic vessels have valves, lymph draining should be done in one direction, toward the heart.

After the brief introduction, Lin demonstrated lymphatic drainage in both supine and prone positions. The sequence of strokes was divided into three segments for supine position -- lateral aspect of upper limbs, lateral aspect of lower limbs, chest and stomach. The sequence for prone position was similar – medial aspect of upper limbs, medial aspect of lower limbs, back and waist. Pressure points were not used in lymphatic drainage even though, theoretically, they are reference points for moving body fluids.

I volunteered to be the on-table dummy so that I could feel Lin's touch for lymphatic drainage. Her pressure was about the same as that for regular massage. She seemed not to recognize that lymphatic vessels and ducts tend to close up with pressure.

Spinal Tuina

Spinal tuina was an "add on" for students who registered for it. Professor Yuan Jianqiang was the featured lecturer. Yuan was probably in his mid-50s, slim in build, short in physical stature and bespectacled. He dressed smartly in custom-made shirt and pants, more like a successful businessman than a professor of Chinese medicine. He came to class with two female assistants, but did not introduce them. He was affable, seemingly attentive to the audience. He even had time to chat with me during the lecture. He spoke through a lapel mike and had the verbal mannerism of saying "ah" in between phrases. His Putonghua had a strong Cantonese accent.

Yuan has been engaged in tuina study and research since 1984. He was one of the star pupils of Professors Long Cenghua and Wei Zheng, a couple of pioneers in the study and teaching of spinal pathology in China. He and Hou Yunshan coauthored the book *Spinal Tuina*.[78] I was given a copy as part of the course package.

Spinal Tuina has six chapters. Chapter 1 deals with the historical development of tuina, including a presentation on the effectiveness of using internal medicine and tuina to treat spinal problems. Chapter 2 describes the distribution of meridians and pressure points, with special emphasis on the regular pressure points on Du and bladder

---

[78] The Chinese title of the book *zhong yi jing luo ji zhu tui na liao fa tu jie*, translated literally, is Chinese Medicine Meridian Vertebra Tuina Therapy Illustration, or An Illustrated Guide to Vertebral (Meridian) Tuina Therapy in Chinese Medicine. The 12-word title might be necessary in Chinese, but it is too wordy and redundant in English. Despite its emphasis on illustration, the book is laden with text and the illustrations are less than 20 percent of the book's content. Thus, I take the liberty to name the book *Spinal Tuina*.

meridians and 16 extra points on the neck and posterior trunk. Chapter 3 is on spinal anatomy and physiology: its bones, nerves, muscles and the spinal cord. Chapter 4 deals with the three-step method of pinpointing a diseased condition. Chapter 5 introduces spinal tuina therapy, including the primary and secondary techniques for treating soft tissues and osteopathy (setting misaligned bones). It also has a section on nutritional treatment of 21 conditions related to spinal pathology. Chapter 6 has three sections: Section 1 is on cervical problems and related internal pathologies, Section 2 is on thoracic problems and related internal pathologies and Section 3 is on lumbar problems and related internal pathologies. The book has 340 pages.

The central theme of the book is that the vertebral column is a very important body organ. On it are traversed the Du meridian and the bladder meridian, which are closely connected with the functions and dysfunctions of visceral organs. When back muscles are over-strained or impacted by negative elements in the environment, or when vertebrae are dislocated, they create congestion or stagnation in the Du and bladder meridians, which, in turn, affect the smooth functions of the visceral organs. Spinal tuina on meridians and pressure points are able to open up the meridians and to adjust vertebral dislocation. In so doing, it restores the body to wholeness.

If the staff and the instructors of the Center of Continuing Education were more creative, they could have taught from *Spinal Tuina* instead of following the standard syllabus or the textbooks. *Spinal Tuina* has much clearer pictures of meridians and pressure points and the text is much fuller. The presentation on muscles, vertebrae and spinal nerves is more comprehensive. The pictures on hand techniques are in color and clearer and the discussion on pathologies is more direct and adaptable. Using *Spinal Tuina* as the main textbook, my classmates and I would have gained much more from our learning. But, the school has to follow central guidelines and we were stuck with the indigestible.

In deceptive simplicity, Yuan introduced the history of spinal tuina through a number of success stories. Without overt emphasis, he shared two important concepts with the audience, that spinal tuina is using external moves to treat internal problems (*yi wai ke zuo nei bu*) and that thorough diagnosis should precede clinical treatment. He also advised us that focusing on working with the sacrum is the preferred route for treating spinal problems. After his spellbinding survey of the field, he showed the class how to read the

X-ray pictures that some classmates had brought. These classmates were ready to be models for demonstration in order to have spinal treatment. Interpreting X-ray pictures of the vertebral column is in fact one of the three steps for pinpointing a diseased condition, what Yuan and Hou wrote about in Chapter 4 of their book. The other two steps are taking health history and doing physical examination.

Yuan showed us how to use the three-step method to locate a problem by interviewing Xiao Wu and interpreting her X-ray picture to the class. Xiao Wu was one of my classmates whose father was a TCM practitioner. With data gathered, Yuan worked on Xiao Wu's vertebrae while she lay prone on the massage table. (She did not undress, just lifted her blouse to her upper shoulder.) He used the index and middle fingers to probe bilaterally and inferiorly along her spinal column, pinpointed the area of misalignment and rock-pushed (shifted) the curvature into alignment. His demonstration reminded me of what I had seen of Erik Dalton's skeletal alignment techniques in a DVD, and I mentioned the association to him. He recognized Dalton, but made no further comments.

We learned how to interpret X-ray pictures of different classmates, palpate along their spinal columns for troubled spots and gently rock the spots into alignment. Yuan underscored that our treatment success would be contingent on the quality of our hand pressure and proper alignment of our hand with the client's curvature. He made us take turns to work on the volunteers, guided by his hands. I don't recall if we did any chiropractic adjustment of our volunteers' vertebrae, but I remember Yuan adjusting, rocking and twisting on a number of them.

Yuan pointed out that vertebral dislocation and deviation can happen laterally (scoliosis), anteriorly (lordosis) and posteriorly (kyphosis). Because hand probing is accurate for 80 percent of the cases, X-ray pictures are needed to provide data for the 20 percent of cases not detected by probing. Thus, X-ray pictures are mandatory in spinal tuina. Yuan also emphasized that to become a good spinal tuina therapist, you have to know the structure of each vertebra intimately so that you can decide which direction to shift, rock or twist. The diagnosis is important also for screening out cases that should not be treated with spinal tuina. For instance, people with herniated disks.

Yuan talked about deviation of the vertebrae as he demonstrated the "rock and stretch" method for treating different volunteers. He discussed four degrees of dislocation: swelling (*peng chu*), slipping (*tu chu*), detaching (*tuo chu*) and floating (*you chu*), and advised that the first two were indicated for tuina therapy, but the last two had to have surgery. "Make sure you know what you should (could) do and should (could) not do as a therapist" was his constant mantra. He emphasized that while X-ray pictures are capable of helping to make a more accurate diagnosis, a therapist must know the difference between normal and abnormal curvature in order to make the proper diagnosis. He also stated that the vertebra superior to the problem area is the marker for measuring dislocation and he further differentiated deviation on the transverse plane and that on the sagittal plane. The talk was straight from Chapter 3 of his book, *Spinal Tuina*.

In his demonstration, Yuan also introduced the three-finger method of probing and treatment, and the foot-lifting test. He drew attention to the impact of lumbar vertebrae on many aspects of life including the reproductive functions. He emphasized to the class the need of constant adjustment in manual therapy as we probe and treat our clients and reiterated the primacy of diagnosis in treatment.

Yuan summarized his presentation with the phrase *shi lu* (train of reasoning). He said he was not so much teaching us techniques as he was teaching us how to think (reason). That comment reminded me of the admonition of Heidi Peña-Moog. Both of them were saying it is relatively easy to learn handwork, but it is harder and more important to learn reasoning. Therapists need to think through why they perform a particular move. That's why we learn anatomy and physiology! I felt the two sessions on spinal tuina were worth the entire tuition cost. Of course, the segment of spinal tuina on vertebral adjustment is beyond the scope of Western massage and its focus on the vertebrae has diminished the role of fascia, muscles and ligaments in body alignment. Nonetheless, the insights from this modality can be incorporated into both Chinese and Western massage practices.

Chapter 19

PRACTICAL TUINA

Before we began learning tuina techniques, we watched a video on *Yijinjing* (*Canon of Muscle Transformation*) to learn how to develop strength in fingers, wrists, arms, muscles in upper back, thighs and legs. In the NOVA training program, there is a lifetime fitness requirement, but it is not specifically linked to massage therapy. The tuina program, in contrast, emphasizes the role of massage in keeping a practitioner physically fit, and fitness as a precondition for treating clients. Everyone in class followed the video to practice "muscle transformation." We learned how to stand still like a piling and how to move meditatively like a fish gliding in water. We learned to develop digital strength and dexterity through the practice of tapping, punching and grasping a small bag of rice. We also learned hand rolling, a technique unique to Chinese tuina. The main point of the exercises was to underscore tuina's use of finger pressure in therapy.

The hands-on techniques of tuina were taught concurrently with the theories of tuina. In these notes, I separate them so as to minimize confusion. The first set of techniques we learned were friction and compression. Lin began with an emphasis of sinking the shoulders, dropping the elbows, hanging the wrists and breathing from *dantian* (the area below the navel) as the desired form for doing tuina. In other words, pay heed to posture and body mechanics and breathe!

Chinese friction is different from the Western notion of friction. It is more like effleurage, moving the palm, fingers or elbow in a straight line or circularly on the client's body surface to generate heat. According to Lin, the preferred frequency for friction is 100-120 strokes per minute (much too fast for my practice). It includes a variety of hand techniques such as pushing with fingers, palm or elbow moving with strength in one direction; smearing with thumb or palm moving in a curve, bilaterally or up and down; rubbing with fingers or palm moving in circular motion; scrubbing with palm pressing down on body surface and moving up and down on it; and kneading with both palmer hands holding the body surface moving briskly in opposite directions.

Compression is using fingers, palms and other body parts of the therapist to press or squeeze the treatment area. It is similar to petrissage in Western massage. The varieties of compression technique include pressing, using thumb, palm, or elbow to press perpendicularly in a light-heavy-light pattern; poking, using tip of thumb, first joint of thumb or second joint of index finger; plucking, like playing a string instrument, using finger tips, base of hand and elbow tip; squeezing, press and release, lift and squeeze, using thumb and two or four other fingers; twisting, using fingers in screwing motion; grasping, using thumb and two or three other fingers to lift; and stepping, using big toes, plantar feet or heels on the lumbar region.

Lin showed us variations of the two basic techniques and supplemented her demonstration with video clips. My classmates and I practiced each technique either on rice bags or on ourselves; we were not sufficiently familiar with each other to exchange practices. I didn't know the extent of my classmate's dexterity in these techniques. I only knew I would have to spend many hours of practice and application before I could feel these fine points in my hands. We did not have a demonstration of the stepping technique.

Lin also shared a 30-word formula to highlight the intended effects of six of the techniques: pushing to move qi and blood, rubbing to smooth qi, grasping to loosen the muscles, pressing to adjust the web of meridians, poking to regulate the branches of meridian, and kneading to enliven blood. These six are probably the basic "strokes" of Chinese massage.

The next set of techniques we learned was swaying, percussion and vibration. Swaying is using fingers, palms and wrist joints to oscillate on a body surface with motion originating from the forearms. It includes the actions of thumb meditation, kneading and rolling. Swaying has no parallel moves in western massage. It is unique to Chinese tuina. Thumb meditation involves using the thumb to move back and forth over a pressure point. Kneading involves using fingers and palm to knead in a circular fashion. Rolling involves using the edge of hypothenar eminence or an empty fist to knead in a rhythmic manner. All these subtle techniques are novel to Western practice. Maria Mercati has developed an alternate form, what she calls Bodyharmonics Rolling, for Western practitioners.[79]

Percussion is similar to tapotement in Western massage. It uses fingers, palmar and dorsal hands, fists or other special tools to pound the body surface rhythmically. Chinese percussion has four variations: patting, rapping, striking and pecking. Patting is done with four fingers close together, dorsal hand, empty palm (similar to Western cupping) or five open digits. Rapping is done with empty fist and the ulna side of the hand (similar to Western hacking). Striking uses fingertips (moving like raindrops), back of empty fists and base of the palmar hand to hit the body surface. Pecking is forming the fingers into a beak to hit the treatment area like a hen picking up grains from the ground. Striking with back of empty fists and pecking are probably unique to Chinese tuina.

Vibration in Chinese massage is almost identical to vibration in Western massage. It consists of shaking and trembling. Shaking uses both hands to hold and shake the distal end of upper or lower limbs. Trembling uses fingers and palms to vibrate over a treatment area. Both techniques utilize internal energy to generate the oscillation.

Lin lectured on each technique and its variations, showed video clips of the technique and then demonstrated it to the class. We practiced each technique on the rice bags and on ourselves.

Joint mobilization in tuina includes flexion and extension technique, which is essentially simple stretching; counter-extension technique, which is stretching a treatment area in opposite directions; and rocking, which is moving joints in circle. All these techniques can be used for treating neck, shoulder joints, elbow and wrist joints, lower-back, knee and ankle joints. The focus is on stretching the ligaments. Lin showed a variation of neck stretching by using two towels, one under the lower jaw and one under the

---

[79]   *The Handbook of Chinese Massage* (1997).

occiput. Concurrently, she pulled the lower-jaw towel superiorly and the occipital towel anteriorly -- a neat trick that I have yet to try on myself or my clients!

Beginner Massage in Supine Position

After we had learned the basic hand techniques, we learned beginner massage in supine position. We followed the protocol for basic full body wellness massage in supine position in the training manual. Lin showed the procedures for massaging head and face, chest and stomach, upper limbs and lower limbs and the methods for locating significant pressure points in each of the body areas. I find using body landmarks is easier for finding pressure points. It is like the difference between telling someone the cross section of longitude and latitude for a location and saying that 7-Eleven at the end of the street is the location! After each overview and demonstration, we watched a video clip on specific techniques from the site www. baojiantuina.com. After the video review, the classmates formed pairs to work on each other. I worked with Chen Jianhua, Guo Jin and Cai Li – all male classmates. Later, I had in-class exchanges with some of the female classmates, who were generally much more reserved than my NOVA classmates.

For head and face tuina, the commonly used hand techniques are kneading, pushing, smearing, rubbing, poking and brushing.[80] The acupuncture points involved are located on the face, head and neck, related to several meridians. They include *baihui* (GV20), *dicang* (ST4), *fengchi* (GB20), *fengfu* (GV16), *jiache* (ST6), *jingming* (BL1), *quanliao* (SI18), *shuigou* (GV26), *taiyang* (EX-HN5), *yintang* (EX-HN3) and *zanzhu* (BL2).

The protocol for head and face tuina has 11 steps and the sequence, I discovered later, must be learned and performed exactly as taught. None of the free expressions or doing what is comfortable for the client as emphasized in Western massage! From the sample test and the actual test for certification, I found several questions on the proper sequence of the protocol. Woe to you if you massage out of sequence! The 11 steps are:

---

[80]   Brushing was not mentioned in any of the hands on techniques. It is simply running the fingers through the hair and scratching the scalp with fingers.

- Smearing from *yintang* (EX-HN3) to *taiyang* (EX-HN5) 5-10 times, and kneading *taiyang* (EX-HN5) several times;
- Treating the eye socket by squeezing *jingming* (BL1) for 30 seconds and then rubbing the eye socket laterally 3-5 times;
- Poking *yingxiang* (LI20) for 30 seconds, then pushing and rubbing along the wings of the nose from *yingxiang* (LI20) to *juliao* (ST3) to *quanliao* (SI18) 3-5 times;
- Pushing and smearing from *shuigou* (GV26) to *dicang* (ST4) 3-5 times;
- Rubbing from the lower jaw to *jiache* (ST6) 3-5 times;
- Kneading from *jiache* (ST6) to *taiyang* (EX-HN5) 3-5 times;
- Poking and kneading (one action) from *yintang* (EX-HN3) to *baihui* (GV20) 3-5 times, then poking and kneading *yintang* (EX-HN3), *shenting* (GV24) and *baihui* (GV20) for 30 seconds each;
- Poking and kneading from *zanzhu* (BL2) to *baihui* (GV20) 3-5 times, then poking and kneading *zanzhu* (BL2) and *baihui* (GV20) for 30 seconds each;
- Hooking[81] and poking (one action) *fengci* (GB20) and *fengfu* (GV16) for 1-2 minutes each, and then kneading them 3-5 times;
- Brushing client's hair as though shampooing it for 2-3 minutes, using finger tips in the morning and finger pads in the afternoon; and
- Kneading client's auricles (ears) 1-2 minutes, pulling the ear lobes inferiorly 3-5 times.

That is quite a routine! And it is just for head and face massage.

<>

The routine of chest and stomach tuina has six steps, beginning with pressing the shoulders and ending with rubbing the stomach, first clockwise and then counter-clockwise. The prominent pressure points are *shangwan* (CV13), *zhongwan* (CV12), *xiawan* (CV10), *tianshu* (ST25), *qihai* (CV6) and *guanyuan* (CV4); all are located on the stomach. Clients are to flex their legs in stomach massage.

---

[81]   Hooking was not taught in any of the classes. It is simply curving the middle finger into a hook and using that to treat a body part, especially the occiput and the mastoid process.

The routine of upper limbs tuina also has six steps, beginning with kneading the muscles from shoulder to hand and ending with rocking shoulder joints. The prominent pressure points are *quchi* (LI11), *shousanli* (LI10), *neiguan* (PC6), *hegu* (LI4) and *laogong* (PC8); all are naturally on the hands and forearms. Actually, since the upper limbs are the thoroughfares of the six hand-meridians, they deserve more attention than what is usually done in Western massage.

The routine of lower limbs tuina has seven steps, beginning with pushing the thigh muscles inferiorly and ending with rocking the ankles. Of the numerous pressure points along the thighs, legs and feet, only three are cited for special attention: *zusanli* (ST36), *xuehai* (SP10) and *sanyinjiao* (SP6) on the thigh and leg. Like the upper limbs, the lower limbs are thoroughfares of the six foot-meridians; they also deserve more attention than what is usually done in Western massage.

Beginner Massage in Prone Position

The routines for basic full body wellness tuina in prone position are symmetrical to those for the anterior body, except that there is no routine for upper limbs when client is in prone position. The tuina routines are for neck and shoulder, back and waist and lower limbs.

In the meridian system, neck and shoulder are the thoroughfares of sanjiao, gallbladder, bladder and Du meridians (all yang channels), and the pressure point *dazhui* (GV14), located at the depression under C7, is the confluence of the six yang channels. The common massage techniques for neck and shoulder are pushing, grasping, kneading, pressing and rolling. Prominent pressure points to pay attention to are *jianjing* (GB21) on the shoulder, *bingfeng* (SI12) in supraspinous fossa and *tianzong* (SI11) in infraspinous fossa.

The tuina sequence for neck and shoulders has five steps. It begins with (1) grasping and kneading (one action) the neck muscles for two to three minutes, (2) finger-pressing along the cervical grooves inferiorly two or three times, followed with kneading, (3) grasping and kneading the scapula region laterally for two to three minutes, (4) pressing (lightly and heavily in turns) *jianjing* (GB21), *bingfeng* (SI12) and *tianzong* (SI11) each for one to two minutes, and (5) rolling shoulders for two to three minutes, followed with rapping a few times.

In the meridian system, posterior trunk, waist and lower limbs are the thoroughfares of bladder and Du meridians, both yang channels. The bladder meridian has 67 pressure points, the most in the meridian system. Several of the points are linked to *zangfu*, visceral organs. The Du meridian has 28 pressure points and all of them are connected to the other yang meridians. Thus, massaging the back, waist and lower limbs is really massaging the Du and bladder meridians and their pressure points. It affects the functions of visceral organs, circulation of body fluids and movement of yin-qi and yang-qi in all the meridians. Thus, if a therapist or her client is short of time, they should focus on working the posterior trunk.

The preferred techniques for massaging back and waist are pressing, kneading, pushing, patting and plucking and the most common pressure points are *shenshu* (BL23) and *mingmen* (GV4). The tuina sequence has eight steps. It begins with pressing and kneading the lamina grooves of the vertebrae and the bladder meridian three to five times, and ends with pushing the lamina grooves three to five times.

The preferred techniques for massaging lower limbs are pressing, kneading, grasping, pushing, patting, rapping and counter-extension, and the most common pressure points are on the hip, leg and ankle, including *huantiao* (GB30), *weizhong* (BL40), *chengshan* (BL57), *chengfu* (BL36), *yinmen* (BL37), *taixi* (KI3) and *kunlun* (BL60), and the foot reflexive zones for heart, lungs, spleen, livers and kidneys. A tall order! The tuina sequence has nine steps, beginning with pushing inferiorly the anterior, medial and lateral aspects of the foot and ending with rotating the ankle.

During one of the practice sessions, I showed my classmates the Virginian Stretch and suggested it might be an alternate way to do back and waist massage. No one can accuse me of hiding my lamp under a bushel! Both the instructors, Ma and Lin, felt my hand pressure was too light for tuina, but Chen Jianhua thought my touch was what his *sifu* referred to as the "palace style," perfect for some clients. I was confident enough of my understanding of the essence of massage that I made no change to my hand pressure. I did not (and do not) accept the notion of "no pain, no gain."

Intermediate Massage

The routines for intermediate massage in supine position involved massaging head and face, chest and stomach, upper and lower limbs. The process was similar to that of the beginner level, with addition or exchange of new pressure points. The intermediate level also has cautions for each body region.

There is more variance in the use of pressure points for massaging head and face, chest and stomach than for massaging upper and lower limbs. Other than the five pressure points of *dicang* (ST4), *shuigou* (GV26), *taiyang* (EX-HN5), *yintang* (EX-HN3) and *zanzhu* (BL2) that were shared with the beginner level, the intermediate level has *shenting* (GV24), *yuyao* (EX-HN4), *sizhukong* (TE23), *chengqi* (ST1) and *sibai* (ST2) as prominent points for massaging head and face; and it has added *qimen* (LR14), *zhangmen* (LR13) and *jingmen* (GB25) for massaging chest and stomach. There is no difference in pressure points usage for upper limbs, and the intermediate level uses one more point (*xiyan* – EX-LE5), in addition to *zusanli* (ST36), *xuehai* (SP10) and *sanyinjiao* (SP6) used in the beginner level, in massaging lower limbs.

In massage techniques for head and face, the beginner level uses six different moves and the intermediate level uses ten. Only four moves (pushing, rubbing, kneading, poking) are common to both levels. Techniques for chest and stomach, upper and lower limbs are practically identical for both levels. In terms of the number of steps in each routine, the intermediate level requires more steps than the beginner level for each body region. Not only that, it also has a routine different from that in the beginner level. The chest and stomach routine is a good illustration of the difference.

For the beginner level, the routine is: press client's shoulders with base of your palm; hold client's thorax with open hand and push laterally from midline to line under armpit, move caudally; use palm-on-palm method to knead client's stomach; lift client's abdominis caudally; poke-press *shangwan* (CV13), *zhongwan* (CV12), *xiawan* (CV10), *tianshu* (ST25), *qihai* (CV6) and *guanyuan* (CV4); place palm on client's navel, rub client's stomach first clockwise, then counter-clockwise.

For the intermediate level, the routine is: press client's shoulders with base of your palm; place open hand on midline of client's chest; push laterally and caudally to edge of ribs; use base of your palm to knead client's *zhongfu* (LU1); poke-knead *qimen* (LR14), *zhangmen* (LR13) and *jingmen* (GB25); push *shangwan* (CV13), *zhongwan* (CV12) and *xiawan* (CV10); poke-press *tianshu* (ST25), *qihai* (CV6) and *guanyuan* (CV4); lift-squeeze rectus abdominis caudally; place hands palm-on-palm on client's navel and knead stomach clockwise; use palm to rub and scrub client's stomach first clockwise, then counter-clockwise.

Thus, for testing purposes, especially in a written test, students need to memorize the respective sequences for beginner level or intermediate level. Since I took only the certification test for the beginner level, I have no idea what testers actually require of students in the practical test for the intermediate level.

The routine for intermediate massage in prone position involves massaging neck and shoulders, back and waist and lower limbs. The common pressure points for massaging neck and shoulder are identical for beginner level and intermediate level. The intermediate level utilizes one more pressure point (*baliao* – BL31-34)[82] than the beginner level for massaging back and waist, and it does not use *yinmen* (BL37) for massaging lower limbs.

Malaises and Diseases

From the syllabus, one might conclude that beginner level and intermediate level of tuina are essentially for relaxation and advanced level of tuina is for therapy because the advanced level of the curriculum devoted nine sessions to general malaises and diseases besides lectures and demos on *guasha* and cupping, lymphatic drainage and acupuncture. The tuina-plus modalities are clearly for therapeutic work.

We learned how to treat headache, nasal congestion, strains in the eye and forehead, aches in the neck and shoulder, chest constriction, aches in the upper limbs, low back strain, back muscle spasm, loss of appetite, aches in the lower limbs, heel pains, mental fatigue, restless insomnia and sports strains. They were all in the training manual. For each condition, the instructors talked about its probable causes, its manifestation, and the tuina techniques and the pressure points to be used for its treatment. They demonstrated the routine for each condition and we practiced on our classmates after each demonstration. We learned to use different configurations of pressure points for different conditions, always going by the textbook.

The diseases we discussed in class included scapulohumeral periarthritis, cervical spondylopathy, osteoarthritis of knee joint, acute and chronic strain of lumbar muscles, lumbar intervertebral disc protrusion, blackout (vertigo), dysmenorrhea, infantile indigestion, insomnia, headache, constipation, stomachache,

---

[82] *Baliao* is made of eight pressure points on the bladder meridians (see Appendix 5).

diarrhea and infantile torticollis. All these are requirements for the comprehensive exam for practitioners. They were included in the curriculum for the advanced level of tuina training. I had prior nodding acquaintances with strains of lumbar muscles, vertigo, insomnia, headache, constipation, stomachache and dysmenorrhea from my classes at NOVA, but knew practically nothing about the other diseases. The instructors described the clinical presentation of each disease, the tuina treatment for it and the pressure points to be used. For instance, pressure points for treating dysmenorrhea are *baliao* (BL31-34), *sanjiao xue* (BL22), kidney *xue* (BL23), *mingmen* (GV4), liver *xue* (BL18), spleen *xue* (BL20), *tianshu* (ST25), *xuehai* (SP10), *sanyinjiao* (SP6), *qihai* (CV6), *guanyuan* (CV4), *zhongji* (CV3), *zhongwan* (CV12) and *zusanli* (ST36).

Stomachache, according to Chen, is the intrusion of cold element into the stomach making the patient weary of cold. There is stagnation in the movement of food. As a result, the stomach feels bloated. Concurrently, the qi of liver intrudes into the stomach, causing pain to the ribs. The qi of stomach becomes congested and blood slows down as though it were bruised. Thus, the stomach dreads pressure. Aching is the result. This prosaic description does not do justice to a 34-word ditty Chen recited. She emphasized that keeping warm is one of the principles of wellness in Chinese medicine.

We learned that diarrhea has an acute form and a chronic form. The acute form is a result of what we eat and its stagnation in the digestive system. The chronic form is a result of functional deficiency of the spleen, liver and kidney. The pressure points for treating diarrhea are spleen *xue* (BL20), stomach *xue* (BL21), kidney *xue* (BL23), small intestine *xue* (BL27), *tianshu* (ST25), *zhongwan* (CV12), *qihai* (CV6), *zusanli* (ST36), *shangjuxu* (ST37), *sanyinjiao* (SP6), *xiajuxu* (ST39) and *mingmen* (GV4).

Chen ended her lecture with a list of requirements for good health. They included keeping open the grain path (digestive system), waterway (urinary system), capillary network (integumentary system), and blood vessels (vascular system); maintaining an open attitude, letting menses flow freely and keeping vertebrae soft and supple. She highlighted *qihai* (CV6) as a significant pressure point for treating numerous disorders.

Chapter 20

CHINESE CERTIFICATION EXAM

Sample Questions

On the first day I reported to the school, I was given a set of sample questions to work on to prepare for the certification exam. The questions were similar to the quizzes I had at NOVA, but much less intensive than the courses on Human Biology and Concepts of Disease. They consisted of only two types of questions: multiple-choice and true-or-false. There were 158 questions that required selecting the right answers and 40 questions that required judgment calls.

The multiple-choice questions were divided into sections, following the headings of the foundation book and the training manual. They included questions on ethics, courtesy, customs, essentials of tuina, yin yang and *wu xing* theories, tissues, anatomy, *zangfu* and massage techniques. I worked through the sample questions diligently, flipping through the foundation book and training manual repeatedly to verify my answers. The sample questions were good for review and preparation. They also gave me more exposure to academic Chinese and "trick questions!" However, I did not have a Chinese Sandy Fritz to explain why the correct answers were correct. Neither did

I have NCBTMB computer feedback on my answers. When I began preparing for the certification exam, I had not yet been exposed to the substances of some of the questions under "essentials of tuina" and "massage techniques." The questions alerted me to what I needed to pay attention to in class or to ask my friends about them. The sample questions also revealed what the testers considered as important. Tissues and anatomy, two of the primary subjects in Western massage, had a total of only three perfunctory questions.

Meng *laoshi* reviewed the sample questions with us. For an older person (but younger than me), her patience was worse than that of a kid. She rushed through the Q&A of the 198 questions as though the classroom was on fire. Even my nimble classmates could not keep up with her. When we interrupted her for clarification, she became agitated. It would have been less frustrating for her and the class if she simply distributed an answer sheet and played Sandy Fritz. After all, the sample questions were more than a trial run. They were learning tools. In that frantic review session, I was fortunate to have a classmate repeating Meng's answers to me. In fact, we went over the entire body of sample questions after the session. That was learning!

Meng reminded us what to bring to the actual test session the following Saturday: a 2B pencil with eraser, one form of identification and the uniform that came with our enrollment for the class. We would have to wear the uniform for the practical test. She also gave us another sample test of 100 questions and instructed us to finish it at home in one 90-minute sitting. That was the final drill for the actual test.

Meng also told us that the test for intermediate level was set for March 25, and the deadline for registration was February 1. Thus, it appeared there was an interval of eight weeks between the basic and intermediate tests. Apparently, a similar time gap existed between the tests for intermediate and advanced levels. So to be certified at the advanced level, one would have to have spent 120 hours in class and four months in waiting. I don't know how many of my classmates followed this route. I had decided I would not spend my remaining days in China studying for intermediate certification. It did not serve any purpose.

The Exam

The Guangdong Provincial Government administered the Certification Exam, which was primarily for the purpose of licensing.

The Government sent a group of external examiners to the school to conduct the written and practical tests.

When I arrived at the school, I received my pass for admission to the examination room, which was just another classroom across from the administration office. It had eight desks. There were 11 of us taking the test, ten classmates and one stranger. We had assigned seats, two candidates to a desk. Before we began the test, we had to show our identification, which, for me, was my passport. The written test had 100 questions consisting of 80 multiple-choices and 20 true-or-false statements. Answers were to be marked in a scanner sheet. The test covered what were in the three textbooks. In addition to the usual "trick questions," I had to contend with nuances of Chinese wording. Quite a challenge!

The practical exam was held in another classroom, the same one where I had my regular lessons. There were 11 live "dummies" for us to work on. The test was done en masse. The external examiners walked about the room as we gave full body massage to our dummies. Due to my hearing problem, I did not hear clearly the oral instruction. I just did my own thing and began to massage briskly in order to cover the whole body. Meng *laoshi* came to my rescue and told me that I had to work on only the left side of the dummy. I had plenty of time to work on him. As I was massaging the dummy's leg, one of the examiners asked me what stroke (technique) I was using. I replied, "Grasping." "Can you please elaborate?" "I am lifting the muscle… " (I wanted to say from adhesion, but I could not think of the Chinese expression). He was apparently satisfied and walked on to the next table. The only unpleasant part of the practical exam was the dummy's body odor and that guy was preparing to be a massage practitioner. I wished I could spray him with a dose of eau de cologne!

While the group testing for practical has its limitation, it offers examiners a fast and probably objective way to test a fairly large group of candidates in a relatively short period of time. I cannot verify if it is true, but the practical test is apparently coordinated with questions on techniques in the written test. I remember there were questions about the sequence of massage strokes and how different techniques were to be applied in the written test. The examiners could have asked me why I was using a particular stroke, what muscle(s) I was working on or what treatment I was giving. I would have been pleased to give them my treatment plan *in English*. As I was unable to recall the Chinese technical terms, I was glad they had no extra questions for me.

Test results were usually available two or three weeks after the test, but since the school was closed for the Chinese New Year's holiday, I could not get the result until the end of February. At that time, Meng *laoshi* informed me that I had passed the test, but the certificate was not ready. I had arranged for the school to contact one of my friends in Guangzhou to pick it up, but, to date, I have not heard from the school or my friend.

<>

On February 1, I said goodbye to my classmates after the morning session. Chen Jianhua, Jaymee Li and I were scheduled to visit the Jianqiang Chinese Medical Clinic to set up our practical training. Jianhua and Jaymee decided to do their practical training at Jianqiang Clinic because they wanted to keep me company! The intensive interaction in the four weeks of classroom learning had drawn most of us close together. Many of my classmates asked if I would return to see them before I leave for the U.S. I did not know it at that moment, but I did return on March 19 to collect my Certificate of Completion (Picture 31). At that time, I saw a male instructor teaching a new class and not one of my former classmates or instructors was there. I felt I had lost something intangible.

Chapter 21

AN OUTPATIENT IN A CITY HOSPITAL

On January 30, the day after Yuan's lecture on spinal tuina, I visited the Guangzhou City No. 1 Hospital as an outpatient. Early that morning, about 7 a.m., while I was working at my computer, my hearing aid went dead. I changed the battery twice and the hearing aid was still not working. I tried using the backup hearing aid, and I could not hear anything either. I concluded that either the hearing aids had malfunctioned or I had suddenly lost hearing in my left ear. I did not know where I could repair the hearing aids or how long it would take to repair them. I also did not know where I could check my hearing condition. I felt desperate. My hosts had already left for the day and I did not want to bother any of my local friends early morning, so I went to school in a muted world. Everything and everywhere was quiet! After asking Li *laoshi* and several classmates about treatment facilities near the school, I left for consultation at the Outpatient Department of Guangzhou City No. 1 Hospital at 9 a.m. The facility was located less than ten minutes from the school. I was on my own.

I made inquiry in the hospital lobby, filled out a registration form, paid for registration and proceeded to the ENT Department. At the registration desk, the clerk gave me a booklet on the cover of which I wrote down basic personal information. That booklet was to be my medical record. The receptionist at the ENT was officious and not very helpful. She seemed impatient to repeat what she said even though she worked in a department that treats people with hearing problems. Directional signs for various centers and offices within the ENT section were obscure. There was no visual sign about which number in line was being served. Patients were called via an intercom. For a medical section dealing with ENT not to have visual signs it is certainly a matter of gross negligence. It is not that the hospital does not have the facility or capability for internal communication. It is just that it does not pay attention to this aspect of patient care.

After waiting for about an hour, I met the attending physician, Dr. Huang Shunde. He did a routine check on my ears and ordered some tests for me. I had to queue up to pay the cashier before I had my first test. After the payment, I went back to the receptionist who directed me to a hearing test center. I waited at the center, met the attending audiologist and had a series of test. The audiologist used modern instruments to do a thorough hearing test, but she did not go through the "repeat what I say" routine. She printed out some impressive charts for me. When I returned to the receptionist, she told me to come back in the afternoon for the second test. I told her I might not be able to do so because I had prior commitment at the school for visiting a site for practical training. She agreed I could return the next day. I pre-registered for next day and left the hospital about 11:30 a.m. Half a day was gone!

When I returned to the school, I discovered that the field visit had been rescheduled for the next day. So, I returned to the hospital at 2 p.m. After about an hour, I still did not get to meet with the doctor. So, I acted like the local people and went into the doctor's office as soon as his door was opened. He looked at my hearing test results and decided I needed another test in addition to what he ordered earlier. I queued up again for more payment.

The receptionist then instructed me to return the next day because the ENT Endoscopic Center would be too busy to see me. I told her I had already submitted my registration form when I came earlier in the afternoon. She said, "In that case, you should check with them where the registration form is." "Where do I go?" "There, go straight and turn left." "How far?" "Just go there!" I went ahead and looked back to check if I was heading in the right direction. Someone waved for me to go on until I saw a corridor-full of people. I sat among them, bewildered. Again, I acted like the locals and barged in as soon as the office door was opened. As it turned out, the center had my registration form. I should have waited there instead of outside Dr. Huang's office earlier.

Another impatient healthcare professional told me to sit down, asked me about my age and whether I wore denture, repeated herself because I did not hear what she said and then, after a while, told me to open my month for her to spray some mists into it. She did not tell me what she was doing. After the spray, she directed me to wait outside. Gradually, I felt my nasal passage and the back of my throat becoming numb. What she sprayed into my mouth was anesthetic. Does it hurt for Chinese healthcare professionals to explain to patients what to expect?

Eventually, I was called again into the Endoscopic Center and I lay on the examination table, waiting for whatever procedures the professionals deemed necessary. The doctor inserted a tube into my nostrils for examination and conducted an ear probe as well. The instruments were sterilized in a basin of antiseptic right after use (the same sterilization process in the Hearing Test Center). After I got the results, I returned to Dr. Huang's office to wait again. For the third time, I followed the example of local people rushing into the doctor's office to turn in my test results and waited for the diagnosis. At 4:30, Li *laoshi* telephoned to ask about the backpack I had left in the classroom. I told her to keep it until the next day. Shortly thereafter, I went in to see the doctor again, reminding him that I had been waiting outside. I noticed my file was next to the last on his desk. I doubted that he worked in the order that the files were received.

After another look at my tests, Dr. Huang concluded that my condition warrant hospitalization or at least intravenous treatment. He felt that my hearing loss had to do with inadequate blood supply to the head (a textbook diagnosis!). I declined the options and asked if he had any drug prescriptions for my condition. He did. More payment! But I could pick up the medication from the pharmacy section of the hospital instead of filling the prescription elsewhere. By the time I paid for and got the medication, it was after 5 o'clock.

When I was at the Hearing Test Center, I discovered that my left ear did not have any blockage (such as ear wax) in the ear canal. The audiologist also told me that she found no signs of infection or inflammation. Moreover, in the actual hearing test, I could hear as well as I heard in the audiologist's office in the U.S. During lunch break, I concluded that the trouble with my hearing had nothing to do with my ear; that the culprit was my hearing aid. Before I looked for a repair center, I decided to try another new battery. Voila! With the third battery, the hearing aid resumed its functions! What is the probability of two new batteries being dead consecutively? Was I silly to go through all the troubles of being an outpatient at the City Hospital? I laughed at myself for my overreactions. With my hearing back, I could have bypassed the tests in the afternoon; but since I had already paid for them, I decided to follow through to get a status report on my hearing condition. I ended up with some test data to share with my hearing doctor after my return to the U.S. and I spent a whole day in the City Hospital!

The infrastructure for healthcare delivery at the City Hospital was very good, but the attitude of healthcare personnel needed much improvement. The general areas of the hospital looked clean, but the condition of the men's room on the third floor was deplorable. The total cost for the tests, medications and consultation was about US $120. I was sure I would have to pay at least four or five times that in the U.S.

If you travel in China, you should stay healthy. Visiting a local hospital is not for the timid. If you have no language proficiency, you are lost. Even with language proficiency, I was lost! If you have any handicapping conditions, you should have a local resident to go with you to act as your advocate. Navigating different offices and centers is a serious challenge.

I did not intend to have this experience, but I tasted a bit of what it was like to live as a local person, without special privileges. In a time like that, I prefer to be in the U.S. The school staff persons were not as supportive as they might be. Neither were my classmates. In a sense, I should not expect them to go out of their way to help me, but I could not help feeling being let down.

Chapter 22

TUINA AND YIN YANG TOUCH

Clinical Training in Tuina

At the Jianqiang Chinese Medicine Clinic, Jaymee, Jianhua and I met with the supervisor for practical training, Dr. Huang Fengqin, a TCM practitioner with more than 30 years of clinical experience. While the "contract" for practical training was for one month, the frequency of attendance was negotiable. Each student could design a schedule according to his needs, but all interns were expected to work from 5 to 10 p.m. on the days they were scheduled. I chose Monday, Wednesday and Friday as my clinic days.

I informed Dr. Huang that I was going to Singapore between February 3 and 12. She assured me it was not a problem, but added that the clinic would be closed the week after my return due to the Chinese New Year's holiday. Thus, my clinic sessions were limited to the last two weeks of February, a total of only five sessions! I thought the initial visit was merely an introduction to the clinic, but we were put to work right away.

My mentor therapist at the clinic was Wu Yingping, a down-to-earth unpretentious woman who had more than ten years of clinical experience. She told me I could observe and work with any of the therapists in the clinic even though she was my primary mentor. Unlike the staff and instructors at the Guangzhou Medical College, both Dr. Huang and Mentor Wu treated me as a colleague. They said they were as eager for me to share with them what I knew of Western massage as they were in showing me practical applications of tuina. At various points in the evening while working on her clients, Wu told me what conditions she found on their bodies and what she was doing to treat them. She also told her understandably curious clients who I was and that I would work on them as needed (none of the asking-for-permission business!). Whenever she needed to take a break, Wu asked me to work on her clients. I was glad to have practice in a clinical setting. Wu used *guasha*, cupping and tuina routinely and she worked practically non-stop. Most of her clients were regular users of the clinic.

While I stayed by Wu, Jaymee and Jianhua were off with their mentors elsewhere in the clinic. The clinic was quite large. On the ground floor, it had ten or twelve massage tables. On the second floor, it had another ten or twelve tables. On its walls were laudatory and congratulatory calligraphic messages from Yuan's patients or peers as well as charts of tuina therapy and spinal tuina. In addition to the massage areas, the ground floor had a reception and treatment area for regular TCM patients, a dispensary of Western drugs and a pharmacy for Chinese medicinal herbs. It was a shop front clinic, with very little privacy. Massage on the second floor had a little more privacy but the massage tables were not screened. Second floor activities were monitored at the reception area via closed circuit. I met up with my classmates toward the end of the impromptu session. Jaymee ensured I caught a cab first before she headed home.

When I began my internship formally on February 18 after my trip to Singapore, both my classmates were not there anymore. However, I felt at home in the clinic environment. I had opportunities to try *guasha* and cupping on clients in addition to doing more hands-on practice. Wu commented that my techniques were good and showed me how I might position my hands in a more effective manner. Clients were generally satisfied with my touch. However, whereas I was unsuccessful with treating a big guy because of his muscle armor, Wu made him cry from pain with her touch! As we were in the Chinese New Year's season, one of the clients gave me a red package of RMB 20 *yuan* (three US dollars) as a New Year's gift. That was my first and only tip in China!

In the next session (February 20), Mentor Wu was sick. I got to work with Lu Yaopan, a middle aged TCM practitioner with vast clinical experience. Lu was very courteous. He discussed with me what he called my energy techniques and my understanding of Western massage. I clarified that Yin Yang Touch, as I conceived it, did not grow out of energy work and I did not belong to any particular "school" of massage. I also offered the idea that all massage is a conversion of energy, from kinetic energy to chemical and electrical energy. The conversation was more like a professional exchange between equals rather than that of a teacher-student exchange. He showed me how to use the *guasha* tools more effectively and allowed me to do head *guasha* for one of his clients. At one point of a massage, he stood on the rail of the massage table to apply weight on a client's back. That seemed to me a viable but precarious way to work on heavy-set clients. That evening, I worked on five clients. The massages were physically demanding and energy draining but emotionally satisfying.

In the third session (February 22), the clinic had a slow day. I worked on Therapist Liang and observed him working on a client from Xinjiang. I also worked on another big guy. I had a good discussion with Liang on differences between Chinese and Western massage practices. If he disagreed with me, he did not mention it. I left for home early.

In the fourth session (February 25), Dr. Huang, the supervisor, was my first client. She felt my gentler touch was exactly right for clients who were afraid of pain. However, our session was truncated because she was called to treat a walk-in patient. I offered to give her a make up session on Wednesday, my last practical session at the clinic.

After treating Dr. Huang, I assisted different therapists working on their clients. Most of the therapists seemed to be steeped in the philosophy of "no pain, no gain." They appeared to be using too much pressure too soon. I had watched older people tearing on the massage table! That approach is certainly not acceptable in the U.S. I had also observed that most of the therapists shared a common supply of massage cream and lotion and several sets of glass cups for cupping treatment. Cross-contamination was apparently not a problem for them. The last client I worked with was a big guy again. In addition to manual work, I knew he needed stretching, a maneuver I was unwilling to do because I might hurt myself. Instead, I put him through a modified iliopsoas stretch. He left, feeling relieved.

In the fifth (and final) session (February 27), I had demo massages with three therapists, including Dr. Huang. Despite the interruption in her previous session, Dr. Huang felt so positive about her experience that she invited Xiao Huang, a twenty-some year old therapist, to observe me when I worked on her. Xiao Huang commented that my techniques could be enhanced by incorporation of pressure points and meridian treatment, exactly what I was learning and trying to do.

Both Dr. Huang and I were annoyed that the second demo massage was again interrupted. She had to treat another walk-in patient. To ensure we could have an uninterrupted session and for me to get the benefits of her feedback, I offered to give Dr. Huang a full massage during the almost sacrosanct lunch break, on Friday, March 1. She accepted my offer. In the final session, I massaged a number of clients, including an older woman who had shoulder problem. To treat it, I gave the shoulders a 360° gentle stretch. She was the only client gracious enough to say thank you to me after the session.

Working with Dr. Huang

On March 1, I massaged both Dr. Huang and Mentor Wu and received a massage from Xiao Huang. I adopted the side-lying position that Xiao Huang showed me when I worked on Dr. Huang and Wu later. While I was working on Dr. Huang, Cai Li, a former classmate at the Guangzhou Medical College came to the treatment area to look for her. Cai had shown up at the clinic with a group of several other former classmates who were starting their internship. Meng *laoshi* was with them. She was probably surprised that I was still at the clinic. My internship had expired the day before.

On March 8, International Women's Day, I massaged Mentor Wu and Therapist Li, in addition to Dr. Huang. Li gave me a good feedback on my practice of synchronization of breathing and strokes and offered to give me a massage when we had time later. When I massaged Wu, I discovered she had hypertonic thigh muscles and I was glad to know how to apply joint movements I learned at NOVA to help release the tightness. After Wu, I massaged Dr. Huang and had a good uninterrupted conversation with her. She alerted me to symptoms of kidney deficiency and inefficient circulation of blood in me and cautioned me to watch out for heart problem. She gave me a copy of the book *Therapy for Spinal Diseases* (2003) by Zhong Shiyuan to further my understanding of spinal tuina. When I scanned through that book, I felt it was quite similar to Whitney

Lowe's *Orthopedic Assessment in Massage Therapy* (2006). Lowe's book covered the entire musculoskeletal structure, but Zhong's book was focused on the spinal structure.

On March 15, I went to the clinic to give Wu a massage, but she was engaged with another client. I ended up with Therapist Li giving me a massage. His was very good. Perhaps in deference to me, he was quite gentle in his pressure, but he did a lot of rocking. After lunch, I worked on Dr. Huang again. I knew the massage was effective because I could feel her shoulder muscles were more relaxed, even though they were still tight. Knowing my interest in the synthesis of Chinese tuina and Western massage, Dr. Huang asked if I might be interested to visit Zhong Shiyuan, a nationally renowned TCM research professor. That was an unimaginably coveted opportunity!

On March 22, Dr. Huang introduced me to Zhong at a community clinic. There was no conversation between us. I just observed how he worked. He treated three patients with a minimum of undressing and prep work. The patients came and laid themselves on the examination table. He worked on them and each treatment was completed in less than ten minutes! Zhong's needle method was active. It included twisting, probing and plucking motions, entirely different from what I observed elsewhere. Despite his hectic schedule, Zhong was courteous and he asked me about Yin Yang Touch as I left the clinic. If I had met him earlier, I might have been able to shadow him for a couple of days. As it was, I was getting ready to leave China the following week and my plate was full.

After the visit to Zhong's clinic, I gave Dr. Huang another massage, my farewell present. It was not as good as my earlier sessions, but she was appreciative. The fact that a veteran TCM practitioner had affirmed the efficacy of my touch by allowing me to work on her on several occasions had boosted my confidence tremendously.

Chapter 23

TEACHING YIN YANG TOUCH

I had my internship at the clinic three days a week and reserved Tuesday and Thursday evenings to work with my friends on Yin Yang Touch and Western massage. Through the efforts of Jane Li (an old friend), I had access to a clinic where I could use one of the treatment rooms to demonstrate Yin Yang Touch and to do massage. I showed my version of Western massage to several friends and taught them the basics of Yin Yang Touch. They were receptive and attentive.

I had asked several friends to read the Yin Yang Touch paper. They were familiar with TCM and I wanted to benefit from their perspectives. Betty Chen in Guangzhou and Amy Leung in Hong Kong were especially helpful. Betty, an accomplished Taiji practitioner, was interested to learn the hands-on techniques. Amy, a TCM student, suggested some more books I might read. I had wanted to discuss the Yin Yang Touch paper with my instructors, especially Chen Shuo, but their English proficiency was limited. A classmate promised she would translate the paper into Chinese, but to date I have not seen the result. I know too well how difficult it is to put that paper into Chinese. That's why I have not tried to do it myself. Coincidentally, an old friend, well versed in sports medicine, affirmed that I was on the right path in my study of Yin and Yang. He engaged me in a conversation during a dinner in a noisy restaurant, listened intensely as I explained to him what I wrote in the Yin Yang Touch paper and reminded me "when pressure is applied, the force of electric current is increased." That was a rewarding discussion!

Beginning in March, I no longer had the use of the clinic, but Betty still wanted to learn more about Yin Yang Touch and practice the massage strokes she had learned. By that time, another friend Lucy Liang had joined us. We decided to practice in the park near where I lived, alongside groups doing their Taiji, fan and sword dances. Mercy was also a learner in that outdoor classroom. In a secluded spot in the park, we worked on massaging the neck and shoulders and forearms and doing the Virginian Stretch. Onlookers were curious about what we were doing and some stayed by to watch us. I also showed several former colleagues the Virginian Stretch when we had a reunion dinner in a restaurant. They were surprised at the effects of the stretch and had fun giving chair massage to each other in the private dining room. I taught wherever I could!

On March 13, while visiting our old friend Sun Yilong in Xiamen, Mercy and I were accorded a unique experience. Sun brought us to meet his friend, Master Chen, a well-known blind therapist, who had treated him for some serious problems. Both Mercy and I had a massage in the simply furnished treatment room in Master Chen's house, which was on the ground floor of a relatively old building along a narrow street. Unless you knew the location, you were unlikely to visit that clinic. I was very glad we did. Master Chen, probably in his late forties, was courteous and gracious. He gave me pointers on hand rolling and breathing, by examples rather than words. His touch is what I try to develop, soft but firm. His vibration touch was electrifying! When he worked on my head, I could feel the vibration down in my toes. His strokes over the abdomen were equally awesome. After the massage, I asked him how he developed the vibration touch. He showed me without hesitation, but cautioned me not to rush or force it. That brief contact with Master Chen was an indelible moment. I learned wherever I could, from whomever willing to teach me.

While I was attending classes at the college, I created opportunities for me to practice massage more regularly. I massaged Lao Jiang, my former office driver; and Lao Zhang, the father of Doris, in their homes on two occasions. Lao Jiang had developed a bad case of involuntary hand trembling since his retirement a few years ago. I had the impression that his right clavicle bone was pressing on the brachial plexus and he needed relief in his right shoulder joint. I even showed his daughter a few basic strokes so that she could help diminish his discomfort. The other "client," Lao Zhang, had a stroke ten years ago. His right side was paralyzed. I massaged him to help improve the flow of his body fluids and stimulate the hypotonic muscles. His wife was familiar with TCM, and had resigned to Lao Zhang's condition. I discussed these cases with Chen Jianhua and he felt that both of them could benefit from using medicinal lotion (especially the one his *sifu* formulated) to complement tuina for better results. However, my increasingly hectic schedule in Guangzhou (which included a stint of intensive treatment for my hearing loss in a military hospital) had kept me from following through with more treatments. I did re-gift the medicinal lotion from Chen to Lao Jiang since I could not bring it back to the U.S. I do have the formula for reformulating it.

In Guangzhou, I also made house calls on Lin Xin and Adam Chen, old friends from my previous assignment. I taught Agnes Ye how to de-stress Xin, and Eva Liu how to apply Yin Yang Touch on Adam, her husband. Eva videotaped the whole process and emailed the recording to me. That gave me a chance to check my posture and the clarity of my teaching. In Guangzhou, I had given massages to 16 different people and taught five friends to use massage to take care of their relatives. In Singapore, I treated three "clients": my high school friend for her stomach congestion, my sister-in-law for her shoulder ache, and a visitor from China for her stiff shoulders and neck. All three of them had relief from their pain, much to my delight. Thus, even though my clinical training was shortened because of my visit to Singapore, I made good use of my time abroad to practice my skill and to help reduce pain. You might say my practice had expanded internationally!

My former Guangzhou colleagues were all delighted that I had a new career in massage therapy. They thought I would have spent my retirement in traveling or pursuing some innocuous hobbies such as painting, gardening or some activities that were not labor intensive. A 70-year old man pursuing a new career was an inspiration to them! Their enthusiasm made me realize that what I had been doing since 2010 was in fact worthy of sharing with a larger circle of people who might be interested in becoming massage therapists. The seed of writing this book was sown.

My friends, old and new, were especially interested in my desire to synthesize Chinese and Western massage practices. They pampered me with gifts, actually, new resources: Ursula Chen gave me the

Chinese version of *Five Element Acupuncture* by Nora Franglen,[83] Mario Mo gave me the *Manuel on How to Use the Human Body* by Wu Qingzhong,[84] Sun Yilong gave me a copy of *Zhou Yi* (a book on divining hexagrams), Dr. Huang Fendqin, as I mentioned earlier, gave me *Therapy for Spinal Diseases* by Zhong Shiyuan, and Betty Chen gave me a video she made of the Guangzhou Motion.[85] All of them wanted me to succeed! I also bought me a small library of 20 other books on TCM for my continuing education and research and spent whatever free time I had in Guangzhou reading those books.

When old and new friends in Guangzhou knew that I had become a massage therapist, they engaged me in discussing the effects of massage. Despite my change in social status, they treated me with the same respect and attention. Two of the friends mentioned they knew tuina experts and they would arrange for me to study with the experts intensively. However, both of that fell through. Another friend, formerly head of the TCM Department in one of the hospitals in Guangzhou, was going to coach me about TCM, but it fell through also. I did not pester these friends because I had adopted the philosophy of "follow the flow." If they could do it, they would have done it. Why should I embarrass them for not fulfilling random promises? Besides, they did not owe me any favor! I was not entirely unhappy with the unrealized opportunities because I knew I could call on my old friend Dr. Grace Wong, a retired expert acupuncturist in Maryland, for more guidance after my return to the U.S. The challenge would be for me to know what questions to ask her and where to begin.

<>

With Mercy in Guangzhou, I resumed exploring massage facilities in the city. We had foot massages and full body massages in a number of spas and wellness centers. Most were adequate, but none was outstanding. The Jinbi Wellness Center that we frequented when we were working in Guangzhou had been completely renovated and we did not meet any of the former employees. It had a different menu of service, with exotic titles and matching prices. The full

---

[83] I am yet to read the English version. The Chinese version is fascinating. It offers many ideas for me to pursue.

[84] Which has led me to explore the role of massage in weight loss and to write the paper on JIANFEI (Chapter 28).

[85] See Appendix 1.

body massage I had there was the best of the whole trip. Generally, I enjoyed foot massages more than full body massages because most of the technicians for full body massage had limp touches (the experience at Jinbi Wellness Center was an exception). I wondered where the technicians had their trainings. I was sure it was not from the program I just concluded. Their touch was completely different from "no pain, no gain." Perhaps those massages were for relaxation and not for therapeutic treatment; that's why they were insipid. Still, it was better to have a massage than not to have one at all. I missed the firmness of the therapeutic touches of my NOVA classmates.

The training in Guangzhou was a once-in-a-lifetime experience. Even though I had reservations about the training program at the Guangzhou Medical College and the teaching style of the primary instructors, I felt the Guangzhou experience had exposed me to what I needed to learn more so that I could be a better interpreter of Chinese massage. I needed the total immersion. If I studied tuina in the U.S., I would have digressed to other activities. Besides, my Guangzhou experience was more than a classroom learning. I had learned at the clinic; from my friends, old and new; and from my reading.

The training program was adequate for its purposes. The school was run as a business and it churned out graduates for employment in spas, wellness centers and private practice. As long as prospective technicians flock to it, it could maintain the status quo in its operation. As one interested in the practical as well as the theoretical aspect of massage, I was disappointed that the training program did not structure more hands-on training or require its students to undertake mandatory exchanges. The instructors had no homework requirements and no quizzes for the students, hence, they did not have to spend time to gauge or grade their progress. The program had tried to meet as much of the external requirements as it could within the four weeks of classes and its focus was on external certification. It did not matter, apparently, whether the students really learned therapeutic massage. All that it mattered was their passing the certification exam and getting their license to work. As it is taught entirely in Chinese and the teaching style is archaic, the training program is not for foreign students.

The tuina training at the Guangzhou Medical College had included lectures and demos on topics that are part of the syllabus for advanced and practitioner's levels, but it left out interesting electives such as sports massage, pediatric massage, esthetic massage, weight loss massage, breast massage, gluteal massage, shiatsu, and massage practices in Hong Kong, Korea and Thailand, management of a massage facility, marketing analysis and continuing education -- all of which are in the *Handbook for Practitioners* that I received on the first day of class. The training also left out materials on reception and consultation at the advanced and practitioner's levels. I told my friends I could easily ace the "reception and consultation" section in the advanced syllabus. I would not need to spend much time to study it because the materials were in English! The fact that English terms and phrases were included in a Chinese massage curriculum indicated that the editors of the textbooks expected that massage therapy would be available to foreign visitors. This emphasis would be unnecessary and unthinkable forty years ago before Deng Xiaoping opened China to the world!

By the time this foreign student was scheduled to return to the U.S. in late March, he was eager and ready. He had only a few more weeks to prepare for the International Massage Therapy Research Conference, which was to be held in Boston, Massachusetts. Sovine and he were co-presenters of a poster presentation on using massage to treat fibromyalgia. They had exchanged emails on the poster's design and he was eager to see the final product.

Part III

MASSAGE RESEARCH

Chapter 24

THE BOSTON CONFERENCE

Poster Presentation

When I completed the class project on treating fibromyalgia, Sovine asked me what I intended to do with it beyond its initial objective. I discovered she had in mind asking me to consider entering the case report contest sponsored by the Massage Therapy Foundation (MTF). However, I had earlier come across a "Call for Abstracts" for the International Massage Therapy Research Conference and was interested in testing with that audience the idea of entanglement of free nerve endings in fasciae as the probable cause of fibromyalgia. The research conference was hosted by MTF on April 25-27, 2013 in Boston (I later discovered it met once every three years; my fibromyalgia study was timely). After some discussion, Sovine and I agreed we could recast the class project for both the case report contest and the conference.

To be considered for presentation at the conference, we had to submit an abstract of 300 words that included introduction, objectives, methods, results and conclusion. The deadline was September 15, 2012. For case report contest, we had to submit a report of 2000-4000 words that had cover page, acknowledgements, abstract/key words, introduction, methods, results, discussion and references. The deadline was October 1, 2013. These formats were quite different from what we learned about doing SOAP notes or the HOPRS Method for gathering and interpreting clinical assessment information.[86] Thus, instead of focusing on preparing for certification exam, I alternated between exam preparation and re-casting the class project into a case report. I did not work on the abstract separately since the case report had a section on abstract and I could use it to meet the requirements of the conference.

The case report was scored according to a rubric. For conciseness and coherence, it got a maximum of six points; abstract/key words, six points; research question, eight points; introduction and literature review, 25 points; profile of client, ten points; treatment plan, 15 points; results, ten points; and discussion, 20 points. I dismembered the class project and re-assembled the data under the relevant sections. I wrote and re-wrote, trimmed and re-trimmed. I tried to include as much data as I could within the 4000-word limit. Sovine read and re-read what I wrote and made suggestions for change. We made the deadline. The process of preparing the case report and abstract was made easier with timely communication from Alison Pittas of MTF.

In late November 2012, MFT informed us that our abstract was accepted as a poster presentation at the research conference. We had to convert the abstract into a poster. Timothy Sovine, a graphic designer, helped us to accomplish that task while I was in China. He delineated sections for signs of fibromyalgia, theory of fibromyalgia pain, criteria for success, treatment model, snapshots of actual treatment, progress and results and conclusion. He also included pictures of free nerve ending, tender points and compress of raw ginger and sea salt on the client. It was an attractive, colorful and well-designed poster (Picture 32).

Five weeks later, in late December 2012, MFT informed us that our case report was not selected for an award. Even though the review committee was interested in our theories on the mechanism of fibromyalgia, it felt the focus of the case was lost. The committee members preferred to read more about the treatment and outcomes with the client rather than the theories about the condition. They advised us to revise the report and submit it to a professional journal.

---

[86] See "The HOPRS Method" in *Orthopedic Assessment in Massage Therapy* (2006). HOPRS stands for history, observation, palpation, range-of-motion and resistance testing and special tests.

I was very impressed with the thoughtful feedback from the review committee. However, as Sovine was busy with her teaching and clinical practice and I was getting ready to go to China to learn tuina, we did not follow through with the committee's advice.

After my return from China, Sovine and I had a preview of our presentation in Boston, Massachusetts. Due to other obligations, she was unable to attend the Boston Conference. I was to be on my own! While we were discussing the presentation, Nancy Crippen joined us. We ended up with an impromptu dry run of the presentation and responded to Crippen's questions as though we were already in Boston. After the encounter, Crippen felt it was important to establish ownership of intellectual property as represented in the poster and decided to apply for a grant to replicate the exploratory case study.

When I arrived at the conference site, I found our poster prominently displayed in the lobby, right outside the main ballroom on the plaza level of Seaport Hotel. There were 16-17 other posters on display, silently inviting viewers to consider their merits. The conference organized poster presentation as an on-going and informal way for attendees to exchange ideas and scheduled a formal reception at which poster presenters and their associates could avail themselves to explain their studies.

During the reception, I stood by our poster to discuss the data with a dozen or so visitors. Most of them were impressed with the positive results and none of them had voiced reservation about the theory of entanglement of free nerve ending. Except for a comment of Jeanette Ezzo, I did not get any new idea to advance our study.

Learning from the Conference

Jeanette Ezzo (Picture 33) was one of the three keynote speakers for the conference. She spoke on "What is needed to prove the effectiveness of massage?" During one of the breaks, I identified myself and asked if she might have suggestions for improving our study. She thought we could use a standardized instrument to measure the effects of massage instead of relying on subjective digital palpation of the tender points. Besides that initial conversation, we had snippets of exchanges in the next two days. Chatting with Ezzo was my most significant encounter at the Boston Conference.

In addition to Ezzo, I met Patricia Benjamin, author of *Tappan's Handbook*, at a reception; Leslie A. Young, (Picture 34) editor-in-chief of *Massage & Bodywork*, in a restaurant (our tables were next to each other); and Ruth Werner, President of MTF, at the registration desk. Meeting them reminded me of a comment a friend made many years ago: "Yes, you know them, but do they know you?" Young recognized me from our prior contacts about my paper on Yin Yang Touch, but Benjamin and Werner did not know me at all. Even though I was a novice and alone, I felt quite at home at the conference. I was comfortable with the "language of research."

Many of the presentations reminded me of the debate between quantitative research and qualitative research in my graduate school days at Northwestern University. As I learned in graduate school, both forms of research were useful if they were done properly. Knowledge is more than numbers and we are always at risk of the "fallacy of misplaced concreteness" (Alfred North Whitehead). Everyone at the conference was interested in evidence and the hierarchy of evidence, and Ezzo reminded us that we needed to ask the clients for their assessments of the effectiveness of massage instead of relying solely on objective measures.

Many interesting ideas were shared at the conference but I caught only a few of them. My notebook has jottings such as "Clinical outcome is how a patient feels, functions and survives," "Mechanism of action is how a treatment produces an effect" and "Touch is one of the basic needs." The notion of practice-based research was of great interest to me. It is a "partnership between researchers and clinicians. Data is collected from patients and medical personnel in a real life setting, and findings are translated to clinical practice." With proper training, I believe a massage therapist can be both a researcher and a clinician and data gathering can be a standard operating procedure in clinical practices. We need to teach student therapists what C. Wright Mills wrote of as "sociological imagination," except that in our context, it would be "therapeutic imagination." We also need to demystify research and to re-orient practical training toward training in clinical research. I felt, as I mentioned in Chapter 10, that with some minor adjustments to our status quo of gathering health history and SOAP notes, we could develop therapists who are savvy in understanding and doing research. I jotted down some questions therapists might ask ourselves: As members of a healthcare profession, what is our self-expectation and self-image? What is our model? What should be our model? Does our strength lie in the interpersonal dimension?

If I recall correctly, it was during a presentation by Cynthia Price on dissociation when Ezzo mentioned the challenge of veterans with posttraumatic stress disorder (PTSD) and my rejoinder that techniques used in treating fibromyalgia might work in treating PTSD. Price spoke at length about "interoception," awareness and processing of inner body sensations. I came to a similar but not identical conclusion as I thought about the possibility of starting a treatment program for veterans with PTSD in the Northern Virginia area.

The conference had several workshop sessions, but these sessions were merely miniatures of the plenary sessions: more talks moderated by the same handful of facilitators. Most of them were reporting on studies done. I would have preferred discussion on the process by which some of the studies were accomplished. Some of the sessions were "feel good" sessions in which presenters and audience were engaged in mutual self-congratulation. Perhaps it was due to the nature of a mass gathering, I had not heard any dissent over any presentation. If I were able to hear better, I would have engaged myself more fully with some critical questions for some of the presenters. I would have raised my doubt about the adequacy of light touch as a control variable to Swedish massage in the study of "mechanism of action of Swedish massage" because I feel light touch is just another way of doing Swedish massage. Joel Bialosky of Florida posed a provocative question: "What if massage worked predominantly through a placebo mechanism?" I would have countered with "What if there is no such a thing as placebo but just different modes of treatment?"

Due to my interest in fasciae, I was particularly attentive in the session on "Fascia Focused Models: Theories and Evidence" presented by Leon Chaitow. His statements on hypertonicity of gluteus maximus (*Hypertonicity of gluteus maximus could explain increased tension on the lumbar region, causing low back pain and [pain in] the lateral region of the knee*) and compression and stretching (*Compression or stretching of almost any part of the body has widespread and local effects, due to tensegrity related responses*) had practical import.

Ruth Werner, MTF President, was a superb communicator. She sent out a steady stream of emails before the conference and kept up contact with attendees with a daily electronic update. I liked especially the information she shared on the "development of a taxonomy" for the massage therapy profession. That paper, accessible from http://www.biomedcentral.com/1472-6882/6/24.3d, is more instructional than some of the in-person presentations.

One benefit of attending the conference was earning 13.5 CEUs even though I was just a listener. I had already collected one-half of the CEUs required for renewal of my NCBTMB certification.

Chapter 25

CASE SERIES ON FIBROMYALGIA

In early summer 2013, the Professional Development Committee of Virginia Community College System informed Nancy Crippen that they had awarded her a grant to study the use of massage therapy in treating fibromyalgia (FM). Along with her, Jennifer Sovine and I were co-recipients of the grant. It was another boost to my confidence.

Actually, with the encouragement of Crippen, Sovine and I had agreed to begin offering students in Massage III the opportunity to replicate the exploratory study on treating FM as a classroom assignment. We wanted to gather a critical mass of data to share with the healthcare profession about the effectiveness of massage. Solace Clinical Massage, a center for the management of chronic pain, had agreed to provide space for students to meet as a group and to treat their clients.

Preparing for the Study

To ensure uniformity and comparability across the cases, we selected the Revised Fibromyalgia Impact Questionnaire (FIQR), a standardized instrument with 21 questions available from www.

myalgia.com, as the measure of success. This was a substitute for the palpation on tender points that we did in the exploratory study.

In the exploratory study, we had found raw ginger root and sea salt produce more lasting benefits and decided to promote using these organic products in the professional development project even though we had not yet isolated their effects on treating FM. We feel that so long as we are mindful of doing no harm, the cross contamination or cross fertilization of different modalities at this stage of finding treatment for FM is not a serious drawback.

Also, since Angela in the exploratory study had reported that abdominal breathing and abdominal massage coupled with joint movements were especially beneficial in helping her to fall asleep and stay asleep, to let go of stress held up in the body and to regulate sluggish bowel movement (conditions that are often associated with FM), we told student therapists to encourage their clients to consider adapting these activities for self-care as preemptive measures for treatment.

To streamline the case series project, we formalized the treatment process in the exploratory study into a set of protocol for eight or 12 treatment sessions, to coincide with the college schedules. In the protocol, we referred to the therapist as female and the client as male, for convenience in communication. It goes without saying that the therapist can be male and the client, female.

In the first session, the therapist is to review with her client the model of entanglement of free nerve endings as the probable cause of FM pains and the use of sustained gliding and rhythmic compression as the treatment mode, to demonstrate the self-care routines of abdominal breathing, abdominal massage and joint movements, to locate and palpate the 18 tender points[87] and to record his reactions. She is then to use Yin Yang Touch to do a full body relaxation massage for her client, beginning with him in supine position and ending with him in prone position. The therapist is to ensure that her client drink at least half-a-pint of water before and after massage.

In the second session, the therapist is to re-demonstrate the self-care routines and use Yin Yang Touch to do a full body relaxation massage, beginning with the client in supine position and ending with the client in prone position. After the full body massage, the therapist is to apply gentle rhythmic compression and sustained gliding over the posterior tender points 1-6 for fifteen to twenty minutes. The

---

[87] Numbering of the tender points is based on *Clinical Massage Therapy* (2005), p. 982.

client is to synchronize his breathing with the compression and gliding. At the end of the session, the therapist is to alert her client that he might feel sorer in his muscles after the treatment and that some of the tender points might feel cold.

In the third and fourth sessions, the therapist is to work through the self-care routines with her client and give him a full body relaxation massage, beginning with the client in supine position and ending with the client in prone position. After the full body massage, the therapist is to apply ground raw ginger root and sea salt compress to tender points 3-6 (to address coldness in tender points). While the compress is on tender points 3-6, the therapist is to apply gentle rhythmic compression and sustained gliding over tender points 7-10 for fifteen to twenty minutes. After that, the therapist is to remove the compress, apply rhythmic compression and sustained gliding over tender points 1-6 for ten minutes and wipe the tender points with a warm cloth.

In the fifth and sixth sessions, the therapist is to work through the self-care routines with the client and give him an anterior full body relaxation massage. After anterior body massage, the therapist is to wrap ginger root and sea salt compress on tender points 15-18 and apply gentle rhythmic compression and sustained gliding over tender points 11-14 for fifteen to twenty minutes. After the anterior treatment, the therapist is to place her client in prone position, apply ginger root and sea salt compress on tender points 3-6, give the client a posterior full body relaxation massage and apply rhythmic compression and sustained gliding over tender points 7-10 for ten minutes. The therapist is then to remove the compress from tender points 3-6, unwrap tender points 15-18, apply rhythmic compression and sustained gliding to tender points 1-6, and apply gentle friction to tender points 15-18. She is then to wipe the tender points with a warm cloth.

In the seventh session, the therapist is to apply raw ginger root and sea salt compress on tender points 11-14 and tender points 15-18 and give an anterior full body relaxation massage to her client, with emphasis on abdominal massage. After the anterior body massage, the therapist is to remove the compress from tender points 11-14 and massage them for ten minutes. The therapist is then to place her client in prone position, apply compress to tender points 3-6 and give him a posterior full body relaxation massage, with emphasis on the lumbar region. After the posterior body massage, the therapist is to remove the compresses from tender points 3-6 and 15-18, apply rhythmic compression and sustained gliding to tender points 1-6, apply gentle friction to tender points 15-18 for fifteen to twenty minutes, and wipe the tender points with a warm cloth. Repeat Sessions 5-7 for clients having the 12-session treatment.

In the eighth (or final) session, the therapist is to work with her client on self-care routines and to do a full body massage with normal pressure. Both of them are to review progress and to plan for follow up treatment.

The steps outlined in the protocol were not to be followed rigidly. Instead, they should be adjusted according to the clients' conditions. However, students were to document variations or deviations from the routine so that results of the treatment could be assessed with due regards to the adjustments. Intake form, consent and release form and SOAP chart were also redesigned specifically for data collection.

The Case Series

Eight students from Massage III class in the summer and fall semesters 2013 participated in the project.[88] They were in the 20-59 age group, six female and two male, all of them college graduates. Each of them spent sixty to ninety minutes in each massage session. The total hands-on time was 118 hours.[89]

All the clients were female. Their ages ranged from 37 to 75: one was under 40, four were in the 40-49 age group and three were over 50. Their FM history varied from 1.5 years to 20 years: one had FM for less than ten years; six had it between ten to nineteen years, and one for twenty years. Seven of the clients had prior surgery and other medical conditions, in addition to FM. Seven of them were non-smokers and six of them did not use alcohol. Only three exercised regularly.

Most FM clients had to deal with sleep problem, stress and pain. Therefore, we collected pre-massage and post-massage data on these problems to measure the effectiveness of massage therapy for FM.

In terms of sleep problem, all but one client showed improvement in their sleep level. On a scale of 1-10, 1 being sleeping extremely

---

[88]   They were Richard, Esi, Amanda, Tansy, Rebecca, Nicole-Sophie, Deborah and Steven.

[89]   Four students completed eight sessions, three students completed 12 sessions and one student completed 11 sessions of 90 minutes each, for a total of 118 hours.

poorly and 10 being sleeping extremely well, the sleep scores in the first session for the seven who had improvement had varied from 2 to 9 points, with an average of 4.71. The scores in the final session for the same group had varied from 5 to 10 points, with an average of 7.29, an improvement of 2.58 points. Individual improvements had ranged between 1 and 5 points.

Client 2_2 was the exception. She reported having worsening sleep conditions between the first and final sessions, from 5 to 2 points. The score of 2 was her worst in the 12-session period. In previous sessions, her scores were 9 for one session, 8 for four sessions, 7 for two sessions, 6, 5, and 4 for one session each, for a total of 70 points, yielding an average of 7.0 points. Thus, one might conclude that issues extraneous to FM conditions before the final session could probably account for her worsening sleep conditions.

In terms of stress, five of the eight clients reported improvement in their stress level. On a scale of 1-10, 1 being extremely low level of stress and 10 being extremely high level of stress, the stress level in the first session for the five who had stress improvement was between 10 and 4 points, with an average of 6.80. The stress level in the final session for the same group was between 7 and 2 points, with an average of 3.40, a difference of 3.40 points. Individual improvements had varied from 1 to 7 points.

The three clients who showed higher stress level between the first and final sessions had other life issues that were not directly related to FM. One was dealing with the effects of a car accident; the other was dealing with issues that kept her from sleeping well and the third one had stressed herself with overwork (which is a common problem of people who found relief for their FM condition). Those issues could account for the increase of stress.

In terms of pain, six of the eight clients reported improvement in their conditions after the first treatment. On a scale of 1-10, 1 being extremely low level of pain and 10 being extremely high level of pain, the individual scores at the beginning of the first session for the six who had pain improvement were between 2 and 7 points, with an average of 5.0. The scores at the end of the first session for the same group were between 1 and 5 points, with an average of 3.0, an improvement of 2.0 points. Individual improvements had varied from 1 to 5 points.

At the end of the final session, all the clients reported improvement in their pain conditions. Individual scores at the beginning of the final session were between 1 and 8 points, with an average of 3.9. The scores at the end of the final session were between 0 and 6 points, with an average of 1.75, an improvement of 2.15 points. Individual improvements had varied from 1 to 6 points. Thus, massage seems to be effective in lowering pain both within a session and over a period of time.

In addition to the discrete problems associated with FM, we examined the overall impact of FM on the clients, whether it was extreme, severe, moderate or mild. In the first session, there was one client each in extreme and severe FM conditions, two in moderate FM conditions and four in mild FM condition. In the final session, the client who was in extreme FM conditions (Case 1_1) had improved to the severe conditions, with a drop of 16.5 points. The client in severe conditions (Case 2_2) had improved to moderate conditions, with a drop of 10.2 points. The clients in moderate conditions (Case 1_4 and 2_4) had improved to mild conditions, with a drop of 16.7 and 16.5 points, respectively. Three of the four clients in mild FM conditions in the first session had also shown improvement, with a drop of 8.3 points (Case 1_2), 9.4 points (Case 1_3) and 23.5 points (Case 2_1). Only one client (Case 2_3) had no significant improvement.

In their evaluation, all but one client were positive about their massage treatment.

Case 1_1 states: *"[Student therapist] is great. I really feel like the massage therapy is helpful, especially since you suggested she try side massage. Now it doesn't hurt my back. The therapy that is done with the breathing is working out painful areas that don't get much attention usually.... I was very glad to be a part of this study."*

Case 1_2 states: *"[Student therapist] is always very professional and explains the techniques he is using. I found this specific protocol... to be very effective.... I was diagnosed with FM 12 years ago and had it at a very manageable level. However, I continued to struggle with the lack of restorative sleep. This treatment really seemed to help with that, which is why [student therapist] and I plan to continue with it on a regular basis. In addition, the ginger root and sea salt compress really seemed to enhance the pain/sensitivity reduction and kept the discomfort from returning. In fact at our last session, we recorded the lowest tender point assessment I've had in 12 years."*

Case 1_3 states: *"[Student therapist] is very professional.... She found many trigger points all over my body and worked to eliminate each one every session.... My pain level has dropped from 80-90% to 15-20%.... My largest pain areas are the sides of my body, making it difficult to sleep for very long on either side. With the messages, I'm finding I don't go from one side to the other as often so I'm getting more optimum sleep."* Since the end of the treatment, Case 1_3 had in fact become a paying client of the then student therapist (now a certified massage practitioner) who informed me that the client *"not only expressed her gratitude for being part of the research, she also expressed 'still feeling great' for the first time in over 20 years."*

Case 1_4 states: *"My experience with [student therapist] and the pilot project was a very good one.... She did explain what she was doing and why in each session... I can't really pinpoint what techniques helped more. I felt like the ginger that she put on my tender points definitely helped. There were days when my knees were actually pain free.... I do think overall my pain level has decreased... I was experiencing some problems with my sleep before the study; however, I am sleeping better now.... I have already discussed continuing the treatment with her in the future...."*

Case 2_1 states: *"Can massage help fibromyalgia pain? Based on my 12-massage session treatment, I can say yes. Many factors about this therapy were helpful. I believe some pain is rooted in the tension we carry in our muscles. These sessions were a conscious effort to not only make time for stress relief, but brought awareness to which parts of the body the stress was manifesting in. The session times were not only a physical relief, but also a mental relief. The assessment of muscle groups that may be out of alignment, overused, or underused by a massage therapist can also help give ideas about reducing pain. The ginger application was also very helpful. The heat produced by the organic compound gave a relief option that did not include adding pharmaceuticals to the care plan of pain. This would be important to many pain sufferers who are trying to reduce or eliminate the cost of or physical damage brought on by prescription medications. The introduction to self-care brought an opportunity to assess stressful areas of my life, come up with strategies to resolve those problems, and give accountability to following through with the plan. Thank you very much for allowing me to be involved in this study."*

Case 2_2 states: *"[Student therapist] explained everything very thoroughly. She explained every session with detail and what she would be working on. I found the compress somewhat helpful in the sense that sometimes it would feel like an icy-hot feeling and other times it felt like a cold cream. The self-care deep breathing helped me relax better during the massage. I will definitely continue with the treatment and with [student therapist] as she is very caring to my needs. My body is very sensitive so of course I was sore after the massage. It would last a couple of hours. The day after the massage I had no aches and pains. I am very happy I participated in this study. Before this study I would avoid massages of any kind. Now I look forward to massage. I've enjoyed working with [student therapist] very much. I have found lots of relief for my aches and pains."*

Case 2_4 states: *"The first massage I experienced during this study felt wonderful. I left feeling relaxed and refreshed…. However, within 24 hours I was having spasms in my back. Within 48 hours my entire body hurt in extreme pain. It was as if the massage woke up every myofascial trigger point in my body and they were all mad. Over the next few weeks, pressure was adjusted and my body seemed to react more positively. I was able to experience longer periods of relief before my body reacted with some type of pain and what pain I did have was less severe. By week six I noticed more flexibility without pain. As long as I was able to keep my daily routine at a slow pace, I felt less stressed and more relaxed…. [My] fibromyalgia flare up of pain, spasm, and extreme fatigue… did not last as long as they normally did prior to the massages…. Overtime, I felt that the massages helped my body be able to return to its normal state of low pain levels more quickly…. What seems to have improved is the duration of my body's reaction."*

The client who made no assessment of the treatment was Case 2_3. She was the one who showed no significant improvement in her FM condition. She was a smoker, using five to ten cigarettes a day;

and she did not exercise. When I visited her for on-site observation, she told me she had monthly acupuncture treatment in addition to trying massage for treating FM. She also did not use the ginger/sea salt compress regularly. Whether these factors had impact on her condition is uncertain.

Seven of the eight clients participating in the project showed improvement in their FM condition, according to the FIQR scores. Most of them appeared to have more energy after the 8-session or 12-session treatment. Evidently, massage therapy can be a viable treatment option for patients with FM.

The summary report of Deborah Wedemeyer, one of the student therapists, captured the dynamics of the treatment process.[90] *In the first session, the client was in distress, therefore, we focused the session on decreasing stress. From self-reporting and manual palpation, the client felt tenderness in six points in the lower cervical, occiput, and trapezius regions. In the second session, the client's hands and feet were cold and she felt great relief upon receiving hand and foot massage to increase circulation. Abdominal and back massage brought heat to mid-region of the client's body. The client's breathing grew increasingly slower throughout the massage.*

During sessions 2, 3 and 12, the client fell asleep. When ginger and sea salt compress was included in sessions 3, 4 and 5, the client felt some tingling, but it did not increase heat on the skin. In session 5, the client received the ginger-sea salt formula for use outside the massage sessions. In sessions 5 and 6, client reported feeling much more grounded and was able to incorporate more strenuous art projects and activities into her life. In session 8, the client received deep tissue massage and reacted well to moderate pressure. By session 12, the client was going to yoga classes three times a week and working with a personal trainer to increase muscle tone. No tenderness was found in any of the 18 points in the final session.

Lessons Learned

The purpose of the professional development project was to replicate the exploratory study on using massage to treat FM. Crippen, Sovine and I had accomplished our goal. While the number of cases is still too small for claiming success, the results do show a success rate of 88 percent (7 out of 8).

---

[90]   Excerpted from the report of Deborah Wedemeyer. Used with permission.

Due to the voluntary and pioneering nature of this project, we had to adapt what we wanted to do to fit with what we were able or capable of doing. We had intended to include palpation of the 18 tender points as a measure for success, but we did not want to subject the volunteer clients to more tests or the student therapists to more demands. Neither did we want to intrude on the treatment process. So, we used the FIQR to measure progress instead of coupling it with palpation of tender points. Retrospectively, it would have been worthwhile for student therapists to spend more time to do both palpation and the FIQR in the first and final sessions.

We also had to forego asking the volunteers to verify their progress with a physician since they were unlikely to be willing to incur new expenses after the eight or 12 sessions of treatment and even if they were willing to have a check up with their doctors, we had no resources to follow up with them. After all, we were in a community college setting and its focus is teaching and not research.

However, the benefits that students get from involving in focused case study might perhaps be gleaned from the report of Rebecca Mayfield, one of the student therapists:[91] *On a personal level, the experience of working with my client in the FM study was very humbling. To date, it has been my experience that after a client gets off the table she or he is elated with the results: pain is reduced, relaxation is increased, and overall wellbeing is restored. Such was not the case with my FM client. I was routinely frustrated by my ability to increase her pain level after a massage even after being conscious of the pressure I was applying. I was frustrated by the inability to provide pain relief in an area before another area caused her pain. There was no linear pattern to the increase or decrease of pain. The "aha" moments I had did not come until I started to look at the data as a whole, following the 12 sessions.* She would probably not gain these insights if she were simply doing routine massages. Her experience shows that research does have a place even in a community college because it improves teaching and learning.

<>

In the mix of using different modalities for treating FM, what, then, is the role of massage therapy? The exploratory study has shown that massage therapy was in fact the primary route through which other modalities made their contributions. Without massage as the

---

[91]   Used with permission.

focus, the potential and real contributions of other modalities were unlikely to find expression. The professional development project had affirmed what was found effective in the exploratory study, that NOVA-S Method, coupled with ginger root and sea salt, was apparently viable in treating FM. Massage has a dual role in treating FM. It is a treatment modality on its own merit, and a mediating channel through which other modalities show their healing effects.

After the project, Sharon Fussell of Solace Clinical Massage wrote to a number of rheumatologists in Northern Virginia about the study and informed them that I was available to help treat their FM clients, but we had received no inquiry. We continued to solicit referrals from friends but persons with FM conditions had not availed themselves of massage therapy. However, the poster presentation Sovine and I made at the Boston Conference did lead me to explore applying the NOVA-S Method and Yin Yang Touch to the treatment of veterans with posttraumatic stress disorder (PTSD). It was a case of serendipity!

Chapter 26

PTSD WORKSHOP

Designing a PTSD Workshop

I have heard of posttraumatic stress disorder (PTSD) in news broadcasts and casual conversations, but I did not pay much attention. In one of the brief chats with Jeanette Ezzo at the Boston Conference (Chapter 24), we exchanged ideas on how massage might benefit veterans with PTSD. Ezzo talked about calming the hyperarousal of brain nerves and I talked about applying the NOVA-S Method for de-stressing. We agreed a pilot project on treating veterans with PTSD might show the positive effects of massage therapy and we could eventually extend it to include the civilian population.

Upon returning from the conference, I broadened my initial interest. I was interested in more than treatment. I wanted a pilot project that includes treatment, research, outreach and teaching (TROT) and I sketched an outline of a two-year project that would involve 168 veterans, 300 family members, 42 massage students, six clinicians and one coordinator, with a price tag of three-quarters of a million dollars. The expected outcomes of the project would include veterans becoming more capable of coping with daily demands of civilian life, family members becoming more capable of supporting veterans in their adjustment to civilian life, massage students gaining the skills and experience of working with people with PTSD, massage therapists becoming more ready to work with people with PTSD and the massage profession and society at large gaining a better understanding of PTSD.

I thought setting up a project with multiple emphases would help fill a gap in healthcare for veterans and provide funds for NOVA to expand the Massage Therapy Program. The Department of Veterans Affairs could provide funds to NOVA to set up a clinic for treating veterans with PTSD and to hire personnel to staff the clinic. Fort Belvoir and Quantico Marine Base, the military facilities close by the college, could refer veterans and their family members to the clinic for treatment and consultation. The college could use funds provided by the Government to give scholarship to senior students in the Massage Therapy Program who are interested in becoming interns at the clinic and to hire certified massage therapists to be clinicians. The college could also hire a coordinator to oversee the project, liaise between the military and the college, monitor and report on the treatment outcome. It was a win-win proposition for all involved.

I called the project "TROT for PTSD" and shared the proposal with three NOVA faculty members. In the first discussion among us in mid-May, we realized we knew of no massage therapists in the Northern Virginia area who had significant experience in working with veterans with PTSD (not that there were none, it was just that we did not know of anyone) and we had no personal contact with the military establishment. We had no potential leads on funding or referral. If we have no clinicians to supervise students and if we are unfamiliar with the dynamics of PTSD, we could hardly convince the VA Department to support a pilot project. Thus, launching TROT for PTSD was not viable. However, we still felt treating veterans with PTSD was a worthwhile project in itself and I was tasked with developing a plan for finding and training clinicians. We could deal with the treatment population and the question of funding later. Personally, I felt I needed to have an in-depth understanding of veterans with PTSD.

In my previous careers as a church worker and a Government employee, I had designed and conducted workshops for leadership training. I thought of using the same model for finding and training clinicians. I surfed the Internet to educate myself about veterans with PTSD and enrolled in an online course on "From the War Zone to the Home Front II: Supporting the Mental Health of Veterans and

Families," offered by the Massachusetts General Hospital (http://www.mghcme.org), for a more organized introduction to the subject. I read reports on PTSD and found "Treatment for Posttraumatic Stress Disorder in Military and Veteran Populations: Initial Assessment" (http://wwe.nap.edu/catalog.php?record_Id=13364)   especially helpful. I gathered information on people and organizations that work with veterans, sources from which I might find presenters and sponsors for the workshop.

I set three objectives for the workshop: to educate the public and healthcare professionals on the scope, impact and symptoms of PTSD in the veteran community, to understand the science of the brain experiencing PTSD and to introduce to healthcare professionals and caregivers a complementary method for treating people with PTSD. I expected the outcome of the workshop to include attendees understanding the warning signs and symptoms of PTSD and the scope and depth of the impact of PTSD on veteran population and feeling more confident in addressing the issue of PTSD; and healthcare professionals and caregivers learning and applying the complementary method to treat clients and family members suffering from PTSD and becoming a continuing network of research and support for testing and promoting complementary and alternate treatments of PTSD.

The workshop design I presented to the NOVA faculty members included presentations on the dynamics of PTSD, a profile of veterans with PTSD and how therapists can treat it with what they had learned in their basic training. The message I wanted to convey to the therapists was simply "You can do it!" with a minimum of extra effort. I included in the design some prospective presenters and the NOVA-S Method as a treatment modality. I customized the intake form and SOAP chart for therapists to collect treatment data and chose the PTSD checklist (PCL-M) and the "symptom domain" of the FIQR as measurement tools for the effectiveness of massage.

PTSD has acquired such a mystique that healthcare professionals are extremely cautious about its treatment. From my point of view, it is all about stress. Extreme stress, undoubtedly; but stress, all the same. Fibromyalgia is one form of stress that Sovine and I have treated successfully with the NOVA-S Method. From what we have read and heard about the reactions of people with fibromyalgia and veterans with PTSD, we find a core of common problems between them, problems such as chronic pain, low energy, poor sleep, high level of depression and high sensitivity to touch. We feel the NOVA-S

Method might help to de-stress veterans with PTSD, just as it works for people with fibromyalgia.

In fibromyalgia, the focus of treatment is on freer flow of cellular fluid so that free nerve endings are de-entangled. In PTSD, the focus is on using tactile sensation to recondition the brain[92] so that it would decelerate its rate of arousal, detach its wiring to past trauma and repair the damaged free nerve endings with proper coating. We would use the same method (and extend the same understanding) to treat a different condition. As sustained gliding (from effleurage) and rhythmic compression (from touch without movement) are basic techniques in Western massage in which every massage student has prior training, and breathing is essential for massage, licensed or certified therapists already have the requisite skills for treating veterans with PTSD. What they need is the assurance that they can help heal this population.

I planned to invite healthcare providers who had direct experience of working with veterans to share their insights on the dynamics of PTSD and massage practitioners who had taught massage therapy to explain how massage might treat PTSD. I wanted to invite therapists who had treated veterans with PTSD to share their first-hand experience. And I wanted to demonstrate the NOVA-S Method as a modality for healing. The total presentation would provide strong stimulus to therapists so that they would feel confident to meet the challenge.

As the Massage Therapy Program at NOVA was an NCBTMB-approved provider of continuing education, it could offer continuing education credits (CEU) as an incentive for therapists to attend the workshop. We decided to offer 8 CEUs for attendance and an additional 12 CEUs for completion of additional assignments, which included doing ten sessions of massage with a veteran, preferably one with PTSD. The price of the workshop was $99, a real bargain!

Initially, we wanted therapists to submit to the college the whole package of health history, consent and release forms, SOAP notes, completed trauma stress checklist and questionnaire on the impact of PTSD. However, to protect client privacy and to comply with guidelines for protecting human subjects in research, we decided that CEU participants needed to submit only a summary form of data collection and the completed checklist and questionnaire. We did not have a central location for the case files.

---

[92]   See *Job's Body* (2003).

As the workshop design unfolded, we thought it was a good idea to expand the audience base to reach out to the family members of veterans and to the general public. In other words, make the workshop an outreach event as well as a training event. Thus, TROT for PTSD might not be launched as initially envisaged, but the workshop has the same emphasis. It was a "Mini-TROT!"

The NOVA faculty members and I agreed to hold the workshop on Sunday, November 10, 2013, a day ahead of Veterans' Day and to run a massage clinic on Veterans' Day. Both events were to express our appreciation to veterans and their family members for their service to our Nation. Subsequently, due to the college schedule, we moved the clinic session to the Saturday before Veterans' Day. Perhaps due to the long holiday weekend, very few veterans signed up for the clinic. The clinic could accommodate at least 24 clients for the day, but only seven veterans had made appointments and four actually showed up.

Earlier in our planning, we decided to invite alumni of the Massage Therapy Program to provide free massage to veterans and dovetail the massage clinic with an alumni reunion. Several alumni responded positively. However, as pre-registration for massage was scant, we informed them not to come for the clinic. Instead, we had the reunion in an evening gathering at a Mexican restaurant close by the campus.

Searching for Presenters

Sovine and I were fairly confident about the theoretical basis for treating PTSD and the effectiveness of NOVA-S Method for de-stressing. However, neither of us had the expertise derived from hands-on working with veterans with PTSD. The workshop would need healthcare providers who had treated PTSD to provide the necessary background for therapists to link what they read and heard about PTSD to the case experience of healthcare providers. I searched the Internet for groups that worked with Veterans with PTSD and reached into my network of friends for persons who might have first hand experience.

The first group I contacted was the Center for Deployment Psychology (CDP), an organization funded in part by the Department of Defense and headquartered at the Uniformed Services University of the Health Sciences in Bethesda, Maryland. Its mission was to educate professionals in deployment-related mental health issues. I provided them information about the massage training program at NOVA, the target audience and an estimate of the number of people who might attend the workshop, the specific PTSD information for which we request a speaker and the length of time we needed from her. CDP did not respond to my request.

Concurrent with my exploration with CDP, I visited the Veterans Affairs (VA) Medical Center in Washington, D.C., about the possibility of providing free massages to veterans at its facilities. I wanted to have first hand experience of working with veterans and to explore how NOVA and VA might have some cooperative programs for treating veterans with PTSD. The Voluntary Services Office accepted my resume and assured me it would call me the next day. I did not hear from them. A few days later, I called the office again, but no one answered my call. Neither did I hear from the primary contact person for PTSD.

In early June, my old friend James (not his real name) responded to my call for help by asking his daughter Karen (not her real name) to contact me. I did not know she was injured with PTSD and TBI (traumatic brain injury) while on a training mission and had to leave the Army. She supported the workshop idea whole-heartedly, agreed to attend as a presenter and referred me to her healthcare providers, Pauline and Patricia, as potential workshop presenters. Pauline was a neuropsychologist and Patricia was a social work case manager. I shared the idea of the workshop with them and requested their participation without remuneration. They agreed.

As Jeanette Ezzo was the one who ignited my interest in using massage to treat veterans with PTSD, I felt she should be the one to share ideas on how massage might be used to treat PTSD. I requested her help in early June, with the audacity of informing her in advance that we did not have money to pay for her services. She too agreed to help! Later, when I previewed the workshop agenda with her, she suggested we phrase her presentation as "What is the role of Massage in PTSD?" She also requested a change in the opening lines of the workshop promotion because she felt it was unduly "hype" to list her as the "main attraction."

In our division of labor, the faculty members at NOVA and I let each other have a great deal of freedom to tackle the assigned tasks. I was primarily focused on the workshop content and the presenters. When the promotion materials (designed by another faculty member) were circulated for comments before their posting on the college website, I had no problem with them. In fact, I was quite delighted that Ezzo was highlighted as the "main attraction." I thought it gave her due credit. In hindsight, I realized I should have consulted with her.

To provide vicarious experience to participants and to further enhance their confidence, we decided to include a panel discussion on "Working with Veterans with PTSD." In the course of searching for presenters, I came across several volunteer organizations that provide wellness service to veterans, many with emphasis on serving "wounded warriors." To my delight and dismay, several people affiliated with these groups were willing to share their experience on what it was like to work with veterans, but most of them demurred about having expertise in working with veterans with PTSD. Nonetheless, we set up the panel and recruited discussants for it. However, due to personal and logistical problems, we had to make several substitutions and the final panel had a membership completely different from the initial lineup. I also scheduled Sovine and me to round off the workshop with hands-on demonstration and practice of the NOVA-S Method and a group discussion on how we might engage in doing cooperative research.

Working with Workforce Development Office

With presenters committed and the agenda finalized, we were ready to launch promoting the workshop. "Not so fast," the Workforce Development Office (WDCE), NOVA, erected a roadblock. It seemed that extra-curricular offerings of NOVA had to be routed through WDCE because it had the expertise for providing continuing education. Our workshop was an infringement on their prerogative. Through the months of July, August and September, the massage faculty members negotiated with WDCE on how the event should and could be advertised, as well as how registration fee should and could be collected and divided between WDCE and the Massage Therapy Program. The workshop publicity was held up because we did not have an acceptable way for receiving and accounting for CEU registration fee. The idea of foregoing the CEU and offering the workshop as a free event was fleetingly discussed, but not pursued. We did not believe therapists would register for the workshop if they did not receive CEU. Eventually, it took an intervention of the Provost's Office to remove the roadblock. Thereafter, WDCE involved six staff persons to work with us to expedite the development of a website with link for registration.

WDCE eventually clarified its role as the vehicle by which participants register for the event and as the processor of participant fees. WDCE would pass the majority of the funds taken in to the Massage Therapy Program and we would handle procurement and payment associated with the workshop. This provided a very clear delineation of duties and allowed WDCE and us to collaborate successfully. It was exactly what we initially requested. The website was finally up and running in early October. We began to recruit therapists to attend the workshop.

Dealing with Complications

In late October, I was informed that some complications had developed that might have impact on the workshop. I suggested turning the workshop into a seminar, but the massage faculty members convinced me that we should go ahead with the workshop even though at that point we only had three registrants. We needed to proceed as planned so that we could establish credibility with the NOVA administration. We streamlined the workshop agenda and reset the target audience of the workshop back to massage therapists but continue to make room for interested persons. I became the contact person for answering inquiries about the workshop and provided daily updates to the massage faculty members. Sovine and I also undertook the task of recruiting NOVA alumni to register for the workshop. Further into late October, the Division Dean interceded with the Provost's Office to provide free lunches to the participants and the Provost approved the request the next day, prompting a staff member to remark that it was the "fastest approval ever!" On November 9, the day before the workshop, we had 17 CEU registrants and 18 pre-registered attendees.

When I met with Ezzo in October, I shared with her drafts of the data collecting instruments I developed. They included a questionnaire on the impact of trauma, an intake form, the consent and release forms and a SOAP note chart. The questionnaire was based on the Post Traumatic Check List (PCL-M) developed by the U.S. Government and the "symptom domain" of the Revised Fibromyalgia Impact Questionnaire (FIQR). The other forms were customized for the PTSD workshop. Regrettably, I failed to note the sources of the questionnaire and Ezzo chided me for plagiarism, a cardinal sin for people doing research. Anyone who is familiar with PTSD and fibromyalgia issues would recognize the questionnaire

I put together as PCL-M and FIQR. Not listing the sources is gross negligence. I was grateful to her for drawing my attention to the plagiarism issue. People who know me would excuse the oversight. People who don't know me would rightfully brand me as unethical and disregard whatever I try to do for veterans with PTSD. Ezzo thereafter insisted that if research were to follow the workshop, we should use validated instruments, with proper acknowledgment of their sources. I had no problem agreeing with her since doing it right is very important for opening a way for massage to advance as a profession.

Esso's keen interest in the workshop was affirming and refreshing. She was assuming ownership of it and I had no trouble sharing or even relinquishing ownership. I have always worked on the principle that the more input I receive for a project, the better the final product will be. At age 70-plus, I do not need another achievement, but my friends at NOVA teased me about the workshop being my baby. If so, Ezzo was its godmother!

Ezzo's insistence on using validated measuring tools ran into the professional concerns of Patricia and Pauline. They felt that "the PCL-M and other measures should only be given by clinicians with training in PTSD treatment (i.e., mental health professionals or with their supervision)." Also, they were concerned that the workshop was leading to a research project that "requires supervision from an Institutional Review Board (IRB)." They stated they would be unable to participate in the research project. While I did entertain the thought that they might refer clients to the research project for treatment, I was aware of their professional boundaries and I assured them post-workshop activities would not involve them. Their roles in the workshop were to highlight the problem and to provide a perspective on it. What the audience decided to do after their presentation was a different issue.

As for the use of measuring tools, my understanding is that they are in the public domain and anyone can use them for whatever purpose. Ours is to establish a baseline on a veteran's PTSD condition before massage treatment and to assess progress or the lack thereof after treatment. We are not into screening, diagnosis or prescription. Veterans who participate in the research project are persons self-identified or medically defined as having PTSD. They participate entirely as volunteers on their own initiative and not referred by any authority. The consent and release for treatment is between them and the therapist. No institution is involved; therefore, no IRB approval is required. However, the observation of Patricia and Pauline had raised the question about the critical point when a project crosses over into research and therefore in need of an IRB approval. They also pointed out that "collection of data in a centralized source that would be published requires IRB approval." Since we could not resolve the issue in time, we had to suspend the post-workshop cooperative research efforts.

Getting to Know Veterans

To test the efficacy of the NOVA-S Method on treating veterans with PTSD, I volunteered with a non-profit organization that supported members of U.S. Armed Services who suffered injuries in the Middle East. I gave seated massages to veterans and their family members, hoping to come across some who have PTSD. Among 33 encounters between July and October 2013, only three were veterans with PTSD. But for the fact they noted the condition in the intake form, I would not have known they were afflicted. Their requests for massage were no different from other "wounded warriors." They wanted work on their neck, shoulder and back and expressed appreciation for the NOVA-S Method, but I did not have feedback on the effects of massage. That organization did not have pre-massage and post-massage assessments. I also volunteered for a wellness event for the Warrior Transition Battalion and gave seated massage to eight veterans in the two-and-a-half hour period. That event also had no assessment on the effectiveness of massage. I wanted to attend a Warrior Transition Workshop organized by another veterans' group to promote massage therapy, but I was denied permission.

Not satisfied with the lack of exposure to veterans with PTSD, I contacted the National Intrepid Center of Excellence (NICoE), a Government entity dedicated to working with returning troops with TBI and PTSD, for the possibility of doing an internship with them. The following is what I stated in my letter of introduction:

In discussion with different groups working with veterans, I found that all of them, for confidentiality and insurance reasons, are not interested in using massage therapy to treat veterans with PTSD because it has no proven record. Thus, therapists who are willing and able to work with veterans are in a Catch-22 situation and veterans who might be helped are denied the opportunity to improve their quality of life.

In order to build a record, a treatment modality needs to have a chance to show what it can do, without doing harm to the client, of course. As a research massage therapist, I am very interested in helping to build a record for massage therapy and to show its positive effects for treating PTSD. I need a population of veterans I can work with, under supervision as needed.

I have heard of the work of NICoE and your work with returning troops for TBI and PTSD and I am wondering if your program can provide me the opportunity to use my skills to treat veterans with PTSD. I am willing to provide free service and commit myself to serve for six months to a year. I enclose a copy of my resume for your reference.

I wanted to know firsthand what it was like to work with veterans with PTSD so that I could share that experience with other therapists. The NICoE contact declined my offer, as "providers who work with [their] patients must be either government employees or contractors who are all credentialed through the Walter Reed Military Medical Center." No room for volunteers until the credentialing issue is resolved!

PTSD Case Study

But I did have an opportunity to test the NOVA-S Method with a veteran with PTSD. The client, Karen (not her real name), was a 48-year old female veteran who received healthcare from VA for PTSD. She was diagnosed as having PTSD for more than 20 years and her goal in massage therapy was to get pain relief.

Between July and October, I had six massage sessions with Karen. In the first session, I showed her partner a routine of the NOVA-S Method for him to apply on her, daily, if possible. Without rehashing the etiology of PTSD, I stated my understanding of the disorder as involving hyperactivity of brain functions. Thus, de-stressing the brain through tactile movement and non-movement was the focus of my therapeutic practice. I showed Karen a routine of arm extension and flexion synchronized with abdominal breathing for relaxation and preparation for sleep.

In the first session, Karen filled out a two-part Traumatic Stress Impact Questionnaire to establish a baseline of her PTSD condition. Part I of the questionnaire is the PCL-M. I augmented it with two additional items on overall impact, whether PTSD prevented

Karen from accomplishing goals for the week and whether she was completely overwhelmed by PTSD symptoms. Part II of the questionnaire is an adaptation of the "symptom domain" of the Revised Fibromyalgia Impact Questionnaire (FIQR). It consists of 8 of the ten FIQR questions. Questions on level of stiffness and level of balance problems were replaced with questions on how well Karen takes care of herself and whether she could move about/drive/travel freely. All the questions in Part II deal with her experience in the preceding 7 days.

Before the 7th session of treatment, Karen filled out the same questionnaire again to assess the progress or the lack thereof of her reactions to the lingering effects of PTSD.

According to the PCL-M guideline for measuring change, "a 5-10 point change represents reliable change (i.e., change not due to chance) and a ten to twenty point change represents clinically significant change." It further recommends "using 5 points as a minimum threshold for determining whether an individual has responded to treatment and 10 points as a minimum threshold for determining whether the improvement is clinically meaningful."[93]

In the PCL-M Index, Karen's score has dropped 25 points, from 66 to 41, which indicates a "clinically significantly change." She was much less bothered by PTSD symptoms after six sessions of treatment. With decrease in the negative impact of PTSD, one might find a similar decrease in the felt intensity of the effects of PTSD symptoms. This expectation is in fact supported in the Index of Symptom Intensity. The score has a 33-point drop, placing the overall impact of PTSD to below the mid-point of intensity.

Before the massage treatment, Karen felt PTSD prevented her "quite a bit" from accomplishing goals for the week and she was "quite a bit" overwhelmed by her PTSD symptoms. After the sixth session, Karen felt PTSD had just "a little bit" of impact on accomplishing her goals and she was not as overwhelmed by her PTSD symptoms. Both indices and the questions on overall impact showed massage therapy had a high degree of efficacy in treating PTSD, even though the data were that of only one veteran. It should also be underscored that the effectiveness of massage treatment was due not to my work alone; but due to the frequent massages Karen received from her partner.

Through the six sessions that extended over a four-month period, Karen's stress level had varied from a high of 7 to a low of 3, with more

---

[93] "Measuring Change," PTSD Checklist, reviewed/updated by National Center for PTSD, June 13, 2013.

recent sessions showing stress level below the midpoint. Generally, she had been able to keep her stress at a low level. Massage seemed to have positive impact.

In the initial interview, Karen indicated that lack of sleep and being unable to sleep was a major issue. It was an outcome of the classic PTSD re-experiencing syndrome. When Karen went to sleep, she re-lived the trauma of the injury. Thus, the primary goal of massage therapy was to de-stress the brain so that Karen was able to have restorative sleep. Over the treatment period, Karen's sleep wellness score rose from 4 (relatively poor) to 8 (relatively high). Massage seemed to be effective in helping her to fall asleep and stay asleep.

In the initial interview, Karen stated she had soreness in her left shoulder, arm, lower back and chest. The left side of her body had persistent pain. This pattern had lasted over the six sessions, but most pains were of relatively low intensity. For each session, her pain had eased off after massage. For the fifth and sixth sessions, I used cupping to treat Karen's left trapezius and pectoral area in addition to using sustained gliding and rhythmic compression for general massage. However, both the massage and cupping did not provide lasting relief. The soreness was still present at the end of the sixth session. Perhaps, the condition might be improved with further sustained massage treatment and cupping and with Karen wearing underwear with broader shoulder strips to relieve the pressure on her shoulders.

The case study was in progress before the PTSD workshop. Preliminary data seemed to show massage therapy done by Karen's partner and me was effective in treating PTSD. Does massage therapy work similarly for other female veterans and for male veterans? Is it as effective without the caregiver's frequent massages? How well might it work? These and other research questions are worthy of further exploration. Continuing treatment of the client and extending treatment to other veterans (and their caregivers) might yield more revealing data on the effectiveness of massage therapy. The real challenges for using massage therapy to treat veterans with PTSD are finding therapists willing to treat the veterans and finding veterans willing to be treated.

Before I started working with Karen, I taught her partner the basic strokes and practice of the NOVA-S Method. The partner had not become a massage therapist (and I was not training him to be a therapist), but he could provide the relief Karen needed. As the

NOVA-S Method is time-consuming and patience intensive, it occurs to me that teaching caregivers to work with their family members is an essential complement to professional massage. This is needed for holistic service.

Workshop Evaluation

As the workshop had included using the NOVA-S Method to treat veterans with PTSD and the emphasis of the method is on intentional deep breathing and deliberate movement, I informed the massage faculty members that I would start the workshop with Guangzhou Motion (Appendix 1) and Virginian Stretch (Chapter 8), two sets of exercise, to set the tone. I wanted the workshop to help participants feel what it was like to slow down. My colleagues allowed me the latitude.

The workshop was launched as planned. From initial conception in late April to final delivery in early November, it took 6 months and 15 days, not a long gestation period. A total of 40 people attended the workshop, including 17 who signed up for continuing education credits, 14 registered attendees, one unsigned walk-in and eight presenters. Of the 32 attendees, 25 were female and seven were male. They included 16 massage therapists, five NOVA students, three NOVA staff persons, six NOVA alumni, six veterans, and seven with other identities (the total exceeds 31 because some attendees have more than one identity. For example, some therapists are also NOVA alumni). Four of the attendees came from Maryland and Washington, D.C.; and 28 were from Virginia, mostly the Northern Region. Of the 17 who registered for continuing education, seven planned to engage in post-workshop cooperative case study.

Of the 31 who registered for the workshop, 25 had completed an evaluation. On a 5-point scale, from excellent to poor (or most likely to least likely), the ratings of attendees can be divided into three groups, 15 rated the workshop as very good to excellent (1:00-1:49), seven rated it as good to very good (1.50-2.49), and three rated it as good (2 with score of 2.5 and 1 with score of 2.67). The usefulness of the presentations, the relevance of the subject matter to attendees' profession, the understandability of technical and practical components of the workshop and the applicability of the workshop to participants' practices or life situations were all in the very good to excellent categories. Life being what it is, it is not surprising that a smaller number of participants reported the subject matter as not relating to them personally and a similar number not wanting to continue training in massage for PTSD clients.

The quiz on PTSD that I designed partially to measure the learning results of the workshop and customized for CEU registrants was meant to assess if attendees have done any pre-workshop reading (as recommended in the workshop announcement) and whether they gained new knowledge in the workshop. The CEU registrants completed identical pre-workshop and post-workshop quiz. Their average score rose from 5.06 to 5.53, not a significant change. The individual scores showed seven registrants had increased recognition of some of the issues associated with PTSD, six registrants had no change, and four registrants had decreased recognition.

Interestingly, some registrants reported having a better grasp of PTSD issues before the workshop than they did after listening to the presentation. To vent her annoyance, one participant noted, *"Several of the questions were related to statistics but not to the condition, symptoms, treatment, etc.... The presentation didn't necessarily cover those numbers, I'm not sure what the quiz was trying to measure."* Perhaps, a vast amount of raw information shared in a short time span had led to more confusion!

Most participants had added comments to their evaluation. They not only assessed the workshop experience, but also suggested improvement and follow-up activities. These voluntary comments were indirect measurements of participants' level of interest.

> *I tried to get 2 friends to come who have PTSD, but they could not make it. This would have really helped them. I will definitely share my handouts/links with them. I look forward to using these techniques with clients and friends. Thank you for the information and resources! #21*
>
> *This workshop was a good review of materials I've had in the past. Due to not needing/wanting CEUs, I didn't feel welcome in the hands-on portion even though I was invited to stay. #20.*
>
> *Totally glad that I took the time to attend. I loved each of the presentations.... I enjoyed hearing two perspectives from survivors and participating with the NOVA-S Method. #19*
>
> *I would recommend more time on the practical part. For therapists, more hands-on time is usually better for them to understand. Also would like to see more info not just for veterans but also for other PTSD and have a presenter for*

other areas of PTSD. For the quiz, have the presentations address the questions. [They] did not address them. #17

Only improvement would be a printout of the protocols (NOVA-S) for people that need to read and see it. Also, better clarity for the 20 CEUs route as far as do we need to use certain techniques/documentation. #15

More techniques for grounding, more hands on skills for coping with PTSD clients when they are triggered, mindful techniques, [and] I liked the hands-on practice and treatment – more. #8.

I would like to have had more time to hear Dr. _____ speak. I would have liked to hear more specifics on PTSD. I also would have liked to learn more about non-veteran PTSD populations. #7

One participant wrote me an email the day after the workshop in these words: *I want to take a brief moment to thank you for the tremendous undertaking of the Workshop on PTSD on Sunday, November 10. It is a huge subject and far too many people suffer from it, probably unknowingly. As I am new to the State of Virginia, I will work my network to find a veteran to complete the 20 CEU requirements. I would love to know who else is committed to the task and meet with them at least twice during the process.... Please put me on your list for "Constant Contact" in any way I can help!*

The workshop had ended and it left a number of follow up activities for Sovine and Crippen. Due to concerns over the lack of oversight by an IRB, the post-workshop practical activities were decentralized. Registrants were free to use whatever modality they preferred to treat their clients with PTSD, and their clients could either be a veteran or a civilian. In order to earn the 12 extra CEUs, they still needed to complete the online course on veterans with PTSD and ten massage sessions with one client. They were to submit a copy of their certificate of completion of the online course, a summary of the massage sessions and the completed Pre- and Post-treatment PTSD checklist and Revised Fibromyalgia Impact Questionnaire (FIQR) to NOVA.

Despite my close involvement with the workshop, I did not ask either Crippen or Sovine about the status of the follow up activities. I knew both of them were stretched thin with teaching and administrative chores since the workshop and they did not need me to intrude into their hectic schedules. I would love for NOVA to be the rally point for therapists interested in using massage to treat veterans with PTSD, but NOVA has other ideas. I might be frustrated about missed or lost opportunities, but I continue to believe in "following the natural flow." More exciting opportunities for service are ahead!

Chapter 27

SCOLIOSIS: A SUSPENDED CASE

Joan, a friend Mercy knew through her network of volunteer activities, was interested in the exploratory case study on using massage to treat fibromyalgia. She felt her friend's daughter might benefit from massage treatment. Before she referred her friend to me, Joan wanted to find out more about my method. So, Mercy and I met her for coffee and I answered all her questions. At the end of the meeting, Joan said, "I know your research interest is not on scoliosis, but, do you think, massage might work for people with scoliosis?" I remembered some classmates at NOVA had success in their case studies on scoliosis and I told her massage might work.

"Could you please find time to work with my daughter? She has a bad case of scoliosis for many years. She has pain all the time," Joan said.

"If your daughter is willing to spend time to explore the possibilities, I would be glad to work with her. Why don't you talk to her about it? If she is interested, bring her to our house for a trial session to see how she feels." That's how I became involved in a case study of scoliosis.

Joan's daughter Pam (not her real name) is an Asian-American, 27 years old, and a mother of three young boys. She first came to see me in late October 2012, right after my NCBTMB certification. Her case has been suspended since early September 2013. In the 12-month period, we had 19 treatment sessions.

In 1994, when she was nine years old, Pam was diagnosed with a case of "lumbar scoliosis convex to the right," her left leg is 6 mm longer than her right leg, and her left ilia crest is 3 mm higher than the right. Since then, she had been in and out of hospitals for a variety of medical problems. She complained of having pain in her neck, shoulders, upper and lower back, pelvis and feet. She also had debilitating headaches. Her goals for massage treatment are headache and pain reduction.

In Pam's first massage, which lasted 75 minutes, I discovered her back muscles were extremely hypertonic, as tight and compact as that of a body builder. I gave her a full body relaxation massage using mainly gliding, friction and light percussion. She felt relaxed post-massage. Joan reported that Pam returned home "upbeat and relaxed in her body; not tensed and expecting pain."

Pam and I agreed to have ten treatment sessions before I left for China (for my tuina study). I wanted to help her body adjust to new patterns of reaction in the ten weeks and she was asked to reinforce the new sensation with self-care routines. My plan was to relax the left quadratus lumborum, iliopsoas and abdominals and to stimulate the same set of muscles on the right; as well as to relax the right erector spinae and transversospinalis muscles and to stimulate the same set of muscles on the left. Her condition gave me an excellent opportunity to apply Yin Yang Touch to Western massage practices.

In the second session, Pam had a posture assessment. Her left shoulder was higher than her right shoulder, her waist was shifting to the left and her left hip was higher than her right hip. Also, her hips were pulling posteriorly. On the massage table, her ribcage showed uneven alignment. Muscles of her shoulders, chest, pelvis and thighs were prime candidates for Yin Yang Touch treatment.

I gave Pam a 90-minute full body massage, focusing on the upper back. I treated the coldness in her upper traps with ground ginger root and moist heat and treated the hypertonicity in her left scapular area with ice. Her body was induced to confusion. It had to react to coldness in one area and warmth in another area concurrently. My theory was that muscle confusion could lead to muscle tension and muscle tension raised to the extreme brings its own release. After the massage, Pam felt her body had more flexibility and less stiffness. I taught her abdominal breathing and abdominal massage and suggested for her to adopt them for self-care. For her, abdominal massage was especially important for strengthening the abdominals so that they could withstand the pulling and stretching of her QL and iliopsoas.

The routine established in the first two sessions was repeated in subsequent sessions and we were able to complete nine treatment sessions before the start of 2013. In Sessions 5 and 6, Pam fell asleep during massage. When she woke up, she remarked, "You definitely have healing hands!" During the ten-week period, she had problems with sore throat, headaches and numb pinky. She had tonsillectomy in early December and flu in late December. As a result, she was highly stressed. In the midst of chronic and acute pains, she still had to take care of her three boys and to assume the tasks of a homemaker.

Three weeks after my return from China, I resumed treating Pam. Between late April and early September 2013, we had ten more sessions, about once every other week. Her headaches had dominated most of the sessions. She did not sleep well. She also had sinus and allergy problems and her body ached all over. My reading of her conditions was that the headaches were caused by scoliosis and stresses from her other ailments and her routine obligations at home. She needed to de-stress and to treat her scoliosis in order to deal with her headache problems, but she was unable to do so. Frequently, she had to reschedule a treatment session because she had to attend to the schooling needs of her boys. Meeting the treatment deadline became a stress for her!

In the 20 weeks before the case was suspended, Pam continued to complain about having headache, sinus infection, stomach problem, sore shoulders, cold and stiff neck. She had visited her primary care physician several times and had been prescribed with a number of drugs. In late August 2013, she felt she might have a case of nerve impingement. In the meantime, I had added cupping to her treatment routine since my return from China and had made several house calls to treat her headache problems. I was also exploring how I might use pressure points to trace the genesis of her headaches.

In early September 2013, Pam told me her neurologist had given her new medications for nerve pain. She was also taking a higher dose of Motrin, every two hours, for headache. She had been referred to a hand specialist for suspected tendonitis and she wished to do acupuncture for her problems. I gave her contact information for an acupuncturist and recommended spinal reflex therapy as an alternative treatment. She agreed to call me to continue massage therapy after her complications had settled. I have no plans to follow up with her conditions.

Despite frequent medical consultations, Pam did not have chiropractic adjustments of her spine conditions. From my observation, I am inclined to believe that pressure on her cervical vertebrae caused by scoliosis is the causal factor for her headache. Thus, treating her headache condition with drugs is unlikely to produce lasting relief until scoliosis has been treated. If she could have a spinal adjustment followed by massage therapy, her headache situation could be improved. As it was, she resorted to drug therapy for her headache and followed a more complicated path of treatment even though that path had not given her much relief. Massage therapy could help improve her conditions, but it is effective only after her spine has been structurally realigned. As I am not licensed to practice medicine, my diagnosis is good only on paper. It is disappointing not to have closure in the case.

Postlude

Chapter 28

RESEARCH -- THE ROAD LESS TRAVELED

I began my journey as a massage therapist not knowing I was heading to a "road less traveled." I became a *research* massage therapist. My incessant attempts at connecting the dots even while I was a student in massage classes had led me to unconventional ideas and practices. My review of established theories in TCM had led me to unresolved issues that I want to have plausible answers. I discovered massage is both bodywork and brainwork, and research is the bridge to connect and express them. Bodywork requires physical energy and stamina. Brainwork requires mental energy and sustainment. Bodywork is yang, brainwork is yin; and I am trying to blend them. I began the massage journey when my physical strength was beginning to decline, but I could draw on my mental strength for compensation. Working from my strength pushed me to develop a softer and quieter touch that calls from my depth to a client's depth. I try to tune in with my client for resonance and harmony.

This focus has helped me to visualize relaxation not as what I do for a client but as what I might help the client do for herself/himself actively. It allows me to differentiate between relaxation and stimulation and to integrate them with Yin Yang Touch, Virginian Stretch, the NOVA-S Method and Guangzhou Motion and eventually develop JIANFEI, a massage routine for weight control. It allows me to refine the art and science of skin-on-skin contact and be alert to the fact that when I touch skin, I am touching the brain. I just have to let my fingers do the feeling and reach beneath the weather-beaten epidermis.

Yin Yang Touch, Virginian Stretch, the NOVA-S Method and JIANFEI have resulted from my reading and reflection as I practice my trade as a massage therapist. That reading-reflection process is the starting point of doing research, to reason out *a priori* why a method might work and to test if the treatment, in fact, might work. It is theoretical massage, as in theoretical physics. It is contrary but complementary to evidence-based research that massage profession is striving toward. The emphasis on evidence-based research is to win massage a hearing in the arena of traditional Western medicine, but massage therapy is essentially complementary and alternative medicine and it makes no sense to ape after traditional allopathic medicine. The model of allopathic medicine is not necessarily the proper model, especially since it is wanting on so many fronts. In any case, from my reading and reflection, I started using massage to treat anterior pelvic tilt, fibromyalgia, posttraumatic stress disorder and scoliosis. I have barely laid the groundwork for systematic gathering of data for each of these conditions and I know not what the future might bring. I have provided details of my treatment methods so that therapists interested in the pursuit of healing might build on or depart from them. I am involved in massage research to help expand the frontier of knowledge and to help advance massage therapy as a routine modality in healthcare. I want to help bring down the cost of healthcare in the U.S. by showcasing a cost-effective treatment modality and advocating for its adoption.

I am eager for other therapists to engage in research and I look for opportunities to engage in teaching and sharing about research. I want to de-mystify it so that more therapists can be involved in a common effort to gather data systematically to show how massage works to treat chronic pain. Writing this book is a step in the journey of a thousand steps.

On the less traveled road, I enjoy travel alone, sometimes. More often than not, I like travel companions with whom I can share what I have found and vice versa. I like to have companions to explore with me: the use of Chinese tuina and Western massage in treating insomnia and headache, conditions that are often associated with chronic disorder and related to stress; the significance of blood pressure, pulse and temperature in therapeutic massage; the blending of cupping and organic compress and the coupling of multiple pressure points for treating specific disorders; the development of Yin Yang Touch as a layperson's massage technique; and the development of better understanding of the relationship between sleep, rejuvenation of blood and weight control (the emphasis of the JIANFEI routine); and the use of massage for weight loss. I am sure other interests will emerge.

JIANFEI, a Massage Routine for Weight Loss

Massage research has many frontiers. No one can reach all of them, but informed therapists know many of them are out there. When you reach the terminus of one frontier, you will find that it will lead you to another and another. As I explored the application of Yin Yang Touch, I discovered several references on weight loss. I decided to follow their trails and synthesize what I have discovered into a theoretical model for JIANFEI, a massage routine for weight loss.[94] The gist of JIANFEI is that you are overweight not because of what you eat or how much you eat, but because of what you don't rid -- what you don't get rid of from your body. You don't rid, despite apparent regular bowel movements and other normal body functions, because the waste disposal system of your body is underperforming.

The waste disposal system of your body is made up of, primarily, the blood, the heart and the acupressure points on the meridians. When your blood supply is inadequate and sub-par, your heart pumping power is below efficiency and your pressure points are blocked, the waste disposal system cannot remove as much waste from your body as it should. The waste becomes fat and it takes up residency in your body and you become overweight.

To lose weight, you need to remove unwanted fat from your body. You can do that by increasing the quantity and quality of your blood. Let's suppose the optimal quantity of your blood is 8 units, but the

---

[94]   The main ideas of JIANFEI are from *The User's Manual for Human Body* (2006) and *The User's Manual for Human Body 2* (2008) by Wu Qingzhong. and from the presentations of Chen Yuqin on the websites www.360doc.com and www.qiaodanjing.com. The materials are in Chinese. *Qiaodanjing* is the Chinese expression for tapping the gallbladder meridian.

actual quantity is 6 units,[95] your blood supply is deficient by 2 units. Let's further suppose that the optimal quality of your blood is 10 units but yours is 8 units. Your blood quality is 2 units below par. If the force needed to remove fat from your body is the function of heart power times blood quantity times blood quality and if 10 units is the optimal heart power, the optimal flushing force would be 800 (10x8x10) units. In our example, heart power with deficient blood quantity and quality would generate actual flushing force of 480 (10x6x8) units. Clearly, deficient blood does not have the full power to accomplish its waste disposal task.

As the organs primarily responsible for blood formation and rejuvenation are the gallbladder and liver (not bones, as commonly taught in Western anatomy and physiology classes), they need stimulation to purify the body fluid and to secrete chemicals (mainly bile) to enrich the blood. The essential way for getting gallbladder and liver to be more active is through sleeping, not just any time, but between dusk and 1:40 a.m., according to Chen Yuqin, the creator of Meridian Massage in China. However, according to the Chinese body clock, the optimal sleeping time is between 11 p.m. and 3 a.m., when the life energy qi is most active in the gallbladder and liver meridians.[96] Regardless of the exact timeframe, giving the body "down time" is critical for the gallbladder and liver to recharge the blood and increase its volume for weight control. Sleep to lose weight is a pre-condition for anyone who wants to lose weight.

Of course, some people find it difficult to fall asleep and stay asleep for many reasons. Those unable to sleep because of stress, they might adopt the routine described in Part Eight of *the Handbook of Chinese Massage* by Maria Mercati or the routine described in Chapter 11 of this book to help them overcome the problem.

In addition to sleep, you need to improve the pumping power of your heart in order to lose weight. Contrary to popular Western medical folklore, overweight is not a causal factor of heart problems. Just the opposite! Heart problems lead to overweight, or, more precisely, a heart that pumps with less than optimal force leads to weight gain.

---

[95] All the numbers are illustrative. They have no direct correlation with what the body actually produces. The concept of "blood volume" is a challenge to laboratory science. Thus far, there is no way to measure blood volume, according to Wu and Chen.

[96] *Tappan's Handbook of Healing Massage Techniques* (2010), p. 363.

The heart is enveloped in the pericardium and the pericardial sac has a thin layer of fluid cushioning it. The pumping power of the heart is inversely correlated with the amount of pericardial fluid in the sac. If the optimal pumping power of the heart is 10 units and the optimal amount of pericardial fluid is 1 unit, the optimal heart power would be 10 units. However, if the actual amount of fluid is 1.5 units, the actual heart power would be 6.7 (10/3 x2) units, a loss of 3.3. The excess fluid absorbs some of the pumping power and renders the heart less efficient in driving the blood through the body.

Using the previous example, a heart that pumps with 6.7 units of power in a body of deficient blood would generate a flushing force of 322 (6.7x6x8) units, a sub-par, sluggish stream that is inefficient in flushing out waste product. Thus, removing excess fluid from the pericardium is essential for the heart to function optimally. Massage along the heart and pericardium meridians can strengthen the heart and remove pericardial fluid.

In your body there is a network of vessels through which the blood flows. Overlying these vessels is the network of meridians through which the vital energy (qi) flows. Along with the driving force of the heart, the vital energy (qi) moves the blood through the pulling of yin-qi and yang-qi (the negative energy and positive energy). On the meridians are 361 regular points and 48 extra points, which, like locks on a canal, channel the flow of qi. When the locks are not completely open, qi flow is impeded. As a result, its pulling action on the blood is diminished. These locks are blocked when waste products present in the interstices of the organs through which the meridians pass are stuck to the locks. Thus, removing the waste products is how to keep the locks open and keeping the locks completely open is necessary for waste products to be moved and removed. Regular and frequent massages on the locks will ensure they are open.

Constipation and indigestion are two conditions that retain waste products in the body. According to *Meridians and Pressure Points*,[97] there are 37 points associated with constipation and five points associated with indigestion (Appendix 6). They are found on the liver, stomach, spleen, bladder, kidney, sanjiao, Du and Ren meridians. In terms of body regions, most of the blocked points are located on the stomach, posterior body, the lower legs and feet.

From the perspective of TCM, weight loss involves actions of the heart, pericardium, liver, gallbladder, stomach, bladder, kidney and spleen, and massage can bring about weight loss through

---

[97]   *Meridians and Pressure Points* (in Chinese, 2012), pp. 39-233.

improving the functions of these organs by stimulating the associated meridians.[98] JIANFEI is a massage routine derived from meridian massage and abdominal massage, set in the stimulation mode of Yin Yang Touch (Chapter 14). The objective of JIANFEI is to agitate the waste disposal system of the body so that waste products can be moved and removed. Thus, stimulation (in contrast to relaxation) is the preferred mode of massage.

To stimulate the heart, the therapist needs to focus on the heart meridian and the pericardium meridian. The heart meridian is a pair of yin channels that start from the heart, run transversely from it to the lungs, then descend and emerge from the armpits, pass along the anterior arms and forearms, and end on the tips of the little fingers. The pericardium meridian is also a pair of yin channels that start from inside the chest, emerge on the chest just beside the nipples in the space between the 4th and 5th ribs. They ascend the chest, curve around the armpits, and run downward along the arms and forearms, lateral (and sort of parallel) to the heart meridian, and end on the tips of the middle fingers. Thus, massaging the heart and pericardium meridians to empower the heart, the therapist should focus on the pectoral muscles, the anterior arms and forearms and the palms of her client.

To increase blood production and rejuvenation, the therapist needs to focus on stimulating the gallbladder and liver meridians. The gallbladder meridian is a pair of yang channels that start from the outer corners of the eyes. They ascend to the corners of the forehead, zigzag across the lateral aspects of the head, curve behind the ears to reach the top of the shoulders. They then pass in front of the underarms, along the lateral aspects of the ribcage, the hips, thighs, knees, lower legs and feet, and end at the lateral side of the tips of the 4th toes. Thus, to stimulate the gallbladder, the therapist should focus on massaging the head (especially the temporal regions) and the lateral aspects of the trunks, thighs, lower legs and dorsal feet.

The liver meridian is a pair of yin channels that start from the big toes, pass the front of the medial malleoli, and ascend along the medial side of the knees and thighs to the pubic region to the lower abdomen. From there the channels run upward, encircle the

---

[98]   Descriptions of the courses of the meridians are synthesized from *Meridians and Pressure Points* (2012), *the Handbook of Chinese Massage* (1997), *The Web that Has No Weaver* (2000) and *An Outline of Chinese Acupuncture* (1975) by the Academy of Traditional Chinese Medicine [Beijing].

stomach, enter the liver, pass through the diaphragm and the chest, ascend along the throat, connect with the eyes, and emerge at the forehead. The courses of the liver meridian are mostly internal and most of the acupressure points are on the medial aspects of the legs and thighs. Thus, to stimulate the liver, the therapist should focus on massaging the legs, thighs and feet.

To keep the pressure points open, the therapist should focus on pressing the salient points (Appendix 6) on the liver, stomach, spleen, bladder, kidney and Ren meridians, skipping *zhigou* (SJ6), *changqiang* (GV1) and *yaoshu* (GV2). The points on the Du meridian are difficult to access and the one on the sanjiao meridian is isolated, therefore, not significant for the task at hand.

The stomach meridian is a pair of yang channels that have several branches. One branch zigzags across the face, ascends along the angles of the jaw, goes upward in front of the ears, along the hairline to reach the forehead. Another descends from the jaw, crosses the neck, chest and abdomen and ends in the groin. A third branch runs from inside the abdomen to the knees and along the lateral aspects of the tibia and ends at the tips of the second toes. The five pressure points to be kept open are on the stomach, lower legs and dorsal feet.

The spleen meridian is a pair of yin channels that start from the big toes and ascend in front of the medial malleoli and up the legs. They then run along the posterior tibia, knees and thighs and upward to enter the abdomen and the spleen. The main branch continues on the surface of the abdomen, runs upward to the chest where it penetrates internally to follow the throat up to the root of the tongue. The seven pressure points to be kept open are on the stomach and the feet.

The bladder meridian is a pair of yang channels that start from the depressions just beyond the outer corners of the eyes. They ascend the forehead, run across the head, pass through *baihui* (GV20), enter the brain, and re-emerge at the back of the neck as two sub-branches lateral to the spinal column. They extend from the shoulders to the gluteus and the popliteus where they run as one branch to end at the tips of the small toes. The 12 pressure points to be kept opened are located on the posterior body between L1 and S5 and the posterior lower legs.

The kidney meridian is a pair of yin channels that start on the soles of the feet. They pass through the heels and ascend along the medial side of the legs and thighs, run upward over the abdomen and chest and end in a depression on the lower edges of the collarbone 2 *cun*[99] to the side of the midline. The nine pressure points to be kept opened are located on the stomach and feet.

The Ren meridian is a single yin channel that coordinates all the yin meridians (Chapter 14). The pressure points to be kept opened are mainly above and below the navel.

When you press the acupressure points on the meridians, you are removing the waste products that block the locks to facilitate the flow of qi, which in turn impact the flow of blood. As noted earlier, most of the acupressure points having significant roles in waste removal are in the stomach, the posterior body between L1 and S5 and along the midline, lower legs and feet. Thus, to unblock the pressure points, all that the therapist needs is to massage the stomach, the posterior body, and the lower legs and feet.

JIANFEI, the massage routine for weight loss, has two levels: basic and advanced. The basic level is focused on the head, face, anterior arms and forearms, hands, abdomen, anterior trunk, posterior and medial thighs and legs and feet. It skips the large intestine, bladder, sanjiao and Du meridian to provide more time for treating the other pressure points. (The advanced level includes treating points on the other meridians.) JIANFEI is a stimulation massage following the principle of yang on yang and yin on yin. On the yang aspects of her client, the therapist strokes downward and inward; on the yin aspects of her client, the therapist strokes upward and outward. Both actions are to be in a brisk tempo, going against the flow of qi. The whole purpose is to wake up the sluggish body and to remove waste products from it.

A full treatment of JIANFEI will take 12 to 16 weeks, at least one massage session per week. It is not an instant fix because overweight is a condition that develops over a period of time and most quick fixes have no sustaining power. One might postulate that every pound over the normal weight requires at least a week to be worked off. The waste disposal system of a highly overweight person will need more time to work off the excess. The advantage of JIANFEI is that other than allowing adequate time for sleep between 11 p.m. and 3 a.m., there are no extraneous requirements.

CRITERIA FOR SUCCESS. Before the treatment of JIANFEI, the client should measure and record his weight and the width of his arm, waist, hip and thigh and the percentage of his body fat. These

---

[99] "*Cun*" is a Chinese unit of client-based measurement. One *cun* is equal to one thumb's width, and three *cun* is equal to the width of four pointed fingers held together.

same measurements, repeated in four-week intervals, will provide the objective indices of weight loss and the success of JIANFEI.

From clinical experience of people undergoing meridian massage and abdominal massage in China, weight loss is usually not apparent in the first four weeks. In fact, some of them might even show an increase in body weight. What is happening is that the body has begun increasing the volume of blood and hastening the removal of waste, but the weight of the increased blood volume is higher than the weight of the waste removed. Besides, some of the dehydrated wastes have also absorbed water to increase their weight. Clients doing JIANFEI can expect similar results. Gaining weight in the first four weeks of JIANFEI is normal.

After the waste disposal system has been reconditioned for four weeks, it should begin to function more efficiently. It should be able to move more waste out of the body while it retains the increased blood volume gained in the initial four weeks. Moreover, increased secretion of bile (through stimulation of the gallbladder meridian) would have improved the blood's quality and continuing stimulation of the pericardium meridian would have drawn out the excess fluid from the pericardium sac. Poor blood would have become rich blood and weak heart would have become a strong heart. As the system becomes more efficient, more waste products are removed. Thus, beginning with the fifth week, people in the JIANFEI routine should start showing weight loss and a slimmer body.

JIANFEI should be skin-on-skin contact on the specified body regions, following a time-specific protocol. The client could undress to his level of comfort and the treatment might begin with the client in supine position. Both the therapist and the client should breathe deeply as pressure is applied or felt. The client is to breathe deeply throughout the entire session and to be actively aware of the placement of the therapist's hand.

The following is the JIANFEI routine that I have developed, based on my reading and massage practice.

- Hold client's forehead for ten to fifteen seconds. Stroke across it gently with palm from *taiyang* (EX-HN5) to *yintang* (EX-HN3) for two or three minutes. Stroke from the top of the head to the forehead -- from *baihui* (GV20) to *yintang* (EX-HN3) -- for two or three minutes. Draw circles from the cheekbone to the jawbone downward for one or two minutes. Press *yingxiang* (LI20) with the thumb for fifteen to thirty seconds. Cradle client's head in both palms and roll it gently from side to side for one or two minutes. Rest client's head in the palms of the therapist and lift and lower the head gently for one or two minutes. Close and open the fists under the client's head for one to two minutes. (The head and facial massage should last ten to twelve minutes. Maintain a brisk tempo.)

- Tilt client's head to open up the neck and upper shoulder area. Use the backhand to massage the neck and shoulder muscles from acromion to mastoid process (yang on yang and with the flow of yang-qi) for three to four minutes. Repeat for the other side of the neck and shoulder.

- Effleurage and petrissage the hand, forearm and arm, using the backhand to massage the backhand, posterior forearm and arm from shoulder to wrist (yang on yang); using palm to massage the palm, anterior forearm and arm, from wrist to shoulder (yin on yin) for three to four minutes. Grasp and lift arm muscles to release stress. Repeat for the other side.

- Effleurage and petrissage the abdominal muscles, using palm, moving counterclockwise and laterally (yin on yin) for four to six minutes. Press each of the ten pressure points for twenty to thirty seconds. Ask the client to place both hands below the navel and exhale as he feels the therapist's hand pressure. Press over the client's hands and exhale with the client for three or four times. (The abdomen massage should take ten to twelve minutes. Maintain firm pressure and sustained gliding.)

- Effleurage the pectoral muscles, using palms, to move laterally from the sternum (yin on yin), starting with muscles inferior to the breasts and ending with muscles superior to the breasts, for three to four minutes.

- Effleurage the linear alba (the Ren meridian) superiorly from the pubic bone to the jugular notch for four to six times (yin on yin).

- Effleurage the lateral aspects of the trunk, using the backhand, moving from shoulder to hip (yang on yang) for one to two minutes. Repeat for the other side.

- Cross fiber friction the gluteal muscles (yin on yin) for four to six minutes.

- Effleurage and petrissage the anterior and lateral thigh and leg with the backhand (yang on yang), moving from hip to ankle for three to four minutes. Effleurage, petrissage and tapotement the posterior and medial thigh and leg with the palm (yin on yin), move from ankle to hip, for four to six minutes. Repeat for the other side. Press the pressure points for thirty seconds each.

- Effleurage, petrissage and tapotement the foot using the palm for the plantar side and the backhand for the dorsal side for one to two minutes. Press *yongquan* (KI1) for thirty seconds. Repeat for the other foot.
- Cradle client's head in palms. Hold this position for one to two minutes. Breathe deeply and quietly. Release the hold to end the session. (Extend the breathing and hold to four to five minutes if the client has sleep problem.)

On Chinese health websites[100], one reads lots of anecdotal success stories about using massage for weight loss. In America, using massage for weight loss has not been tried in any systematic way and its effectiveness is not known.[101] Moreover, the restriction on the scope of practice of a massage practitioner tends to keep the massage profession from venturing into untried territories.

What prompted me to explore the use of massage for weight loss is the same force that prompted me to write this book. I have read about a seemingly plausible solution to the epidemic problem of obesity in America and I want to share it so that younger and more capable minds can build on it or depart from it. JIANFEI is, in fact, a theory in search of facts, but it is worth exploring. The massage routine as I have developed here is not a prescription and no one is required to try it. In fact, anyone considering using JIANFEI for weight loss should consult a medical professional before doing it.

I am aware that I make a number of claims for which there is no laboratory evidence. For instance, must one really sleep according to the Chinese body clock to allow an increase in blood volume? What is the correlation between blood volume and digestive efficiency? What is the correlation between blood quality and digestive efficiency? Do gallbladder and liver really play the role of blood formation and

---

[100] Using *jianfei anmo* (massage for weight loss in Chinese characters), I found no fewer than 150 Chinese websites on using massage to achieve weight loss, as of January 27, 2015.

[101] On the Internet, you can find some references on massage for weight loss and on facilities that offer the service. However, only a few are about using techniques from traditional Chinese medicine.

rejuvenation? Does regular and frequent massage of acupressure points facilitate weight loss? Is sleep really a precondition for weight loss? Can you really eat whatever you want and however much you want if you just focus on developing an efficient waste disposal system? Does the stimulation mode of massage work better for weight loss than the relaxation mode? Should we wait for laboratory science to validate the claims before we try JIANFEI?

I have no answer for all but the last question. Confronted with the epidemic of obesity, I believe waiting for laboratory evidence is not an option. As long as no harm is done, any method for weight loss or weight control should be tried and reliable success stories should be shared for the greater good. Since JIANFEI as a massage modality for weight loss has no negative side effects, whoever is committed to schedule his/her sleep according to the Chinese body clock and is willing to spend the necessary time to recondition their body should try it. It is arguably a less expansive alternative to conventional methods of weight control and weight loss and it can be a new tool for overcoming the problem of overweight.

JIANFEI is one of my emerging research interests. Teaching lay people to use Yin Yang Touch to care for themselves is another. There are many other intriguing ideas. Each of them offers the promise of an exciting adventure. How marvelous it was that I was encouraged to pursue professional massage as a new career! Yes, the best is yet to be, and you too can become a massage therapist at age 70 or whatever age!

Appendices

1

GUANGZHOU MOTION

This set of exercises was originally known as "Eight Moves for Health." Since I learned it initially from a DVD that Betty Chen of Guangzhou gave me, I decided to call it Guangzhou Motion instead of its original name. To simplify learning and teaching, I rename the various moves in bold letters after their original more exotic names.

When I do these exercises, I focus on the sensations on my finger tips whenever possible. The sensations are from the *dantian*, the area of the body below the navel. I exhale whenever I move my limbs or my body and I inhale whenever I rest. I pause to breathe a full cycle of exhaling and inhaling whenever I need to. Chen told me that her teacher, Master Xue Anri, taught his students not to hold their breath while doing the exercises. Instead, they should allow their breathing to lead the movements.

I have italicized my deviations and observations and enclosed them in square brackets in the translation. Since I am interested in promoting health and wellness rather than promoting a certain school of practice, I believe my adaptations are in tune with the monastic origin and the Buddhist spirit of these exercises.

According to Chen, Xue wrote the article "Eight Moves for Health" and published it in a magazine on Chinese martial art in

1997 or 98. However, the magazine has been defunct since 2006. Xue is Deng Jintao's student and Deng is the original promoter of Guangzhou Motion.

The benefits of these exercises are not evidence-based according to Western standards, but the exercises have stood the test of time. The challenge is for laboratory medicine to show that the benefits are unfounded.

<>

Introduction

Master Deng Jintao was the teacher of Guangzhou Motion. He learned it from Master Kuanyong of the Huanan Temple in Shaoguan (in Northern Guangdong Province) in the 1930s. The set of exercises has eight moves divided into five breathing cycles. You can practice as many sets as you wish according to your interest, strength and time available. It is best to increase the number of sets gradually.

This set of exercises is energy work done without moving the feet after their initial parting. It uses physical movements and deep breathing to tone the body.

Characteristics of the Exercise

Being relaxed and quiet are the first principles of the exercises, similar to other energy work. The exercises blend movement and stillness, as well as toughness and gentleness. They have incorporated the essence of *Baduanjin* and *Yijinjing* [*the "Eight Brocades" and the "Canon of Muscle Transformation," respectively. These two are time-honored traditional Chinese exercises.*]

The sequence of stretching, raising and lowering as well as opening and closing [*of the body frame*] in the eight moves harmonizes with the qi flow in the meridians from the three yin hand meridians (from the chest to the hands) to the three yang hand meridians (from the hands to the head) to the three yang foot meridians (from the head to the feet) and to the three yin foot meridians (from the feet to the abdomen). You do not need to visualize the qi flow in the meridians. The sequence of moves leads the qi flow naturally.

The exercises involve relaxation and openness. Muscles, joints, ligaments, bones and blood vessels are stretched and released alternately. The gentle and slow movements are coupled with deep and long abdominal breathing to reach the dual goals of toning external skin and flesh and developing internal breathing. They are excellent for doing energy work.

The exercises are especially beneficial for developing muscle strength of the lower limbs.

Benefits of the Exercise

Repetitions of stretching, releasing, bending, straightening as well as opening and closing [*of the body frame*] inherent in the eight movements require broad and full body engagements that strengthen the bones, muscles and ligaments. The exercises are therapeutic for arthritis, neck and shoulder pains, back pains and sore legs.

The eight moves put the weight of the whole body on the lower limbs. They elicit a counter force that helps to strengthen the venal pumping action in the cardiovascular system. It helps to regulate the blood pressure and the metabolism of triglycerides.

Deep and even abdominal breathing can increase the pulmonary functions and capacity. It is beneficial for improving the functions of the respiratory system.

Abdominal breathing creates an orderly internal pressure in the abdomen to massage the visceral organs and reinforce the local circulation of blood and the physiological functions of the organs.

The discipline of quiet movements inhibits activities in the cerebral cortex and the relaxation allows the brain to improve its blood flow.

The exercise is practiced with eyes looking afar. It helps to improve the eyes' acuity and to retard deterioration of the eyeballs.

Method

PREPARATION. (Normal breathing) Stand erect with arms hanging. Relax and part your feet. Move your left foot laterally one step to align with your left shoulder, with toes pointing forward, both feet straight and parallel and eyes looking forward. Breathe quietly and think peacefully. Focus your thoughts on the *dantian*. [*Dantian is the body region below the navel. I find it easier to move my feet 30° to 40° from the medial line for me to bend and I remain in the preparation stance with bended knees until my breathing has quieted down before I begin the first movement.]*

1. TWO DRAGONS RISING FROM THE SEA -- Breathe in. Use abdominal breathing throughout the exercise. [**REACH OUT**] Straighten your knees. Keep your upper trunk relaxed. Lift your hanging arms up and forward and reach out as far as you can. Let the palms face downward. Point the fingers forward. Breath in. [*My adaptation involves breathing out rather than breathing in, to synchronize exhaling with movement. It is contrary to what was taught by the masters. I also begin to focus on my fingertips to attune to the flow of qi.*]

2. TWO TIGERS HIDING THE DRAGONS -- Breathe out. [**REACH IN**] Rotate both your hands inward until the palms face each other. Bend the elbows to pull the forearms toward the body until both wrists touch the ribcage, to stretch the shoulder joints and pectoral muscles and to compress the back muscles.

3. SOAR TO THE SKY -- Breathe in. [**PULL UP**] Point the fingers upward. Press the fingertips against each other. Cross the thumbs. Form hands in steeple-form over the *shanzhong xue* [*CV17, midpoint on the sternum between the nipples*]. Push hands along the midline upward toward the sky and over the head, leading the body upward. Tiptoe both your feet and raise the head to look skyward, allowing the joints of your ankles, knees, hips, vertebrae, shoulders, elbows, wrists and fingers to be pulled upward toward the sky. [*Instead of breathe in as instructed, I breathe out in this move. I imagine this move as someone pulling the hands skyward rather than I pushing them upward.*]

4. COURTYARD IN THE SEA BOTTOM -- Breathe out. [**PULL DOWN**] Let your heels touch the ground. Flex (withdraw) the elbows behind the head with the little fingers resting on the hairline. Bend upper trunk anteriorly *(lower the body)* and keep your knees straight. Part both hands and stroke the neck. Put the palms downward to reach the ground in front of the feet. Lift the head to look forward. Let the fingertips touch each other. [*I imagine this move as someone pulling my body downward. I find it easier to lower my body with bended knees than straight knees. However, Chen pointed out that the purpose of this move is to stretch the joints and ligaments and keeping the knees straight is a better way to accomplish the purpose.*]

5. CRADLE THE MOON IN YOUR BOSOM -- Breathe in and out. [*LIFT UP*] Maintain the previous posture. Let both arms reach outward in semicircles to reach the front of the feet. Breathe in. Turn the hands upward, with the middle fingers touching each other [*as though you were balancing a trophy*]. Raise the body from the waist and draw in the buttocks to stand erect. Raise the forearms skyward. Rotate palms upward as though you are lifting a heavy load. Breathe out. [*This is the most difficult move for me. I do it in bits. Each time I move, I exhale. Each time I rest, I inhale. I raise my body with the thigh and waist muscles.*]

6. SUPPORT THE FIRMAMENT -- Breathe in. [*REACH UP*] Connect with the previous movement. Move both hands inwards to meet at the *shanzhong xue* (CV17), rotate the wrists and palms forward and let the middle fingers touch each other. Raise the arms upward, with the palms facing skyward and the middle fingers touching each other. Look up to the raised palms. [*As the hands and arms move, I breathe out. This move does not require you to tiptoe.*]

7. THREE TRAYS FALLING TO THE GROUND -- Breathe out. [*LEVEL OUT*] Stretch the raised arms backward and extend them laterally (outwardly). Bend your knees to lower the body. Look forward. Lower the arms to brush the thighs with your hands. Turn the palms skyward and extend your arms forward, align your arms with your shoulders.

8. LEAD THE GOAT HOME -- Breathe in and out. [*LEVEL IN*] Raise your body. Keep your head erect. Look forward. Breathe in. Turn the wrists inward for the palms to face downward. Press both hands to hang by your thighs. Stand erect. Look forward and afar. Focus on the *dantian*.

CLOSING. In the final round, drop your wrists, point the fingers downward and relax the whole body. Move the left foot close to the right foot. Breathe naturally.

2

NOTES ON CHINESE WORDS

Chinese words and phrases in this book are in pinyin,[102] the standard phonetic system for transcribing Chinese words spoken in Mandarin or *Putonghua* into Romanized writing. Chinese words (characters) are monosyllabic and tone sensitive[103]. Each word in a term or phrase has its own syllable and tone and each Chinese syllable is made up of a vowel (final) and a consonant (initial).

Chinese language has six simple vowels: *a, o, e, i, u, ü,* which can be combined to form compound vowels. It has 21 consonants: *b, p, m, f, d, t, n, l, g, k, h, **j, q, x, z, c, s, zh, ch, sh, r**.* The first 11 of these consonants have sounds similar to those in English. The rest of them (in bold letters) are sounded as *jee (j), chee (q), see (x)* (mouth closed, with wisdom teeth touching each other, long "ee"); *dzee (z), chee (c), see (s)* (mouth closed, with wisdom teeth touching each other, short "ee"); *zher as the word judge (zh), cher (ch), sher (sh) and rer (r)* (with curled

---

[102] With the exceptions of the Cantonese words *dumgwat* in Chapter 1 and *Kung Hey Fat Choy* in Chapter 16.

[103] For a fuller introduction to Chinese language and pinyin, consult *Beginner's Chinese* (1997) by Yong Ho; *Integrated Chinese*, 2nd Edition (2005), by Tao-chung Yao and Yuehua Liu *et al.*; and "Pinyin," in Wikipedia.

tongue). According to Wikipedia, "most native speakers of English find [the consonants in bold letters] difficult" to pronoun. They are also difficult for me whose mother tongue is Cantonese.

In terms of writing, syllables starting with *u* are written as *w* in place of *u*; *i* are written as *y* in place of *i*; and *ü* are written as *yu* in place of *ü*.

With notable exceptions for key terms, the emphasis of these notes on learning Chinese tuina is not on pronunciation. It is on the meaning of the Chinese word in pinyin and tonal rendition. However, if you could "master" the sounding of the following twelve words: *an* (as "ahn"), *gun* (as "gwun"), *han* (as "Hahn"), *he* (as "her" without sounding the "r"), *men* (as "muhn"), *mo* (as "mou" as in ought), *qi* (as "chee"), *song* (as "soong"), *tang* (as "tahng"), *wang* (as "wahng"), *tong* (as "toong") and *yang* (as "yahng"), you will have an air of sophistication to show you have been exposed to real Chinese! You can mumble other Chinese words and phrases and no one will notice the difference.

The vowel-consonant combination produces only 400 possible sounds, creating a vast number of homophones and consequent ambiguity. To overcome this problem, Chinese language uses tones (pitches) and context to increase the capacity for communication and to define the meaning of a word or phrase.

Chinese language has four tones (pitches): high level, rising, rising-falling and falling. In language textbook, the four tones are usually marked with diacritics such as -, /, ^, and \. In these notes, when absolutely necessary, we use superscript [1] after the sound to indicate high-level tone, superscript [2] to indicate rising tone, superscript [3] to indicate falling-rising tone and superscript [4] to indicate falling tone to define the meaning of a sound in pinyin.

Variation in tone changes the meaning of a word (vowel-consonant combination). For example, the sound *wen*: *wen[1]* means warm, gentle, review; *wen[2]* means writing, language, hear, smell; *wen[3]* means steady, disorderly, cut one's throat, kiss; and wen[4] means ask, wipe, crack. According to the *New Age Chinese-English Dictionary*, there are at least 20 Chinese words with the sound *wen*. Despite ambiguity, most words in pinyin in this book are not marked with superscripts. Otherwise, the text will look too geeky and cumbersome! There are exceptions; as readers will find or have found.

Chinese language is contextual and ideographic. It is difficult to ascertain a word's meaning without the proper context even when the word is written in ideogram. A word formed with vowel-consonant combination may have different meaning in biology, philosophy or traditional Chinese medicine. In this book, most Chinese words are related to the theory and practice of traditional Chinese medicine, Chinese history and pressure points. I have appended superficial meanings to isolated words according to their usage. I have also stretched the names of pressure points (usually expressed in two- or three-word phrases) to bring out some elements of meaning, but they are not gospel truth. They might be good for association. Syllables of pressure points are usually written as two- or three-word phrases, but I have separated them into distinctive words so that readers might have a feel for the meaning of each word. Thus, when you come across *shang*, you can assume the phrase has something to do with "above," and *xi*, to do with "stream;" most of the time, but not always. That's the folly and fun of the Chinese language!

3

A GLOSSARY OF CHINESE WORDS

Term	Literal Meaning	Context
An	Press	Massage
An	Press	Tuina stroke
Bu	Replenish	TCM
Ca	Scrub	Tuina stroke
Cuo	Knead	Tuina stroke
Dian	Point, hit	Tuina stroke
Dou	Shake	Tuina stroke
Du	Governing	Meridian
Gu	Bone	Anatomy
Guan	Pass, gate	General
Gun	Roll	Tuina stroke
Han	Perspire	TCM
He	(group name)	Pressure Point
Hu	Door, interior	General

Ji¹	Muscle	Anatomy
Ji³	Squeeze	Tuina stroke
Jing	Essence	TCM
Jing	(group name)	Pressure Point
Jinye	Fluid	TCM
Ke	Check	Wu Xing
Kou	Pluck	Tuina stroke
La	Pull	Tuina stroke
Lin	(family name)	General
Ma	(family name)	General
Men	Gate, door	General
Ming	(dynasty name)	History
Mo	Touch	Massage
Mo²	Rub	Tuina stroke
Mo³	Smear	Tuina stroke
Na	Grasp	Massage
Nian	Twist	Tuina stroke
Pai	Pat	Tuina stroke
Qi	Air, energy	Philosophy
Qi	Air, energy	TCM
Qia	Pinch	Tuina stroke
Qie	Palpate	TCM
Qin	(dynasty name)	History
Qing	(dynasty name)	History
Qing	Cleanse	TCM
Ren	Conception	Meridian
San	Disperse	TCM
Sha	Sand, grain	TCM
Shen	Spirit	TCM
Sheng	Give birth	Wu Xing
Shou	Hand	General
Shu	(group name)	Pressure Point
Song	(dynasty name)	History

Tang	(dynasty name)	History
Tong[1]	Open	TCM
Tong[4]	Pain	TCM
Tu	Throw up	TCM
Tui	Push	Massage
Tui	Push	Tuina stroke
Wang	Observe	TCM
Wen[1]	Warm	TCM
Wen[2]	Smell, hear	TCM
Wen[4]	Ask, question	TCM
Wu	Five	Philosophy
Xia	Discharge	TCM
Xiao	Reduce	TCM
Xie	Leak, discharge	TCM
Xing	Walk, travel, journey	Philosophy
Xing	(group name)	Pressure Point
Xue	Blood	TCM
Xue	Point, cavity	Pressure Point
Yang	Masculine, light	Philosophy
Yin	Feminine, shadow	Philosophy
Yuan	(dynasty name)	History
Yuan	Chinese currency, dollar	General
Zhen	Vibrate	Tuina stroke
Zhuo	Peck	Tuina stroke
Zu	Foot	General

Note: Words in bold are pronounced differently in English.

4

A GLOSSARY OF CHINESE PHRASES

Phrase	Meaning	Context
A shi xue	"ah yes" point	Pressure Point
Anmo	press & touch	Massage
Bahuixue	(group name)	Pressure Point
Bamaijiaohuixue	(group name)	Pressure Point
Beihuoji	latissimus dorsi	Anatomy
Beiyuxue	(group name)	Pressure Point
Chijiu	lasting	Tuina
Dantian	pubic region	Anatomy
Dieda	orthopedic medicine	TCM, external
*Dumgwat**	pound bones	Massage
*Fat choy**	strike rich	General
Gonggong	maternal grandfather	General
Guasha	scrape "sand"	Massage
Jiaohuixue	(group name)	Pressure Point

Jingshen	spirit	General
Jinye	body fluid	General
Jiya	finger pressure	Tuina
Jueyin	third degree yin	Meridian
Junyun	even	Tuina
Koujue	pithy formula (rhyme & oral)	Tuina
Kuaile	happy	General
*Kung hey**	congratulate, wish	General
Laoshi	teacher (form of address)	General
Long zhui	vertebra prominens	Anatomy
Luoxue	(group name)	Pressure Point
Muxue	(group name)	Pressure Point
Pengchu	swelling	Spinal Tuina
Putonghua	Chinese Mandarin	General
Rouhe	gentle	Tuina
Sanjiao	three burner	Meridian
Shaoyang	third degree yang	Meridian
Shaoyin	second degree yin	Meridian
Shentou	penetrating	Tuina
Shilu	train of reasoning	Spinal Tuina
Shujiji	erector spinae	Anatomy
Sifu	teacher, master	General
Taiyang	second degree yang	Meridian
Taiyin	utmost yin, first degree yin	Meridian
Tuchu	protruding	Spinal Tuina
Tuina	push & grasp	Tuina
Tuochu	dislocate	Spinal Tuina
Wuxing	five elements	Philosophy, TCM
Xiahexue	(group name)	Pressure Point
Xiefangji	trapezius	Anatomy
Xinnian	new year	General

Xixue	(group name)	Pressure Point
Xueqi	life	General
Yangming	first degree yang	Meridian
Yijinjing	Canon of Muscle Transformation	Tuina
Youchu	slip off	Spinal Tuina
Youli	with strength	Tuina
Yuanxue	(group name)	Pressure Point
Zangfu	internal organs	Anatomy

* Cantonese

5

SELECT PRESSURE POINTS

Name	Nick Name	Alpha Code	Location (Gross)	Traditional Reference
Bai hui	hundred meet	GV20	top of head, midpoint between ears	
Ba liao	eight space	**	S1-S4 foramen	zutaiyang
Bing feng	hold wind	SI12	midpoint of scapular spine	shoutaiyang
Cheng fu	support hold	BL36	middle of gluteal fold	zutaiyang
Cheng qi	hold weep	ST1	directly below pupil on lower eye socket	zutaiyin
Cheng shan	support mountain	BL57	mid posterior leg	zutaiyang
Ci liao	second space	BL32	sacrum, 2nd depression (foramen)	zutaiyang
Da heng	big horizontal	SP15	mid stomach, off to sides of navel	zutaiyin
Da zhui	big vertebra	GV14	between C7 and T1	
Di cang	earth warehouse	ST4	corner of the mouth	zuyangming
Feng chi	wind pond	GB20	lateral depression of occiput	zushaoyang

Feng fu	wind home	GV16	mid occiput	
Guan yuan	pass base	CV4	four fingers width below navel	
He gu	join valley	LI4	depression between posterior thumb and index finger	shouyangming
Huan tiao	ring jump	GB30	mid point between hip bone and coccyx	zushaoyang
Jia che	cheek carrier	ST6	depression on masseter	zutaiyin
Jian jing	shoulder well	GB21	medial scapula	zushaoyang
Jing men	capital door	GB25	below 12th rib	zushaoyang
Jing ming	eye clear	BL1	medial corner of eye	zutaiyang
Ju liao	huge bone-space	ST3	directly below pupil on cheek bone	zutaiyin
Kun lun	descendant order	BL60	between outer ankle bone and Achilles tendon	zutaiyang
Lao gong	labor chamber	PC8	middle of the palm	shoujueyin
Ming men	life door	GV4	between L2 and L3	
Nei guan	inner pass	PC6	two thumb width midpoint above wrist crease	zujueyin
Nei ting	inner court	ST44	dorsal foot, between 2nd & 3rd toes	zuyangming
Qi hai	energy sea	CV6	two fingers width below navel	
Qi men	phase door	LR14	between 6th and 7th ribs, below nipple	zujueyin
Qu chi	crooked pond	LI11	lateral elbow crease	shouyangming
Quan liao	cheekbone space	SI18	cheek	shoutaiyang
San yin jiao	three dark exchange	SP6	four finger width above tip of inner ankle	zutaiyin
Shang ju xu	upper big empty	ST37	lateral leg	zuyangming
Shang wan	upper abdo-cavity	CV13	palm's width above navel	
Shen shu	kidney acupoint	BL23	L2 process	zutaiyang
Shen ting	god courtyard	GV24	one finger width above anterior hairline	
Shou san li	hand three mile	LI10	upper forearm, radial side	shouyangming
Shui gou	water ditch	GV26	furrow below nose	
Si bai	four white	ST2	neck SCM	zuyangming
Si shen cong	four god wise	EX-HN1	top of head, surrounding GV20	
Si zhu kong	silk bamboo empty	TE23	depression at outer tip of eye brow	shoushaoyang

Tai chong	supreme rush	LR3	depression between 1st & 2nd metatarsals	zujueyin
Tai xi	supreme stream	KI3	mid point between inner ankle and tendon	zushaoyin
Tai yang	supreme bright	EX-HN5	depression on temple	
Taibai	supreme white	SP3	root of the big toe	zutaiyin
Tian shu	heaven pivot	ST25	Stomach	zutaiyin
Tian zong	heaven source	SI11	midpoint infraspinous fossa	shoutaiyang
Wei zhong	entrust center	BL40	mid posterior knee crease	zutaiyang
Xi yan	knee eye	EX-LE5	depression below knee cap	
Xia ju xu	lower big empty	ST39	3 x four finger width on lateral leg	zutaiyin
Xia wan	lower abdo-cavity	CV10	two thumbs width above navel	
Xue hai	blood sea	SP10	two thumb width above med patella	zutaiyin
Yin bai	hide white	SP1	distal phalange big toe	zutaiyin
Yin men	dark-red door	BL37	posterior thigh, between BL36 and knee crease	zutaiyang
Yin tang	seal hall	EX-HN3	between eye brows	
Ying xiang	welcome fragrance	LI20	depression lateral to nostril	shouyangming
Yong quan	bubbling fountain	KI1	depression on sole, two thirds from heel	zushaoyin
Yu yao	fish waist	EX-HN4	mid point between eye brows	
Zan zhu	collect bamboo	BL2	medial end of eye brow	zutaiyang
Zhang men	chapter door	LR13	below 11th rib	zujueyin
Zhi gou	branch ditch	TE6	lower forearm	shoushaoyang
Zhong fu	central mission	LU1	upper chest	shoutaiyang
Zhong ji	center extreme	CV3	one thumb width above pubic bone	
Zhong wan	center abdo-cavity	CV12	four fingers width above navel	
Zu san li	foot three mile	ST36	four finger width below kneecap	zutaiyin

** **Ba liao** is made up of shang liao, BL31; ci liao, BL32; zhong liao, BL33 and xia liao, BL34.

6

PRESSURE POINTS FOR THE JIANFEI ROUTINE

For this routine, locations of the pressure points are identified only in the general body regions. Readers interested in more exact locations are advised to consult a standard meridian chart. "*Cun*" is a Chinese unit of client-based measurement. One *cun* is equal to one thumb's width, and three *cun* is equal to the width of four pointed fingers held together.

Constipation

LI4	*hegu*	dorsal hand, web between the thumb & index finger
ST25	*tianshu*	stomach, lateral to the navel
ST36	*zusanli*	leg, inferior to the patella, gap between the fibula & tibia
ST37	*shangjuxu*	leg, inferior to the patella, gap between the fibula & tibia

ST41	*jiexi*	foot, gap between the extensors
ST44	*neiting*	foot, gap between the second and third toes
SP2	*dadu*	foot, medial side of the big toe
SP3	*taibai*	foot, medial aspect of the foot
SP5	*shangqiu*	foot, the medial malleolus
SP6	*sanyinjiao*	foot, posterior tibia, 3 *cun* above the malleolus
SP14	*fujie*	stomach, 1.3 *cun* below *daheng* (SP15)
SP15	*daheng*	stomach, 4 *cun* lateral to the navel
SP16	*fu'ai*	stomach, 3 *cun* above *daheng* (SP15)
BL25	*dachangshu*	back, 1.5 *cun* lateral to L4 (large intestine xue)
BL28	*pangguanshu*	back, level with second posterior sacral foramen
BL31	*shangliao*	back, in the first posterior sacral foramen
BL33	*zhongliao*	back, in the third posterior sacral foramen
BL34	*xialiao*	back, in the fourth posterior sacral foramen
BL38	*fuxi*	back, below knee, gap of the heads of the gastrocnemius
BL51	*huangmen*	back, 3 *cun* lateral to L1
BL53	*baohuang*	back, 3 *cun* lateral to the posterior midline, near BL28
BL54	*zhibian*	back, 3 *cun* lateral to the posterior midline, near BL34
BL57	*chengshan*	leg, inferior gap of the gastrocnemius
KI1	*yongquan*	foot, sole, depression below the middle toe
KI4	*dazhong*	foot, depression on the medial calcaneus
KI8	*jiaoxin*	foot, the posterior tibia
KI14	*siman*	stomach, 2 *cun* below the navel, 0.5 *cun* from midline
KI15	*zhongzhu*	stomach, 1 *cun* below the navel, 0.5 *cun* from midline

KI16	*huangshu*	stomach, level with the navel, 0.5 *cun* from midline
KI17	*shangqu*	stomach, 2 *cun* above the navel, 0.5 *cun* from midline
KI18	*shiguan*	stomach, 3 *cun* above the navel, 0.5 *cun* from midline
KI19	*yindu*	stomach, 4 *cun* above the navel, 0.5 *cun* from midline
SJ6	*zhigou*	arm, posterior, 3 *cun* from the wrist
GV1	*changqiang*	pelvic, midpoint between the tip of coccyx & the anus
GV2	*yaoshu*	pelvic, junction between the sacrum and the coccyx
CV6	*qihai*	stomach, 1.5 *cun* below the navel, abdominal midline
CV21	*xuanji*	chest, midline of the sternum

Indigestion

CV10	*xiawan*	stomach, 2 *cun* above the navel
CV12	*zhongwan*	stomach, midpoint between xiphoid process & the navel
CV13	*shangwan*	stomach, 5 *cun* above the navel
BL19	*danshu*	back, 1.5 *cun* lateral to T10
BL20	*pishu*	back, 1.5 *cun* lateral to T11

7

A GLOSSARY OF ACRONYMS

ABMP	Associated Bodywork and Massage Professionals
Ach	acetylcholine
AIS	active isolated stretching
ASIS	anterior superior iliac spine
Ca++	calcium
CAM	complementary and alternative medicine
CDP	Center for Deployment Psychology
CFF	cross fiber friction
CMT	Certified Massage Therapist
CNA	Certified Nursing Assistant
CNS	central nervous system
CPR	cardiopulmonary resuscitation
ELI	Extended Learning Institute
ENT	ear, nose and throat
FIQR	fibromyalgia impact questionnaire, revised
FM	fibromyalgia

HOPRS	history, observation, palpation, range-of-motion, special testing
ITT	iliotibial tract
MET	muscle energy technique
MTF	Massage Therapy Foundation
MTrP	myofascial trigger point
NCBTMB	National Certification Board for Therapeutic Massage and Bodywork
NCTM	Nationally Certified in Therapeutic Massage
NCTMB	Nationally Certified in Therapeutic Massage and Bodywork
NOVA	Northern Virginia Community College
NVCC	Northern Virginia Community College
PCL-M	posttraumatic [stress disorder] checklist, military [version]
PNF	proprioceptive neuromuscular facilitation
PNS	peripheral nervous system
PSIS	posterior superior iliac spine
PTSD	posttraumatic stress disorder
QL	quadratus lumborum
RMB	Renminbi (People's money – Chinese currency)
ROM	range of motion
SOAP	subjective, objective, assessment, plan
TBI	traumatic brain injury
TCM	traditional Chinese medicine
TFL	tensor fascial latae
TMJ	temporomandibular joint
VA	Veterans Affairs

Index

Edwards Brothers Malloy
Oxnard, CA USA
March 11, 2015